Marine Archaeology

The present work, edited by Miss Joan du Plat Taylor, Librarian of the University of London Institute of Archaeology, has evolved from the collection of studies, *Le Plongeur et l'Archéologue*. Published in French by the Technical Committee of the Confédération Mondiale des Activités Subaquatiques under the supervision of its Director of Publicity, M. François Clouzot, this was produced in collaboration by Cmdt. Jacques-Yves Cousteau, Cmdt. Ph. Tailliez, MM. Fernand Benoit, Frédéric Dumas, Guy de Frondeville, Yves Girault, Alex Sivirine, Jacques Dumas, and François Clouzot, and Miss Honor Frost.

Marine Archaeology

Developments during sixty years in the Mediterranean

EDITED BY

Joan du Plat Taylor
F.S.A.

FOR

C.M.A.S.
(World Underwater Federation)

THOMAS Y. CROWELL COMPANY
NEW YORK
Established 1834

First published in the United States of America in 1966

Library of Congress Catalog Card Number 65-20609

List of Contributors

FRÉDÉRIC DUMAS President of the Archaeological Section of C.M.A.S. Member of the Groupe d'étude et de recherches sous-marines. Co-author of *The Silent World*; author of *Deep-water Archaeology* and *Épaves antiques*.

FERNAND BENOIT Member of the Institut de France. Director of Antiquities for Provence and Corsica. Curator of the Musée Borély, Marseilles.

PROFESSOR GEORGE KARO Formerly Assistant Director and Director of the German Archaeological Institute in Athens, 1905–20 and again 1930–36. Directed excavations at Tiryns and in Athens. Settled in U.S.A. in 1939.

GUY DE FRONDEVILLE Engineer. Organizer of the excavations at Mahdia. Author of *Visiteur de la Mer*.

PROFESSOR NINO LAMBOGLIA Director of the Istituto Internazionale di Studi Liguri, Bordighera, and founder of the Centro Sperimentale di Ricerche Sottomarina, Albenga.

YVES GIRAULT Colleague of Commandant Cousteau in several of the voyages of the *Calypso*. Took part in the excavations at Mahdia, Île du Levant and Dramont as well as Grand Congloué.

COMMANDANT PHILIPPE TAILLIEZ First director of the Groupe d'étude et de recherches sous-marines of the French Navy at Toulon. Author of *Plongées sans câble*, *Nouvelles plongées sans câble* and *Aquarius*. Director of excavations at Mahdia, 1947; vice-president of the Technical section of C.M.A.S.; president of the Technical section of the Fédération Française d'étude et de Sports sous-marins.

CLAUDE SANTAMARIA Discoverer of the Dramont wreck. Member of the St. Raphael Diving Club.

ALEX SIVIRINE Secretary-general of the Office Française de Recherches sous-marines. Engineer who prepared the plans of the O.F.R.S. expeditions to the Fontaine de Vaucluse and Port Miou. Took part in the Dramont excavations.

LIST OF CONTRIBUTORS

DOCTORS ALEXANDER PEDERZINI AND GIANNI ROGHI
Founder members of the Centro Italiano di Ricercatori Subacquei, Genoa, and now members of the Centro Sperimentale di Ricerche Sottomarina, Albenga.

GEORGE F. BASS Research Associate, University Museum of Pennsylvania, Philadelphia, U.S.A. Excavation experience in Greece.

NICHOLAS FLEMMING Research student, Department of Geography, Cambridge.

WILLY HAAG Treasurer of C.M.A.S. President of Centre de Sports Subaquatiques de Neuchâtel.

JOAN DU PLAT TAYLOR Librarian, London University, Institute of Archaeology. Formerly Assistant Curator, Cyprus Museum, Nicosia. Author of *Myrtou-Pigadhes. A Late Bronze Age sanctuary in Cyprus* and other papers.

DOCTOR JOHN WAECHTER Archaeologist. Lecturer, London University, Institute of Archaeology.

DOCTOR W. D. NESTEROFF Sedimentologist of Laboratoire Géologie Physique, Paris.

Contents

Plates

Acknowledgements

The editor wishes to express her thanks to Mrs. Sheilah Dorrell, Mr. J. W. Franklin, Miss Honor Frost, Signor Luigi Guido, Miss E. M. Horsley, Mrs. Gillian Spenser, and Dr. John Waechter for assistance with translations and in the preparation of the text, and to Prof. J. D. Evans for reading the proofs: also to the undermentioned persons for permission to translate and reproduce their articles and reports:

To M. Fernand Benoit for 'Premier résultats des fouilles sous-marines. Typologie des amphores et construction navale', *Actes du Congrés des Sociétés Savantes, Aix-en-Provence*, 1958.

To the Editor of *Archaeology* for the section on Antikythera from Professor Karo's 'Archaeology from the Sea'.

To Dr. Gianni Roghi for the report on Spargi from *Bolletino e Atti*, Centro Italiano di Ricercatori Subacquei, 1958–9.

To Dr. Alessandro Pederzini for the survey of Gallinaria Island in *Bolletino e Atti* (C.I.R.S., 1957).

To Professor Nino Lamboglia for the report on Albenga in *Rivista di Studi Liguri*, 18, 1952; for the articles in *Forma Maris Antiqui*, 1961; also to him and M. Santamaria for the report on Dramont and to Cmdt. Tailliez for the report on Titan in *Atti del II Congresso Internazionale di Archeologia Sottomarina* (Albenga, 1958.)

To the Editor of the *American Journal of Archaeology* for the 'Cape Gelidonya Wreck' from Vol. 65, 1961.

Foreword

The development of underwater archaeology is closely linked with that of diving techniques. Before the Second World War, in the era of the old-style diving helmet and lead-weighted boots, there were only two archaeological finds, although they were of major importance!

With the advent of the free-diver, ancient wrecks have been located almost everywhere, rarely properly exploited, though sometimes pillaged. The invasion of the sea by thousands of divers has brought an unhoped-for 'census' of sites, but has at the same time struck terror into the archaeologist. This fear is theoretically justified, but is in fact only a proof of how far the archaeologist lags behind the diver. It is now up to the governments concerned to prevent the development of a serious conflict: legislation must be amended and scientific departments enlarged and given larger sums for excavation. Not a day should be lost. Divers, whose good faith is unquestioned, refuse to be scapegoats and take the responsibility for the defects of the ministries.

And now, my friends and fellow-divers, let me tell you my favourite daydream: You know that by a miracle a submarine television camera seeking the wreckage of a Comet aircraft in the Mediterranean came upon a deposit of amphorae at a depth divers cannot reach. But we have been able to make constant use of our latest invention, the 'diving saucer', up to depths of 300 m. Imagine our feelings if we were able to uncover in the twilight of our new domain an ancient wreck—completely untouched!

J.-Y. COUSTEAU

Map showing principal sites mentioned in this book

1

Underwater Work
and Archaeological Problems

As a professional diver whose life has been devoted to the development of new techniques, I am happy to have the opportunity of introducing this collection of reports on underwater excavation. Form dictates that these reflections should appear as Chapter 1, but the practised reader will realize that 'Introductions' are better read after the text has been digested! The reports in this book date from 1900, when art treasures were salvaged by sponge-divers from a wreck at Antikythera, to the 1960 excavation by archaeologists and free-divers of a Bronze Age wreck in Turkey. As historical documents and under the scholarly editorship of Miss du Plat Taylor, these reports can hardly fail to impress upon their readers both the growing importance of this kind of research and the archaeological value of sites each containing a closed group of contemporary objects.

Despite their apparent merits, accounts of submarine excavation provoke disquieting questions. Readers ignorant of underwater techniques may find much that is hard to interpret. Why, they may wonder, have so many wreck excavations contributed so little to our knowledge of the structure of ancient ships? They would be wrong to conclude that, because accounts of pioneer research can be misleading, it will not be possible to develop a controlled method of underwater excavation—that is to say, a method which will permit, for instance, of the eventual reconstruction of ships, as well as of their cargoes.

Many reports in this book were written at a time when there was no comparative knowledge of wreck-formation, or indeed of any other kind of submarine site. Others record how men of undoubted skill and experience were forced, by lack of time and money, either to rush their work or to abandon it in its early stages. On land, where the excavator's problems are self-evident, no such considerations need colour our judgement of his achievements. In normal conditions archaeological methods have been standardized and suitable formulae evolved for reporting results; marine archaeology, by contrast, is still in the experimental stage.

The means at the disposal of the men whose work is recorded in these pages varied from bare hands, and perhaps a camera in a leaky case, to heavy digging and lifting machinery, television and film cameras, sizeable boats, and all that these imply in terms of highly skilled personnel. Some of our authors worked on their sites for a few days, while others continued over a period of years, but in every case the time individual divers spent on the bottom was less than one working hour per day, for depth curtails the duration of a dive and well-preserved wrecks are found *only in deep water*.

New methods are now being developed which will allow almost unlimited diving time. After several hours on the bottom, divers will, for instance, instead of surfacing, go to an 'underwater house'. They should be able to work day after day in the sea. I shall revert later to the implications of this rapid technical advance. Meanwhile, past excavations and, more important, the marine sites to which they refer have to be assessed in terms which I shall try briefly to enumerate.

Experience shows that reports of underwater work, if they are to be useful, must include at least:

A geological analysis of the site and its marine environment.

A statement of the total working time spent on the bottom.

A description of the machinery used.

The gross and net weights of objects lifted (especially when these represent the cargo of a ship).

Insistence on detail may seem tedious, but only this kind of data will show whether, by land standards, an excavation has been satisfactory or whether it should merely be considered as a sounding.

Reports should also contain full analytical descriptions of the difficulties encountered in the course of excavation, so that similar pitfalls can be avoided in the future. Dr. Roghi, for instance, has described how, during the first season's campaign on the Roman wreck at Spargi, the cargo of amphorae was lifted to expose the wood of the hull. The following year, when work was resumed, he was surprised to find that this wood, because it had been left unprotected, had disintegrated and disappeared. After such a valuable lesson any archaeologist who repeated the same mistake would deserve the severest censure.

Amateur and professional divers

Amateur divers may well remain unaware of their mistakes, and repeat them in all innocence. This is a very real danger. It is axiomatic that excavation, whether on land or underwater, should be conducted by an archaeologist, but, since no archaeologist can be a professional diver as well, he will be at a disadvantage in marine conditions. Only a man grounded in the skills and disciplines of his craft, who dives regularly throughout the year, is in a position to notice how certain operations could have been carried out more efficiently, and then to correct his own mistakes. Archaeologists devoting two months to field work would have to experiment for years (perhaps on ancient wrecks!) before reaching the same degree of proficiency. Since the controlled excavation of a buried wreck-formation is more difficult than the salvage of a modern ship, it is evident that both kinds of specialist should collaborate.

Even when this ideal collaboration exists it is essential that the techniques that have been used should be recorded in detail, for it is only from precedent that satisfactory methods of excavation will eventually be developed.

The word 'diver' is itself misleading, since it covers both professionals and men who have merely learned to use autonomous apparatus. The confusion particularly affects archaeologists, because their finances usually force them to rely on unpaid helpers. At this juncture the Confédération Mondiale des Activités Subaquatiques can be of service. A world confederation with a membership of amateur and professional divers, it is the aim of C.M.A.S. to maintain standards of work. Acting in an advisory capacity, the Confédération can help to resolve some of the problems that beset archaeologists by putting them in touch with competent divers familiar with conditions in specific parts of the Mediterranean.

When methods of marine excavation have been standardized, it will then be possible to increase the proportion of amateur helpers without endangering the efficiency of a 'dig'. It may, however, take some time, and many competent pilot excavations, before this stage is reached.

The varying aims of specific excavations

The most obvious basis for evaluating any kind of research is a clear realization of the researcher's aims. Applied to the following accounts, even this criterion can be confusing. Let us, for example, compare the reports on Antikythera and the Bronze Age ship at Cape Gelidonya. At Antikythera in the early years of this century the very expert Greek sponge-divers were not expected to do more than salvage art treasures. At that time neither archaeologists nor divers had sufficient knowledge of buried wrecks to be able to analyse the site and guess at the preservation of the ship's hull.* This is in contrast with the recent excavation at Gelidonya, where the archaeologists' and indeed (as head diver to the expedition) my own terms of reference most certainly included the reconstruction of the ship as well as of its cargo. Readers may therefore be astonished to see that the result we achieved remained similar to those at Antikythera.

This disappointing state of affairs in no way reflects on the progress of

---

* I dived on Antikythera myself in 1954 and uncovered a portion of the hull which still lies buried in the mud, under 60 m. of water. At this depth, of course, archaeological recording would be out of the question for physiological reasons, but fifty years earlier underwater recording was not even considered in the excavator's terms of reference.

B

underwater archaeology; it is explained by the atypical marine environment of the Bronze Age cargo. The ship had foundered on a rocky bottom, where there was not a sufficient depth of sand, and where the water was not calm enough to produce conditions favourable to preservation. Some scraps of organic matter were fortuitously preserved because they had been pinned under the weight of the cargo itself. The hull must have disintegrated and been washed away a few months after sinking. A basket and some twigs had found chance shelter and had been well preserved, but such morsels of ship's timber as remained on the site were spongy and insignificant. They had not benefited from the kind of sand-burial that usually occurs as soon as a wreck settles on the bottom, and which accounts for the amazing state of preservation of so many classical hulls. Nor, as the twigs and basket demonstrated, did the earlier date of the Bronze Age wreck explain the bad preservation of the other bits of wood on the site. It was the marine environment that was unusual.

So strange was the appearance of this wreck that at first sight I could make neither head nor tail of the place. My preliminary analysis was further complicated by the fact that all the surface finds (reported to me before I arrived on the spot with the expedition) had been removed by looters. Only the ghostly imprints of ingots which had been prised off rocks bore witness to the hand of man—ancient and modern. Knowing from experience that the greater part of an antique cargo is always camouflaged by the sea, I nevertheless persisted in my examination of what seemed to be a natural stretch of bottom: the slightest anomaly might betray the presence of artifacts that had been metamorphosed.

Eventually I distinguished two piles of cargo (weighing approximately 1 ton) incorporated with the bedrock; by chipping off a sample, I confirmed that bronze objects were indeed embedded in the stone-hard concretions. In these circumstances, there could be no digging in the accepted sense. I therefore advocated that the rock-bound cargo should be broken into the largest possible lumps, and that these should be raised and put together again on land. Only in this way would it be possible to reconstruct the relationships of the finds as each one was chiselled free.

Working on the bottom, the usual methods of archaeological recording were out of the question. Artifacts were not only invisible, but the shape of the enclosing concretions (whose position shifted with every break we had to make) bore no relation to their contents. If the finds had been held in sand, they would naturally have been drawn *in situ*; then excavated layer after layer. The draughtsman's grid and other machinery I had designed for this expedition (for a second, Byzantine, wreck which I knew to be buried in sand) were useless on this uneven, rocky bottom.

Early experiments

Other more typical wreck-formations where sand-burial preserved a significant relationship between hull and cargo have already demonstrated certain structural details of Greek and Roman ships. They should yield much more information in the future, for pioneer experiments cannot be taken as conclusive. Keeping excavations in historical perspective, we should remember, for instance, that the Congloué wreck was the first to be dug solely by free-divers. The wreck at Albenga, though it was discovered at about the same time as the Congloué, has only been sounded, and a plan made of the surface layer of cargo. The evidence produced by Dr. Lamboglia from this preliminary work is impressive, but there is every reason to believe that the best is yet to come.

It is no criticism of pioneer free-divers to say that up to now the results of their research have been misleading. To understand why such exceptionally able scientists and free-divers made what we now regard as mistakes, we must imagine what it was like for them to be confronted with a wreck-formation for the first time. When these men saw a few amphorae scattered on the sea-bed they could not possibly have known that these indicated the presence, under the sand, of a complete cargo and a considerable portion of a wooden ship.

To lift the visible amphorae was a natural reaction. This done, pioneers were astonished to see other jars peeping out of the sand below. They had to dig down into the bottom to extricate the second layer, only to find that its removal revealed yet a third layer. At this point they introduced an air-lift* to assist their labours. The hole that was dug became a huge, inverted cone. Since sand only reaches equilibrium underwater on a gentle gradient, it is impossible to cut a trench with vertical walls, as on land.

As the hole got deeper, amphorae went on appearing out of its sides in all directions, so that it had constantly to be enlarged. Every now and then the sides gave way and cargo cascaded downwards. Mud raised by the divers' movements clouded the water, which, being contained within the hole, could not disperse and be cleared by current. In reduced visibility, excavation got out of hand; divers lost control and grabbed what they could where they could. When, at the bottom of the hole, the air-lift eventually came into contact with hull timber, the very force of the machine shattered the waterlogged wood. In any case, portions of structure showing at the narrowest point of an inverted cone would be too small for identification on a photograph or a drawing, even if records could be made in such muddy water.

Since then a comparative knowledge of wreck-formation has been built up and more rational methods of excavation have been evolved. A shallow, sandy

---

* This machine, already well known to standard-apparatus divers, works like a powerful underwater vacuum-cleaner.

tumulus and other abnormalities on the sea-bed can now be interpreted by an expert as indications of a buried wreck. He can also estimate the extent and limits of this wreck under the sand without digging a hole. Once the significant area has been established, it follows that he will isolate the wreck, raising it above the level of the surrounding bottom by means of a peripheral trench. The air-lift, which has such devastating effects when used on finds, is ideally suited for trenching in virgin ground. When part of a wreck is free standing, its contents can be recorded and then removed in layers.

Hard lessons, learned at the expense of a certain amount of destruction, must now be put to use by pilot excavations undertaken jointly by archaeologists and expert divers.

The time element: its importance in uninterrupted excavation

Time and continuity are important factors in marine excavation. On the large Congloué wreck work lasted, almost without interruption, for eight years. Despite the length of this campaign and the number of divers who worked in teams, portions of cargo and hull still remain on the bottom. On other wrecks, such as the Titan, excavation aims were deliberately restricted to finding the answers to a limited number of specific questions. Available funds are bound to restrict the archaeologist's aims, but brief or intermittent excavation is of necessity destructive. This is because a wreck, when it settles on the bottom, is metamorphosed, and within a relatively short period of time becomes a stable geological formation. If this natural stability is not upset, wrecks will be preserved almost indefinitely. If, on the contrary, the geological balance is disturbed, decay sets in immediately. Digging causes a cargo to shift, while, as Dr. Roghi discovered, freshly exposed organic matter soon disappears.

Harbour excavation

For more obvious reasons, the effectiveness of shallow-water excavation is also related to the duration of a campaign. The size of ancient harbours and their functional unity impose lengthy, though not necessarily continuous, work. In the Bronze Age, before men learned how to build walls underwater, harbours were made by cutting into and adapting offshore reefs and islands. Being dictated by local geography, the resulting structures could, and frequently do, stretch over 5 km. Their size alone would make aerial photography a necessary preliminary to excavation; its uses, however, are more than topographical. Hydrographic factors (which before the invention of dredging were of paramount importance in harbour design), the almost inevitable overbuilding of later date, and, finally, the silting that occurred when installations fell into disuse are a few of the problems discussed in Père Poidebard's excellent reports. His prolonged labours at Tyre and Sidon are of unique value to archaeologists wishing to embark on similar research.

I have no personal experience of ancient harbours, but as a diver I must stress the distinction between the two phases in shallow-water work—namely, *survey* and *excavation*. After aerial photography has shown the extent and nature of submerged installations, architectural survey can begin. In shallow water, *surveying* will be no more than an extension of methods used on land; it will present no insuperable difficulties to inexperienced divers.

The second phase covers both the *excavation* of silted constructions and, in certain areas, of artifacts within the sand of the bottom. In some places, therefore, the *depth* of burial of a sherd or a lost anchor has the same kind of significance as on land: they are stratified.

Submarine stratification

Large and ill-defined stretches of bottom, however, can neither be trenched, as on land, nor examined in layers in the same way as a compact wreck-formation. They constitute a new technical problem. Nor is there any standard method of removing silt from architectural remains, for digging in shallow water (where lack of depth makes air-lifts less efficient) is very different from digging in deep water. Dredging is the current method of excavating harbours, but a more controlled and less costly alternative will have to be devised to meet archaeological requirements. Naval and industrial engineers overcome greater difficulties in the normal course of their work, but they are never consulted on archaeological matters.

Evidence of ancient trade routes: a new category of site

The reports in this book show that during the past sixty years submarine arch-aeology has been restricted to wrecks and harbours, but divers in Mediterranean waters have long been familiar with other kinds of sites. When archaeologists are able to recognize such places and appreciate their significance their excavation will yield new evidence, complementary to wreck and harbour research. I refer to the various kinds of offshore mooring.

Antique anchors of differing periods are found in quantity on certain reefs and shallows out to sea. They mark places where sailing ships moored when the wind fluctuated, and where they had to wait until it again turned to a favourable direction. If these sites were charted and the lost anchors dated we would gain valuable information about early sea-lanes and methods of navigation.

Another type of site that has so far escaped attention is the provisional shelter. Storms in antiquity would drive ships into bays, where their stops are still marked on the bottom by sherds and other ancient refuse. Beer bottles and tins mark the anchorage of a modern steamer in much the same way. Some of these sheltered coves may also have been used as bases for trading with the hinterland. The remains now visible at such places may have been dragged out of the sand by modern fishermen's nets or anchors, but it is important to remember that, in sheltered conditions, ancient artifacts will normally be stratified in the bottom. No such offshore mooring has been excavated, so no method of examining stratification has yet been devised, but once the problem is set its solution should not be beyond human ingenuity.

Unfortunately, there is a real danger that both offshore anchorages and sheltered moorings may be destroyed before a single one is properly excavated. Ever-growing hordes of tourists, divers for pleasure, and amateur archaeologists lift any artifact they notice underwater; even if these finds are presented to a local museum, their significance is diminished because they are out of context. Further, once all surface marks have been removed, archaeologists with a better understanding of marine problems will be unable to find the spot again.

Conclusion

Readers of this book may feel that marine archaeologists must belong to one of two schools: the optimistic, who, in the face of immense and quite evident technical problems, claim that there is no difficulty at all; and the pessimistic, who, faced with the same problems, consider that there is not (and probably never can be) any solution to the difficulties. To both it should be brought home that many problems that daunt the diving archaeologist have already been solved by professional divers working in controlled or experimental conditions. Thus the crippling limitation of working time on the bottom is already being overcome by the use of submarine 'houses', while depth itself is being conquered by the exploitation of lighter gases that can be substituted for compressed air. In this sense, excavation problems are becoming not so much technical as economic, since most innovations are as yet the prerogative of professional divers, and their use involves vast expenditure on equipment and the suitable training of personnel.

The inevitable difficulties attendant on the birth of submarine archaeology do not detract from the ultimate importance of this new form of research. Everyone is now aware of the treasures to be found on the sea-bed. However, such is the progress of diving proper that there is a risk that it may outstrip its practical application to archaeological excavation. Meanwhile, the most inexpert wearer of an aqualung wields considerable power for good or evil in relation to antiquities. The situation is a familiar one, for there are many other ways in which science has provided man with dangerous powers even over nature itself. It is, for instance, possible to divert currents and change the climate by melting polar ice, but were this to be done the sea-level might rise to such an extent that many capital cities would be flooded! The scientist's present duty is not so much to exercise his power, but to continue to investigate the balance of natural forces and get a better understanding of the way in which they work.

Anyone who has a taste for it can wrench antiquities from the sea-bed, but if such persons are not to destroy the thing they love they must first get down to the humbler tasks of charting, of making a comparative study of marine sites, and of keeping abreast with technical progress, by seeking the advice of appropriate experts in underwater work. Only in this way will excavation not be accompanied by destruction.

2

Mediterranean Trade

Off the coast of Provence at least twenty wrecks have been confirmed and in-spected,[1] in spite of the diving limit being only 40 m. Their excavation would necessitate the use of the elaborate techniques experimented with at Mahdia, Albenga, Grand Congloué, and Île du Levant, for they are covered in sand, mud, and marine concretions; but a methodical examination would yield new informa-tion for the history of trade, as well as of marine construction. On land sites amphorae have commonly served for secondary domestic or funerary purposes, but on board a wreck a whole collection will be in use for the first time as cargo containers and so establish the date.

The amount of information yielded by an underwater excavation is not com-parable to that obtained from land sites, since the objects found on the latter are seldom intact, and come from many sources. The principal cargoes consisted of wine, but amphorae also served as containers for pickled fish (portions of tunny on the Île du Levant wreck), olives (Cap Dramont), almonds, nuts, and even lime. Several ships also carried pottery (Etruscan, Campanian, or Late Roman) and have provided lamps or coins—important dating material. Since all objects on board a wreck must have been in contemporaneous use, there is obviously an urgent need for exhaustive excavation to reassemble them in their entirety.

Amphorae

Most of the amphora wrecks belong to the end of the Republican era, when the export trade in wine from south Italy to Gaul was at its height, but they cover a period extending from the sixth century B.C. (the Etruscan and Massaliote am-phorae of Fig. I.I) to Late Roman times—for example, the wrecks at Anse St. Roch, near Antibes, and at Cap Roux.

The synchronism of different types of whole amphorae in the same wreck permits a more precise dating and typology than was made by Dressel in *Corpus*

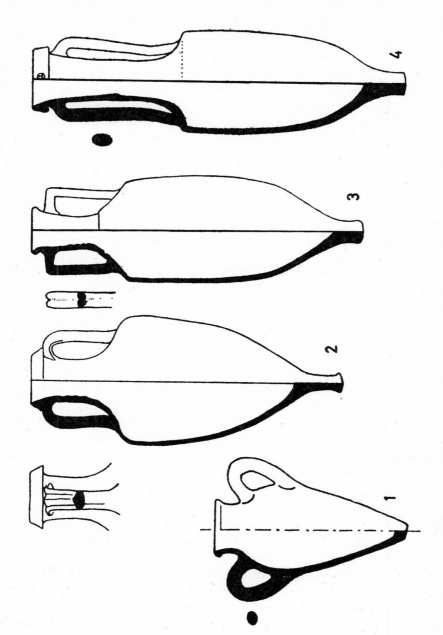

FIG. 1. 1. Etruscan amphora; 2. Republican I, Graeco-Italic amphora;
3. Republican II amphora with rounded lip; 4. Republican III, Italic amphora. Dressel 1A
Scale 1 : 10

Inscriptionum Latinorum, XV (1899), from the excavation of land sites (Fig. 2). This catalogue was based mainly on material from the camps of the *Limes Germanicus* (the Roman frontier lines running from Bonn to Regensburg), whereas the typology derived from underwater excavation applies to the trade expansion of Italy after the Second Punic War.

Moreover, since certain types are missing from the Dressel catalogue, it is necessary not only to establish a new typology to simplify his classification and date it more precisely, but to add a pre-Roman series containing some types unknown to him.[2] Preceding Dressel 1, abundantly represented on land sites of the first century B.C., there is now a Republican series of amphorae in the Greek tradition, but of the Roman period, comprising:

Republican I. This Graeco-Italic amphora type is transitional between the round-shouldered Greek in the shape of a top and the Italo-Roman with angular shoulder (Dressel 1). It is known from the towns (*oppida*) in the western Mediterranean of the third to first centuries B.C., such as Magalas, Ensérune, Pennes-Mirabeau, and Genoa, and has been found at sea in wrecks at Grand Congloué, off Marseilles (Fig. 1.2), Anthéor, La Ciotat, and the Lavezzi Islands of Corsica, and elsewhere.[3]

Republican II. This type of amphora, with rounded lip, is in the true Greek tradition, and has plain or double handles (Dressel 2–3, Fig. 1.3). The oldest examples, about 95 cm. high, have been found on the Genoa-Pegli wreck, associated with Campanian pottery, and the latest come from such *Limes* camps as Augst, Oberaden, and Mandeure.[4] One place of origin seems to be in the region of Pompeii, if one can attribute to this type the double amphora handles of Alesia, Carthage, and Ampurias with the name of *L. Eumachus*, of the middle of the first century B.C.

Republican III. This Italic type amphora with a folded rim, either oblique or vertical, some 110–20 cm. high, was known on the Rhine in the middle of the first century B.C. (Dressel 1), but had a prototype which did not exceed 1 m. in height and contained about 19 litres. An example of the latter is the specimen bearing the name of *Sestius* from the 'deposit' of the Grand Congloué (Fig. 1.4). It is necessary, therefore, to subdivide Dressel I into A and B.[5]

The excellent state of preservation of these amphorae draws attention to the relatively high proportion of stamps, these being very rare in land excavations before the second century B.C.; the same amphora may bear two different stamps, on the rim and on the handle, quite apart from that impressed on the surface of the clay stopper.

It is not established whether these stamps indicate the name of the potter, producer, or exporter, but their varied placing demonstrates that it would be too simple a solution to attribute them uniformly to the potter.[6]

The wreck of La Ciotat contained Graeco-Italic amphorae (Republican I), which enabled us to date the terracotta slipper-bath found among the cargo, and yielded a great number of stamps on the shoulder or at the attachment of the

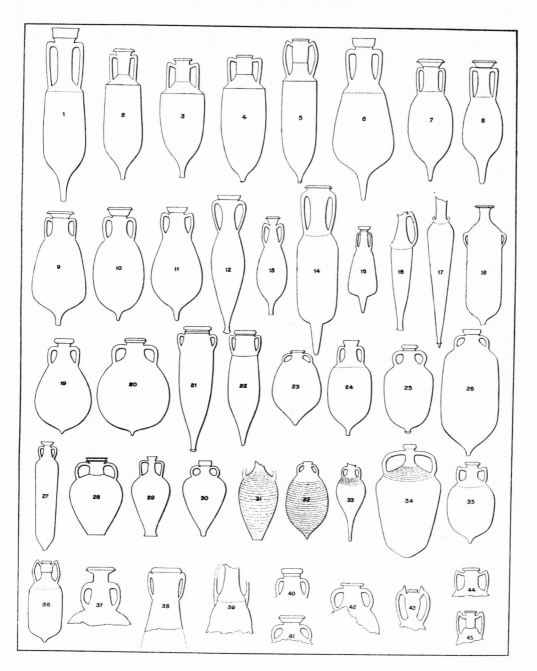

FIG. 2. Table of Dressel amphora types
(*Corp. Inscr. Lat.* XV)

handle: *Bal*(*bus*), *Dec*(*ember*) or *Dec*(*ens*), *Sal*(*vius*), [*V*]*ar*(*us*) or [*C*]*ar*(*us*), *Sato*(?).
These certainly represent an incomplete series which, it is to be hoped, can be
increased from examples dispersed by looters.

The Dramont wreck, containing Italic amphorae from 1·15 to 1·26 m. high
(Dressel 1B), is astonishingly rich epigraphically. Some amphorae bear two different
stamps, one on the lip and one on the shoulder. It had not been possible to establish this combination of two different stamps on one amphora from material from
land excavations. The Dramont stamps are: *Bac*(*chius*), *Eutac*(*tus*), *Onel*(*lus*),
Heracli(*us*), *Pilip*(*us*), *Herm*(*a* or *es*), *Dam*(*a* or *es*), *Moc*(*conus*). The same
piece sometimes associates different marks on the lip and on the shoulder, alternating the position and the coupling. *Pilip*(*us*) is reproduced twice on one amphora,
but on other examples is associated with *Dam*(*a*) or *Herm*(*a*), and *Bac*(*chius*) is
associated with *Eutac*(*tus*) and *Onel*(*lus*). Moreover, several stamps from the
Dramont wreck carrying different names are associated with a square counter-
mark 'S', followed by an anchor without a stock—a combination which is found
only on the lips of amphorae.

If the ships of Dramont and La Ciotat each contain amphorae of the same
type, but bearing different stamps, there is no reason to see in these stamps either
the name of the potter or that of the exporter. No doubt they indicate the names of
associated wine-producers who have displayed both their marks at Dramont, on
the lips and on the shoulders of amphorae—producers whose family names are
found on Campanian inscriptions at Capua, Pompeii, Herculaneum, Pozzuoli,
Naples, Misenum, Terracina, and so on. But the countermark 'S' followed by
an anchor on the neck of the Dramont amphorae, associated with stamps of
different producers, has another significance: perhaps it is the mark of a 'whole-
saler' or middleman. In this case, if one takes into account the symbol, it represents
perhaps the exporter who had purchased, direct from the press on the estate, the
harvest of several landowners of the region, and who had prepared the 'packaging'
at the pottery for its disposal on the Gaulish market.

It seems probable that this would be the meaning of the symbolic anchor or
trident associated with the name of Sestius on the Italic amphorae (Dressel type
1A) of the Grand Congloué wreck. In this group the majority—more than 1,000
examples—carry the name of *Sestius* abridged to three letters SES, followed exclusively by the sign of an anchor or trident. Seven examples bear the mark
DAV. ATEC stamped on the shoulder, doubtless the name of the producer, followed
by that of his slave, vine-grower, or potter—that is, *D*(*ecimus*), *Au*(*fidius*) or
Ar(*ilius*), *Atec*(*hnos*?). The latter is a contemptuous surname which might well
belong to the Greek slave on the estate, associated with the proprietor. Even so,
certain amphorae marked with the stamp *Sestius* retained their clay stoppers,
stamped with the name *L. Titius C*(*aii*) *f*(*ilius*), producer or vine-grower, whose
function must therefore be different from that of *Sestius*.[7] The presence of a

'symbol' impressed after the name *Sestius* on the same stamp is an anomaly in the repertory of the Roman marks before the second century B.C. These stamps follow, not a Roman, but a hellenic tradition, exemplified by the regular occurrence of a sign associated with a name on the amphora stamps of Rhodes, Thasos, Cnidos, Cos, and elsewhere in the third and second centuries B.C.

The firm of *Sestius* is the most important known to us, his stamp having been found in thirteen land and three underwater excavations, not only on the coast of Provence, but at Cosa in Etruria, at Ventimilia, at Vada Sabatia, in Liguria, at Nîmes, old Toulouse, Ruscino, and in the Rhodanian region at Nyons, Alesia, Mont Beuvray, Basle, and Besançon.

The trade mark is also the richest in scribal variations on the name which sometimes consists of four letters, the T being linked to the s(SEST) or to the E(SETS), and in the symbols. These include the anchor (the trident is only represented on the Grand Congloué wreck), and also new signs—the cadeceus, a star with five or eight points, palmettes, crowns, double axes or perhaps a hatchet—all signs which figure equally on the stamps of Rhodes, Cos, Cnidos, and Thasos.

If the firm of *Sestius* originated in the south of Italy, like that of all the wine-producers exporting to Gaul at the end of the Republican period, it follows a hellenic tradition, which would account for the presence of the two signatories on the Italic amphorae of the Grand Congloué wreck among the *Romaioi* of Delos in the second century B.C., *Marcos Sestios* of Frégelles in southern Latium and *Dekmos Aufidios* or *Avilios*.[8]

Since the excavations are unfinished, this can only be a hypothesis, but it is supported by the presence in the wreck of Rhodian amphorae bearing marks known in Delos about 180 B.C., fragments of so-called Megarian bowls with hellenistic reliefs and a large quantity of Campanian pottery belonging to the first half of the second century.

The typological and epigraphic variety of the mark of Sestius implies a 'long chronology': it existed during several decades, and it is to the successors of the Sestius of the Grand Congloué wreck that the stamped amphorae of this name, found on sites of the first century at Basle, old Toulouse, Alesia, and Besançon, must be attributed. Only such an assumption can explain the anomaly of the survival, into the middle of the first century B.C., of a stamp bearing a symbol unique in the epigraphy of amphorae of the Republican period.

Ship construction and tonnage

The salvage of the boat itself poses a complex problem of clearing and raising, of conservation of the wood in a laboratory equipped for that purpose, and of recording, which is far more difficult to resolve than in land excavations, where much less equipment and fewer laboratories and archaeological stores are required.

Parts of the keel and ribs from the wrecks of Grand Congloué and Île du Levant (Titan) have been brought to the surface by Commandants J.-Y. Cousteau and Philippe Tailliez with the aid of the French Navy. The two wrecks are of different types and date (the first belongs to the second century, the second to the mid-first century B.C.) and have yielded, in spite of their bad state of preservation and the dismembering of the sections, the first evidence which we have for the construction and loading of a merchant ship. They show, in comparison with the pontoon-ships of Lake Nemi,[9] a tradition of technical construction which continued from the hellenistic period until Imperial times. Before this, the only records consisted of illustrations (bas-reliefs, mosaics, frescoes)[10] which had no scale and gave no indication of the shape of the ship's hull below the waterline, and some rare literary and epigraphic texts.[11] Most important is the regulation for the port of Thasos of the third century B.C. In order to prevent crowding, the shore was reserved for the beaching of large merchant vessels of more than 3,000 and 5,000 talents—some 78–130 tons weight—the smaller ships being obliged to moor in the port.[12] These figures correspond to those given by Herodotus, Cicero, Pliny, etc.; the vessels of a tonnage of 10,000 amphorae (260 tons) mentioned by Strabo seem to be exceptional. The law of 218 B.C. limited the size of the merchant ships armed by the Senate to a tonnage of 3,000 amphorae.

It can be seen how interesting the salvage of a merchant ship with its complete cargo and timbers would be, allowing its dimensions and tonnage to be calculated and its loading to be studied. From the first two wrecks, the Grand Congloué and Île du Levant (Titan), of which some timbers have been raised, only a part of the very flat-bottomed hull remained, the sides having entirely disappeared from above the angle of the ribs. The length of the section of keel raised, including the ends of the attached ribs, did not in fact exceed 2 m. for the first and 10 m. for the second. These sections of the hull cannot, therefore, give us any indication of the shape of the vessel either longitudinally (had the ship a symmetrical or asymmetrical bow and stern?) or of the transverse section. It is usually accepted that the length of the keel equals about three-quarters that of the ship, including stem and stern, and the width one-quarter, if not more, than the total length taken at deck-level.[13] Such indications as we have, however, are of great interest for the method of construction, and can usefully be compared with the evidence furnished by the Nemi vessels and the remains of ships found at Marseilles, in Italy, and in London.

Although the frame of the Grand Congloué ship (Fig. 23), like, no doubt, that of Mahdia, had only one keel (section: 17 cm. high, 12 cm. wide), to which the ribs were articulated separately, supported by strong triangular floor timbers which ensured the transverse rigidity of the bottom, the keel of the Île du Levant ship (Fig. 35), 22 cm. high by 19·5 cm. wide, was doubled by a counter-keel or keelson. The ribs were made up of single crosspieces fitted into the lower part of the keelson. This was the type of construction of 'Caesar's Galley', the best-preserved wreck from Marseilles, extracted from the mud of the Lacydon.[14] The absence of bottom prevents our knowing if the main keel was supplemented by secondary or 'bilge' keels which reinforced, longitudinally, the rigidity of the hull below the waterline—as, for example, in the ships of Nemi, and as has been suggested for the reconstruction of the flat-bottomed ships of the Veneti.[15]

The hull of the first ship was sheathed with lead as a protection against the boring of the teredo worm, as were also the wrecks of Albenga and Mahdia; lead sheathing was, no doubt, used as part of boat-building techniques on the Nemi ships, though this protection would be unnecessary in the fresh water of the lake, which is free of wood-boring worms.

The planks, none of which is thicker than 4–6 cm., were assembled in the manner common in the Greek and Roman periods—that is, the planks were caulked and joined, edge to edge, by tenons dowelled into mortices. This type of carvel building preceded clinker building, characterized by the overlapping of the planks, which was to appear with the *drakkars* of the Vikings. The nails, of pure copper, were of appropriate size to the thickness of the pieces to be joined, from the tacks with broad, flat heads for fixing the sheathing of lead to the great copper nails, sometimes more than 25 cm. long, which were riveted at the ends and driven into the oak dowels, so passing through ribs, planks, and knees.

These underwater deposits and the examination of the wrecks along the coast have also yielded pieces of the rigging, some of which it has not been possible to identify. All are of lead, which is the only metal used for equipment so far found on the wrecks: anchor stocks with square socket for the wooden shank (the earliest example comes from the Etruscan wreck at Antibes of the sixth century B.C.), and junction pieces for the flukes[16] of the types shown on a red-figure vase from Kertch;[17] brailing rings sometimes have a lug pierced by one or two holes for the lines used in handling the sails; pipes, net-sinkers, and large weights with a loop (*catapirates*, leads for sounding lines); square boxes of lead, lined with oak, and crucibles in the form of conical mortars similar to the type from Albenga, but having a loop at the base, or else holes for fixing, as in the examples from Grand Congloué and Île du Levant.

Paintings and mosaics are incapable of giving an explanation of these pieces of rigging,[18] which cannot be identified until their position is exactly established on the wreck and it becomes possible to compare them with their modern counterparts. The scientific importance of the methodical uncovering of a ship on the grid system is clear. In spite of the difficulties inherent in the disturbance of the site and its occasional dispersal on a sloping bottom, this must be done by methods learned from land sites, with technical methods adapted for an underwater excavation.

NOTES

Chapter 2 is a translation, by permission of M. Fernand Benoit, of his paper, 'Premier résultat des fouilles sous-marines. Typologie des amphores et construction navale', published in *Actes du Congrés des Sociétés Savantes*, Aix-en-Provence (1958).

1 F. Benoit, 'L'archéologie sous-marine en Provence', in *Rivista di Studi Liguri*, 18 (1952), 237–307; 'Épaves de la côte de Provence. Typologie des amphores', in *Gallia*, XIV (1956), 23–34; and 'Nouvelles épaves de Provence', in *Gallia*, XVI (1958), 5–39.

2 N. Lamboglia, 'Sulla cronologia delle anfore romane di età repubblicana', in *Rivista di Studi Liguri*, 21 (1955), 241–70, and F. Benoit, 'Typologie et épigraphie amphoriques', in ibid., 23 (1957), 247ff.

3 F. Benoit, 'Amphores et céramiques de l'épave de Marseille', in *Gallia*, XII (1954), 37, Fig. 2, Series III, and XIV (1956), 25, Nos. 21–2.

4 *Gallia*, XIV (1956), 24, Nos. 6–10.

5 'Typologie', in *Rivista di Studi Liguri*, 23 (1957), 247ff.

6 E. L. Will, 'Les amphores de Sestius', in *Revue Archéologique de l'Est* (Dijon), VII (1956), 241; cf. F. Benoit, 'Typologie et épigraphie amphoriques', loc. cit.

7 Cf. F. Benoit in *Gallia*, XI (1953), 105, and XII (1954), 35–54.

8 J. Hatzfeld, 'Les Italiens résidant à Délos', in *Bulletin de Correspondence hellénique*, 1912, 19 and 77.

9 G. Ucelli, *Le navi di Nemi* (1950).

10 Cf. Commandant Lefebvre de Noëttes, *De la marine antique à la marine moderne* (1935), 67–87; J. Hornell, *Water Transport* (Cambridge, 1946); P. M. Duval, 'La forme des navires romains dans la mosaïque d'Althiburus', in *Mélanges d'Arch. et d'Histoire*, 61 (1949), 119–49.

11 Cf. F. Miltner, 'Seewesen', in *R.E.*, Suppl. (1931), 921–2.

12 M. Launcy, 'Inscriptions de Thasos', in *Bulletin de Correspondence hellénique*, 57 (1933), 395; cf. H. de Saussure, 'De la marine antique à la marine moderne', in *Revue archéologique* (1937), II, 90–103; L. Casson, 'The Isis and Her Voyage', in *Transactions of the American Philological Association*, 81 (1950), 43–56, and, by the same author, 'The Size of Ancient Merchant Ships', in *Studi in onore di Ar. Calderini e R. Paribeni* (Milan), I (1956), 231–8.

13 This report of a quarter is based on the description of the *Isis* (Lucian, *Navigum*, 5), and cannot be taken as reliable; cf. the 'navire du Musée des Thermes', J. le Gall in *Rev. Arch.* (Mél. Ch. Picard, 1948), II, 609.

14 The preserved length of the keel is about 3·8 m.: M. Clerc, *Massilia*, II (1929), 173, Fig. 2. Now dismantled in the store of the Musée Borély.

15 Cf. Commandant Y. Creston, 'Considérations techniques sur la flotte des Vénètes et des Romains', in *Annales de Brétagne* (Rennes, 1956), 92.

16 F. Benoit, 'Jas d'ancre,' in *Rivista di Studi Liguri*, 21 (1955), 11.

17 Mladen Nikolanei, 'Quelques objets et monuments maritimes de la Dalmatie centrale', in *Vjesnik* (Split), 55 (1953), 170, Fig. 4.

18 But see the interpretation of a *roue de manœuvre* on the Albenga wreck with the aid of a mosaic from Sousse (N. Lamboglia, 'La nave romana d'Albenga', in *Rivista di Studi Liguri*, 18 (1952), 195, Fig. 48), and of the sounding-lead from a mosaic at Themetra (L. Foucher, 'Navires et barques', in *Notes et Documents*, XV (Musée Alaoui, 1957), 13 and Fig. 4).

For more recent studies on amphorae see:

F. Benoit, 'Amphores grecques d'origines ou de provenance Marseillaise', in *Rivista di Studi Liguri*, 21 (1955), 32ff.

Martin Almagro, *Las necrópolis de Ampurias*, 2 vols. (Barcelona, 1953–5).

Otto Uenze, *Frührömische amphoren aus Zeitmarken in Spätlatènezeit* (Marburg, 1958).

E. B. Zeest, *Pottery Containers from the Bosphoros*, Materials and Studies in Archaeology in the U.S.S.R., No. 83 (Moscow, 1960) (in Russian).

V. R. Grace, *Amphoras and the Ancient Wine Trade*, American School of Classical Studies at Athens; Excavations at the Athenian Agora; Picture Book No. 6 (1961).

C

3

Some Notable Wreck
Excavations

In the past sponge-divers have brought to the surface several notable pieces of sculpture, such as the Bronze Boy from Marathon, the Zeus from Artemision, and, more recently, the Demeter recovered from one of their trawls off the Turkish coast. The positions of ancient wrecks carrying such treasure have become known, but only in a few cases has a deliberate attempt been made to raise the cargo.

The following reports have been chosen to show what has so far been achieved in the excavation of wrecks by divers, sometimes with the assistance of archaeologists, but only in the last case with an archaeologist actually diving.

The salvage of the sculptures from Antikythera and Mahdia at the beginning of the century is a classic story, but further discoveries and subsequent exploration, as well as further study of the objects, have added new information. At Albenga in 1945 the first attempt was made to recover objects from a cargo-boat carrying amphorae. This was followed by the extensive salvage operations by Commandant Cousteau's team on the mixed cargo of pottery and amphorae at Grand Congloué in 1952, on which work still continues. In 1958 Commandant Tailliez, while in command of G.E.R.S. in Toulon, worked on the wreck at Titan (Île du Levant), with Service divers, as part of a training programme. Though partly looted, a method of planning and recording for the remainder of the cargo was organized. When the amphorae were cleared the keel was found in position. This was carefully recorded and sections brought up for study and reconstruction.

On the Dramont wreck in 1959 M. Dumas attempted to cut a section across a cargo of amphorae down to the hull and to demonstrate the method of loading. In 1958–9 Professor Nino Lamboglia and Dr. Gianni Roghi set out to develop a method of recording an amphora wreck in detail, using grid squares: part of the cargo has been raised, but the experiment is not yet complete.

The Bronze Age ship from Cape Gelidonya, excavated in 1960, was not typical of a well-preserved ancient wreck, which is usually found embedded in silt. The find consisted of a cargo of copper ingots which had sunk on a rocky platform, and all that remained of the ship was held down by the weight of metal and the subsequent growth of marine concretion. But for the first time a joint archaeological and diving team worked together.

(*a*) Antikythera

This was the first cargo from an ancient ship for which a deliberate attempt was made to salvage the objects. It was accidentally found by Symiote sponge-fishers returning from North Africa. The position of the wreck is about one hour's distance from the principal roadstead of the island (Livadia), near the place called Pinakakia (Fig. 3). It lies some 25 m. offshore at 25–34 fathoms. Professor Karo tells the story:[1]

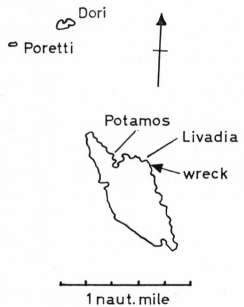

FIG. 3.   Map showing position of Antikythera wreck

'The Aeginetan *sphoungarades* have a good name, but those most renowned for their skill and daring hail from the small island of Syme in the Dodecanese, now at last happily reunited with Greece. Such men are heroes, and as such die young; their exploits are told, suitably embellished, in the seaside taverns where fishermen congregate. And their code of honour and courage is high.

'Shortly before Easter, 1900, such a Symiote crew left the Tunisian waters for home in two *caiques*—cutters which, in size, shape, and equipment, hardly differ from similar craft that have plied the Mediterranean for the last 3,000 or 4,000 years. (The revolutionary innovation of outboard motors was not to reach the Aegean for another quarter of a century.) There were six divers and a complement of twenty-two oarsmen for calm days, when sails would be useless.

'A gale drove the Symiotes off their course to the barren, almost uninhabited islet of Antikythera (or Cerigotto, in the Italian lingua franca of the Mediterranean). As they lay some 25 yds. off the headland which borders the little harbour of the island they thought they might as well look for sponges on the rocky bottom. When they got down, one of the divers, Elias Stadiatis, to his great amazement, sighted the remains of a large ship and an enormous heap of bronze and marble figures and various other objects, at a depth of about 9 fathoms. To prove that he was not romancing, he brought up a bronze arm larger than life.

'The skipper, Demetrios Kondos, himself an old master-diver, promptly corroborated this stunning discovery. Then he took some measurements and sailed home to Syme. After prolonged consultation with the notables of the island, he decided to go to Athens and inform the Greek Government, taking Stadiatis and the bronze arm along. There an agreement was reached, which gave the sponge-fishers adequate compensation for the treasures they might recover and hand over. A vessel of the Hellenic Navy, with the necessary machinery for hauling up heavy weights, was to assist them in their difficult task. A government archaeologist would be on board.

'Delays ensued. When operations at last began towards the end of November, stormy weather put a stop to them after only three hours, and similar aggravating interruptions occurred after every fresh attempt. So the work dragged on for nine months in those peculiarly unfavourable waters. Only six divers were available, and they could not bear the strain of diving more than twice a day. Nor could they work for longer than five minutes on the sea-floor with the very primitive equipment at their disposal: thus their collective efforts only amounted to one hour's work a day.

'And what work it was. Standing insecurely on the slanting bottom, they had to dig and scrape the sculptures out of sand and mud, tie stiff, wet ropes around slimy, slippery bodies of bronze and marble, knot them firmly and return to the surface, breathless and exhausted, while the crane of the attendant ship wound up the load. If a rope slipped, at best a day's work would be lost; but the statue might also roll into deep, inaccessible water, and the recoil of the rope could be very dangerous. Under such conditions, it seems almost miraculous that during those three hours of the first day's work a life-size bronze head, two large marble statues, and several smaller objects were recovered.

'This unique archaeological enterprise was doggedly carried on by fits and starts, with incessant interruptions by storms, extraordinary technical difficulties, and the growing exhaustion of the divers. Some days proved rich in results; then a long, disheartening, sterile spell would follow. Much time was lost in clearing away fallen rocks in the hope of precious finds under them, and in digging through hard, silt-encrusted shale. Such excavations had to be accomplished within a few minutes in the eternal submarine twilight. The weather continued to be vile. After a time, four new divers were added to the small original group, and all worked indefatigably, heroically; two were permanently disabled, and one died.

'Yet these illiterate fishermen, totally ignorant of archaeological techniques, treated the finds with remarkable care and delicacy. I had occasion to examine them very soon after their arrival in Athens, and was amazed at the insignificant amount of recent damage. Not only had the sculptures been handled with evident gentleness, but even pottery and glass vases had been brought up intact. The results filled a long gallery in the National Museum at Athens. The bronzes comprised a splendid nude statue of a young god or hero, larger than life, an excellent work of the fourth century B.C., a couple of fine fifth-century statuettes, and remains of what may have been a group of five or six draped men, hellenistic portraits, of which one head was found the first day [Pl. 1]. All of these must have been looted from some Greek sanctuary—the lead castings under their feet show that they had been torn from stone bases. The missing heads and bodies are undoubtedly still lying on the sea-floor, probably at a depth unattainable by Greek divers.

'The marbles are far less satisfactory. They have nearly all been terribly corroded by sea-water and defaced by encrusted shells. Some are just formless lumps; others have spindly stumps instead of limbs. They look like lepers in advanced stages of the hideous disease [Pl. 1]. They are mostly commercial copies of famous originals, probably made at Athens for the export trade in the last decades B.C. The date is assured by a broken and incomplete bronze instrument [see page 38], for its inscriptions prove it to have been made shortly after 30 B.C. We owe a debt of gratitude to the divers for having carefully collected what must have seemed to them to be insignificant bits of broken metal.

'The discoveries of Antikythera caused a great stir in archaeological and artistic circles; there was a general feeling that the most modern diving equipment should be procured to carry the search into deeper waters. But nothing came of it. The only adequately equipped and manned salvage ship of those happy times— when the Mediterranean sea-floor was not yet littered with wrecks of two world wars—belonged to an Italian company which demanded half of all the expected artistic finds. The Greek Government was forbidden by law to offer works of art as compensation. The negotiations ceased, the initial excitement soon cooled off, and after a few years the sculptures from Antikythera were just a part, and not even the most precious part, of the National Museum's treasures.'

The site of the wreck was again visited by Commandant Cousteau in the *Calypso* in 1953. M. Frédéric Dumas writes:

'During a cruise in the *Calypso* for underwater exploration in Greek waters, we dived on two occasions on the ancient wreck of Antikythera.

'16 August. The island fishermen took us directly to the site. The cliff is practically vertical and continues under water to almost 20 m. in depth. A slope of scree starts from there and ends on sand at a depth of 50 m. This sand forms a step with a gentle slope some 40 m. wide ending in a submarine cliff; this begins at 62 m., and the foot is at some 70 m. Thence there is another gentle slope of sand, which I explored to a depth of 80 m. without finding anything of importance.

'At first sight, there is nothing to indicate the presence of an ancient wreck, but on careful examination of the sand at the foot of the rock-fall some pieces of pottery could be distinguished, and in some places a little digging with the hand revealed more numerous sherds.

'Some 15 m. from the base of the rock-fall a great rock, more or less cylindrical, stands isolated in the sand, with *poseidonia* weed growing on the top. As far as I could judge from the sherds, the wreck lay in the sand at the base of the rock-fall, parallel to the shore of the island. One end was between the isolated rock and the rock-fall, whence the debris extended eastward for a distance of about 40 m. I found no remains among the rocks.

'A young Greek, speaking a little English, who accompanied us, said that the Greeks had dynamited the cliff to bring down a large rock on to the wreck, and that under the rock there was a bronze horse and bronze figures of women and children!

'24 August. We returned to the wreck to make some *sondages* with a portable air-lift. A team of divers found the bodies of two amphorae in the sand. I positioned the air-lift at the edge of the rock-fall, some 2 m. from the last rocks. After finding some fragments of pottery, I struck the hull, perfectly preserved, about 40 cm. under the sand. It is probable that the bottom of the ship is in good order and still contains many small objects in the sand.'

The care with which the sponge-fishers worked is shown by the number of smaller finds which they brought up. These objects, which must have belonged to the equipment of the ship, included four pottery amphorae, four terra-sigillata dishes, Megarian bowls, lagynoi, plain jugs, cooking-pots, and a casserole, a fusiform unguentarium and an alabastron, a lamp, some glass vessels, a gold earring; and the bronze instrument, previously thought to be an astrolabe, but now believed to be the earliest known computer. Two tiles, one of them stamped, may have come from a deck-house. Lead weights and some parts of the ship's timbers were brought up, also a modern iron grapnel.

New studies of several categories of minor objects[2] are being undertaken. The first to appear is Mr. Derek Price's report on the 'computer', with his conclusions as to the nature of the mechanical device and its date[3] (Pl. 2).

For the date of the shipwreck, studies of the amphorae and hellenistic pottery now in progress indicate a date in the second quarter of the first century B.C., with a preference for the early part of the second quarter. This accords with Mr. Price's conclusions.

The purpose of the voyage would seem to have been a commercial shipment of bronze and marble sculpture, which was presumably a single loading at one port. The marbles included a large number of copies and contemporary originals, produced in the same workshop.

The port of origin of the ship and possible source of the sculpture is the Aegean in general, with some possibility of Paros for the marble, or east Greece for the pottery. The final study of the pottery should prove decisive in ascertaining the port of origin.

NOTES

1 This account first appeared in 'Art salvaged from the Sea', *Archaeology*, I (1948), 180. Reports on the Antikythera wreck may be found in the following publications: J. N. Svoronos, *Archeologiki Ephemeris* (1902), cols. 145ff., and 'Die funde von Antikythera', *Das Athener National Museum* (Athens, 1908), I, 1ff.; V. Stais, *The Finds from Antikythera* (1905) (in Greek); Fr. Studnicza, *Archäologischer Anzeiger* (1921), 334ff.; O. Rubensohn, 'Parische Künstler', *Jahrbuch des Deutschen Archäologischen Instituts*, 50 (1935), 60.
2 G. Roger Edwards, 'Hellenistic pottery from the Antikythera wreck', A.I.A. meeting, *American Journal of Archaeology*, 64 (1960), 183.
3 Derek Price, 'An Ancient Greek Computer', *Scientific American* (June 1959).

(b) Mahdia

The discovery and study of the wreck at Mahdia was the most brilliant early success of underwater archaeology, resulting as it did in the recovery of a cargo of works of art.

It was in 1907, three miles out from Mahdia (Fig. 4), that Greek divers exploring the depths for sponges found a pile of columns and blocks of marble lying on the bottom of the sea at a depth of 39 m. The columns were laid out in parallel rows in six main groups, forming an outline like that of a ship. Searching among the columns, the divers discovered pieces of sculpture, which they brought up and offered for sale, and it was the sudden appearance of ancient statues in the markets of Tunisia that aroused the suspicions of the authorities. The Director of Antiquities, at that time M. Alfred Merlin, asked the Navy to carry out an examination, using divers. Then, with the help of rich patrons, the Administration organized five very costly campaigns, each of two to three months' duration, between 1908 and 1913. The work was carried out by Greek divers, the number varying from four to eight at different times; their combined diving time totalled 1,340 hours.

Work was often interrupted by bad conditions. The position of the wreck

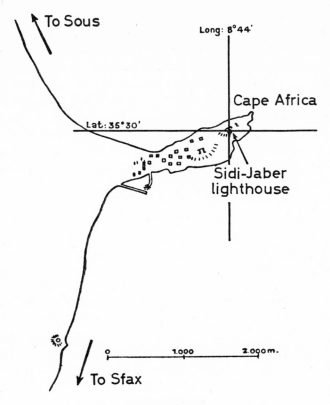

To Sous

Long: 8°44'

Cape Africa

Lat: 35°30'

Sidi-Jaber
lighthouse

0   1.000   2.000 m.

To Sfax

FIG. 4.   Map of Mahdia Peninsula
(Tailliez. *Nouvelles Plongées sans câble*)

offered no protection against the swell, the current sometimes carried away the
marker buoys, and mud hampered work on the bottom. The excavations were
also made more difficult by the fact that they were directed by people who did not
dive and who had to take decisions on the basis of the vague and ill-informed
reports of the Greek divers. At that time decompression tables were not yet
known, and several accidents are recorded.

At the same time as the divers were working on the surface of the deposit, with
the help of the Supervisor of Buoys of the Public Works Department, they went
ahead with raising some of the columns and searching the mud thus disturbed.
At the time M. Alfred Merlin was able to write: 'Digging under the columns . . .
it was not long before we came upon a layer of wood about 20 cm. thick. . . . Then,
once we were through that, we found some delicate trinkets; fine bronze statuettes,
fragments of marble with charming reliefs . . . the layer of wood may have once
been the deck of the ship. The columns and some more fragile material had rested

40

on this floor. . . . Between decks had been the smaller and more precious goods; the hold was full of works of art of metal or of marble.'

Towards the end of the work discoveries became less frequent and the divers claimed that they had reached the keel, after having gone through several layers of wood and penetrated deeply into the mud.

The marble columns lying in the mud, from which they protruded slightly, were protected where the mud covered them, but the uncovered remainder was badly eroded by boring algae and lithodomes (stone-borers).

The finds from Mahdia may be seen in six rooms of the very fine Alaoui Museum in Tunisia. In particular, one may see there a magnificent bronze statue of a young man personifying Agon the spirit of games (Pl. 3) and a 'Herm' of Dionysius, with a long beard and fine features, both signed by the famous sculptor, Boëthos the Chalcedonian. Two fine bronze cornices which were surmounted by busts of Dionysius and of Ariadne (Pl. 5) must have decorated a votive offering in the form of the prow of a ship. There were also small bronze statues and some less well-preserved marbles—busts of Aphrodite, Pan, satyrs—and some statuettes.

The cargo also contained the remains of several bedsteads, which it was possible to reconstruct, and all kinds of inlaid work, candelabra, and two-handled kraters as tall as a man, decorated with Bacchic scenes (Pl. 4).

Inspired works of the finest Greek art were brought up in profusion, alongside neo-Attic examples already showing signs of decadence. Solomon Reinach said that 'no such remarkable discoveries have been made since those of Pompeii and Herculaneum'.

The examination of the inscriptions on the lead ingots, amphorae (Pl. 6), and oil lamps led to the supposition that the wreck was that of a Roman ship carrying from Athens, doubtless to Rome, a cargo ordered by Sulla four or five years after his victory over Mithradates in the year 86 B.C. The correctness of this hypothesis has never been definitely established.

The position of the four lead anchors, found more or less in line a few metres south of the wreck, led M. Merlin to suppose that they had been dropped as the ship foundered. But the anchors were only a short distance from the bow, nearer than one would normally expect, since the chain or hawser holding the anchor is always stretched by the current to a greater distance than this. If the ship had dropped her anchors they would have been found at least 60 m. from the wreck. When the ship foundered, the anchors must therefore have been on board.

It was obvious that the efforts of the Greek divers had not resulted in the re-covery of the whole cargo. The Underwater Study and Research Organization (G.E.R.S.) at Toulon organized an expedition in 1948, directed by Commandant Cousteau and Commandant Tailliez, with the aim of locating the remainder of the wreck and carrying out a preliminary reconnaissance.

After numerous difficulties,* the divers of the organization succeeded in locating the wreck on the sixth day (Fig. 5). They could not then give as much time as they had expected to the actual work on the site. They tried to widen a gap made by the earlier divers by moving four columns and a number of capitals, scraping the sand with their hands from under the columns in order to lift them, and removing the mud with an ordinary water-jet (Fig. 6). Besides the columns, they brought up two beautiful Ionic capitals, and a millstone, as well as fragments of wood containing copper rivets. Altogether, they made 106 dives, a total of thirty-two hours, of which twenty-one were taken up in prospecting alone. M. Merlin wrote at the end of the season: 'The first results obtained show that there is every likelihood that the site has not by any means been worked out, and that a resumption of work would lead to important discoveries.' The divers were of the same opinion, and Commandant Cousteau wrote: 'If our predecessors, in their diving helmets, have very carefully taken the plums, they were not able to do more than scratch the surface of the cargo.'

This expedition represented an important milestone in the history of self-contained diving apparatus. It was here that diving without a piped air supply passed the stage of being a sport and a holiday pastime and became an effective method of investigation that could be placed at the service of archaeology. Thus an experimental method for underwater investigation was introduced, and it has been used ever since, notably at Anthéor in 1950, at Saint-Tropez in 1951, at Grand Congloué since 1952, and in 1954 and 1955 in renewed work by the Club for Underwater Studies of Tunisia at Mahdia.

* 'Tavera's report positioned the wreck from three cross-bearings: the first on the angle of the ancient citadel, the Bordj of Mahdia, through a tooth-shaped piece of wall belonging to a former oil mill on the beach; the two others involved an isolated tree, the roof of a mosque, or Arab *koba*, a hillock, and the angle of a copse, part of whose foliage was of a different colour from the rest. Forty years later ruins and *kobas* were dotted around; the tree and the copse were no longer there. A general search at 6 km. from the shore was fruitless, even with an aquaplane.

'As the landmarks on which the map was based had disappeared, it was necessary to find their position by calculation, and to replace them with signs visible from the sea. With the help of charts, compass and sextant, a party set out to re-establish the position of the *koba* and the oil mill. By chance, an old man remembered and pointed out the site of the mosque and, further on, the foundations of the mill. The position corresponded with the surveyor's observations and the survey poles were erected.

'The navigator of the *Elie Monnier* took sights on the points and dropped a buoy at the position given by Tavera's bearings. Around this a rectangular area of search was marked out with buoys [Fig. 5]; on the bottom, the sides were defined by lines marked off every 25 m. with numbered floats at 1 m. from the bottom. Teams of divers searched the area, metre by metre, navigating from float to float by compass. However, this also was abortive, and the wreck was not there.

'As a final resort, the method used was to search along the bearing on the Bordj of Mahdia, which seemed the most reliable, starting from the area already outlined, and to work towards the shore, back to a depth of 37 m. To economize time and energy, the divers were drawn along on a weighted line at slow speed. After a further long day's diving, the wreck was sighted by Tailliez some 200 m. from Tavera's position.' (Ph. Tailliez, *Nouvelles plongées sans câble*, 85ff.)

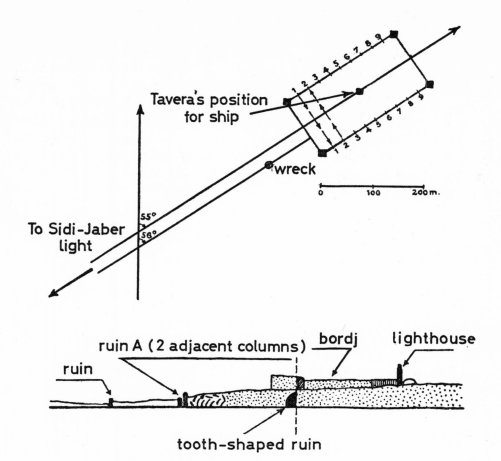

Tavera's position
for ship

wreck

To Sidi-Jaber
light

55°
58°

0   100   200 m.

ruin A (2 adjacent columns)   bordj   lighthouse

ruin

tooth-shaped ruin

FIG. 5.   Diagram of search for Mahdia wreck
(Tailliez. *Nouvelles plongées sans câble*)

The investigations undertaken by this organization in 1954 amounted to sixty-four hours of diving, of which ten were spent in locating the wreck. The divers discovered the wreck after searching for two and a half days, using only the clues provided by the Toulon expedition.

This season showed clearly how effective the use of self-contained diving apparatus could be, compared with the use of diving suits and helmets. Lieutenant Tavera pointed out in his report in 1908 that 'in the period from 3 to 19 August, it was possible to dive on only ten days, and on these days for only thirty-seven hours forty-one minutes in all. Of this diving time, only nine hours twenty-five minutes was spent in useful work. The average duration of a dive was nine minutes twelve seconds, and only a third part of this time could be spent working at the

43

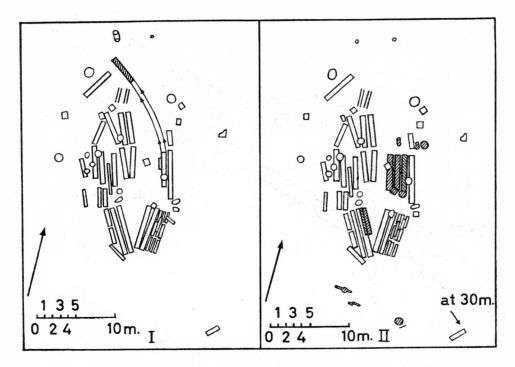

FIG. 6. Plan of Mahdia wreck: I 25 June 1948, before exploration by
G.E.R.S. II 1 July 1948, after excavation by G.E.R.S.
(Tailliez. *Nouvelles plongées sans câble*)

bottom, so that in fact, during sixteen days, work on excavation proper totalled
two hours twenty-eight minutes.'

On the other hand, omitting the time spent in locating the wreck, the 1954
season consisted of nineteen days' work out of twenty-one, during which 217
dives were made, lasting on an average fifteen minutes, i.e. fifty-four hours underwater, of which at least thirty-six to forty were spent on effective work at the
bottom, since the time spent to go down and come up was much less than for
divers with full professional equipment.

The plan of the assemblage was established (Fig. 7), but it was not possible
to obtain a photographic record because of a bottom current, which constantly
disturbed the water at this depth. The most important job undertaken was to lift
and move to a distance of 20–30 m. fourteen large marble columns and several
smaller ones. These together represented a weight of about 60 tons, and were
moved to clear a large working area in the centre of the wreck. Two air-lifts were
tried in succession, served by a 70-h.p. air-compressor. The two devices used were
handled by ropes from three fixed points situated on the perimeter of the working
area, but they were affected by the rocking of the boat through their supporting

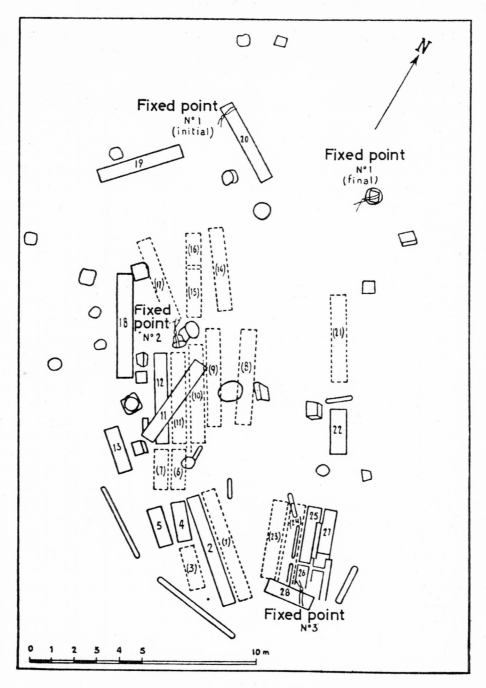

FIG. 7. Plan of Mahdia after the excavation of 1954 season
(*Bulletin Archéologique*, 1955–6)

cables; furthermore, they were intended for use in soft, free-flowing mud. For these reasons, they were not of much use in working in the space cleared by the removal of the columns. In particular, the mud, contrary to previous reports, proved to be extremely compact and of a clay-like consistency.

The archaeological finds were, as a result, not very plentiful: pieces of marble vases, bronze semicircular handles made of two twisted strands, fragments of beds, the entablature of the capital of an Ionic pilaster, a fragment of marble relief representing a female shoulder with part of the breast and of the arm. Fragments of the ship itself were brought up, notably pieces of wood and planking.

At the end of this season, the Club's report expressed doubts about the composition of the cargo as it had appeared from earlier evidence. The report states:

'It ought perhaps to be remembered that the total weight of marble carried must have been more than 200 tons. It is difficult to imagine that such a cargo could have been transported on the deck of a ship of such small tonnage (judging from its dimensions, its displacement has been estimated as from 500 to 600 tons). And in fact nothing has been found to confirm the opinions so far held that this was a decked ship.'

The work of the Club in the 1955 season was directed to following up what had been achieved in the previous year. It was decided to abandon the attempts to move the marble columns, and the divers instead undertook the task of clearing the mud from the deposit itself. The method adopted involved the use of a motor-boat belonging to the Public Works Department, and of a tug carrying the compressor for the air-lift and equipped with a derrick.

Since the previous season, a new air-lift had been devised, and was put into operation by the Club's engineers (see Fig. 8). This apparatus consisted of three metal tubes each 6 m. long, forming a vertical column 8 cm. in diameter, at the lower end of which was connected a flexible metal tube ending in a short pipe, to which the compressed air was fed. The whole thing was about 25 m. long. The air-lift, which did not weigh more than about 150 kg., was supported by two balloons fixed to the top section, which ensured that it remained vertical, and was held in place by cables passed round two pulleys on the sea-bottom. It remained in position underwater for the whole season and could be used over a wide area simply by paying out the cables. The diver, using the suction pipe at the end, controlled the air supply by a tap, and could thus work in any direction in the area surrounding him.

The 1955 season consisted of twenty working days between 14 July and 7 August, during which twenty-eight hours of diving were carried out, more than three-quarters of which represented effective work 40 m. below the surface.

The composition of the mud proved to be the same over the whole area of the wreck: a soft surface layer 20 cm. thick, then 50 cm. of clay resting on a compact bed of pebbles and shells, the natural sea-bed.

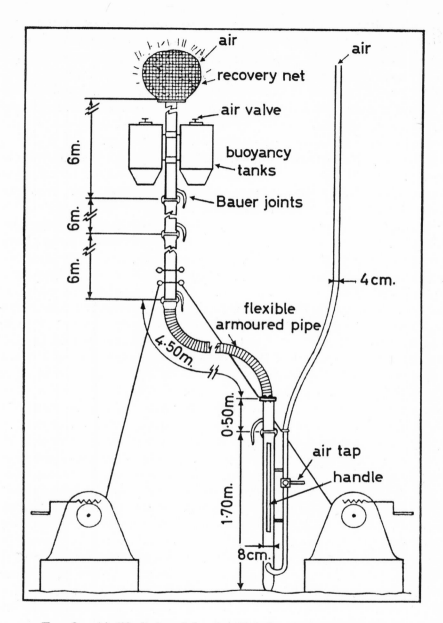

air

recovery net

air valve

buoyancy
tanks

Bauer joints

6m.

6m.

6m.

air

4 cm.

flexible
armoured pipe

4·50m.

0·50m.

air tap

handle

1·70m.

8cm.

FIG. 8. Air-lift designed for the Club for Underwater Studies
of Tunisia for use at Mahdia
(*Bulletin Archéologique*, 1955–6)

The most important discovery this season was the keel of the ship. Its upper surface, 50 cm. across and barely covered by the mud, was followed and exposed for its whole length; measured by tape, it proved to be 26 m. long. This discovery upset previous ideas. Since the keel, which was not more than 40 cm. beneath the mud, had been unable to penetrate the pebbly layer 70 cm. down from the top of the mud, obviously neither could the remainder of the wreck or its cargo. The columns, buried not more than 30 to 40 cm. deep, could not have rested on a deck, but must have been in the well of the ship.

The size of the keel justified an estimate of 30 m. or so for the maximum length of the ship. The earlier assumption of a greater size had been based on the presence of isolated blocks of marble scattered around the periphery of the main deposit, which had fallen off the ship as it went down.

By the end of the season, a plan of the ship had been made, as in the previous year (Fig. 9). The limited size of the wreck suggested that its cargo could not have weighed more than 200–50 tons. The marble columns alone represented 200 tons. The capitals, blocks of marble, and statues already in the Bardo Museum might be estimated as another 20–30 tons. It seemed, therefore, that no great part of the cargo could remain buried in the mud. In spite of more systematic excavation over a wider area than in the previous year, the archaeological finds had been slight: an Ionic capital in good condition, a rounded marble column like that of the bronze Herm in the Bardo Museum, representing the shoulders and neck of a figure whose head could not be found anywhere in the vicinity, a marble leg, the base of a column 1 m. across, an eroded Corinthian capital, fragments of kraters, pieces of bedsteads, sherds, whole amphorae (Pl. 6), and a bulbous urn with a ribbed neck and with narrow, rounded handles attached to its sides.

So far as the ship itself was concerned, the surface coating of mud made the recovery of any of its superstructure hopeless. Effort was concentrated on the keel and its constituents. Nine metres of the keel were brought up; this represents a most valuable archaeological specimen (remembering that the galleys at Nemi were only ceremonial ships, while that at Mahdia was certainly a merchant ship of the period). The structure of the keel proved rather complicated and of astonishingly careful workmanship (Fig. 10). Two panels of planks were set in lateral grooves (the rabbets), a narrow one on the outside and a wider one on the inside. Between these panels were found wide bands of caulking material, of which the weave could still be distinguished. This material between the two layers of wood which constituted the hull of the ship must have ensured that it was watertight, and this was further reinforced by an external sheath of lead to protect the hull from attack by marine organisms.

Several broad panels from the hull were recovered. The length of the planks was noteworthy, and above all the preponderance of ribbing, usual in a round ship; in the sections from near the centre line, the clamps set into the timbers

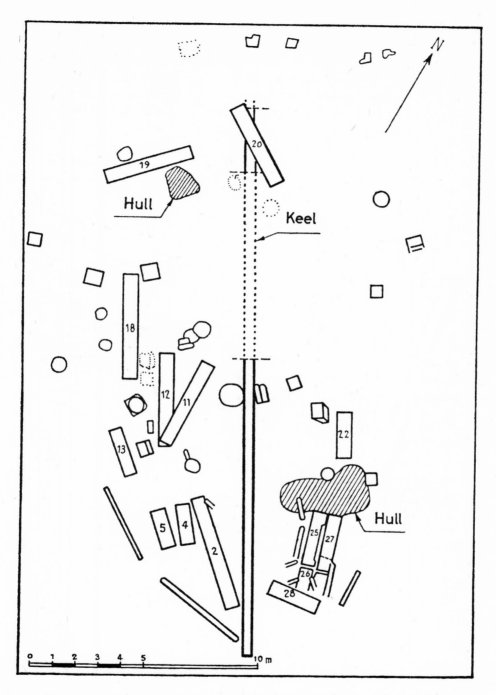

FIG. 9.   Plan of Mahdia wreck after the excavation of the 1955 season
(*Bulletin Archéologique,* 1955–6)

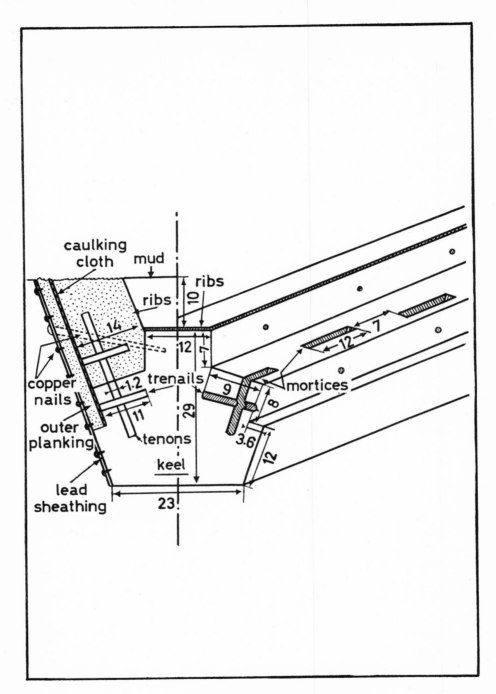

FIG. 10. Mahdia wreck: diagram of keel
(*Bulletin Archéologique*, 1955–6)

were lighter and more widely spaced. Fragments of wood from the keel and the hull were analysed, and it was established that both were of the same wood, a deciduous tree of the elm family.

All traces of the hull where it joined the keel had disappeared. This may be explained by the hypothesis that when the ship came to rest at the bottom, the keel buried itself only 40 cm. deep, and the part of the hull immediately surrounding it remained in the water exposed to rapid attack, and had therefore disappeared. Further out, the weight of the columns made the hull warp until it broke up and was buried, and thus preserved by the mud.

This season, then, provided several lessons. Contrary to previous beliefs, the cargo of the *corbita* of Mahdia, 30 m. by 10 m. in area, was carefully stowed in a regular fashion. The marble columns, sixty-odd in number, weighing about 200 tons, were laid out in five or six parallel rows, carefully secured to the hull. The capitals and blocks of marble, large kraters and marble and bronze statues, weighing perhaps 30 tons, were placed between the rows of columns and on top of them, and fastened with rope or wedged with logs.

What can be deduced about the sinking of the ship? She foundered more than three miles out from the shore, in 40 m. of water, and had certainly been disabled, perhaps by losing either her rudder or her mast. She must have drifted considerably, which explains the distance from the Italian coast—her most likely destination. Coming within sight of Africa and meeting a strong gale, she must have taken in so much water that hand-pumps were not enough to clear it. Without dropping anchor, she would have been broadside on to the wind instead of heading into it. The wind must have been from the north-east, and it is not unusual in summer off the Tunisian coast to find a strong, persistent wind from that direction.

The ship was overwhelmed and went down right side up, heading south-east. Quite a number of marble objects were damaged as she hit the bottom, but the columns did not shift. The deck and part of the hull, projecting well out of the sea-bed, were rapidly destroyed, while that part of the cargo and the hull that went down with it were preserved by the mud. To the accumulation of sediment, which may reach the rate of a few centimetres in 1,000 years, was added the weight of the cargo as it settled, and probably the current also played its part.

The numerous shapeless lumps of stone brought up by the divers, assumed to have been ballast, were in fact derived from the natural sea-bed 60 cm. below, marking the lower limit of penetration by any part of the wreck. They had been brought to the surface in the course of excavation.

The last season, then, revised many ideas about the Mahdia wreck. The remarkable dimensions of the ship, the astonishing disposal of the cargo, with the heavy columns on the deck and the precious objects in the hold, the successive layers of wood representing the deck and between-deck and not the hull, the keel deeply embedded in the mud, the anchors dropped as she sank—all of these were legends springing from the imagination, uncurbed at that time, of the Greek divers.

NOTES

This report first appeared in *Le Plongeur et l'Archéologue*, under the title 'Mahdia: Un Musée au fond de la mer'. Other accounts of the wreck are to be found in the following bibliography:

A. Merlin, 'Les fouilles sous-marine de Mahdia', *La Revue Tunisienne* (1911), 113ff.

—— *Associations pour l'avancement des Sciences*. C. R. de la 42e session (Tunis, 1913), 32.

—— *Revue Scientifique* (21 June 1913) 777ff.

—— *C. R. de l'Académie des Inscriptions et Belles Lettres* (1907), 317; (1908), 245ff., 386ff., 532ff., 610; (1909), 122, 650ff.; (1910), 585ff.; (1911), 206ff., 556ff.; (1913), 469.

—— 'Lingots et ancres trouvées en mer près de Mahdia', *Mélanges offert à René Cagnat* (1912).

—— 'Submarine discoveries in the Mediterranean', *Antiquity*, IV (1930), 405ff.

A. Merlin and L. Poinssot, 'Découvertes sous-marine près de Mahdia', *Klio*, IX (1909), 259.

—— 'Bronzes trouvées en mer près de Mahdia', *Monuments Piots*, XVII, 29ff.

—— 'Statuettes en bronzes trouvées en mer près de Mahdia', *Monuments Piots*, XVIII, 5ff.

—— 'Marbres trouvées en mer près de Mahdia', *Revue Archéologique* (1911), II, 92ff.

—— 'Statuettes trouvées en mer près de Mahdia'. *Mémoires de la Société des Antiquaires de France*, LXX (1911), 211ff.

—— 'Épotides de bronze trouvées en mer près de Mahdia', *Ve Congrés Internationale d'Archéologie* (Algers, 1930), 227ff.

—— 'Cratère et candelabres de marbres trouvées en mer près de Mahdia', *Notes et Documents* (Tunis, 1930).

—— 'Éléments Architecturaux trouvées en mer près de Mahdia', *Karthago*, VII (1956), 59ff.

—— *Guide de Musée Alaoui*, 3rd ed., 59ff.

—— *Catalogue du Musée Alaoui*, 1st and 2nd Supplements.

R. Cagnat, in *Revue de l'Art ancien et moderne* (1911), I, 321ff.

—— 'Naufrages d'objets d'art dans l'antiquité', *Annales du Musée Guimet: bibliographie de vulgarisation*, XXXVI (1912), 91ff.

—— *À travers le monde romain* (1912), 240

J. Carcopino, 'Sylla et les fouilles sous-marine de Mahdia', *Mélanges offerts à Nicolas Iorga* (1933).

E. Condroyer, 'L'exploration sous-marine de la galère de Mahdia', *Neptunia*, 4th quarter (1948), No. 12.

R. Dain, 'Inscriptions attiques trouvées à Mahdia', *Revue des études grecques*, XLIV (1931), 290ff.

W. Fuchs, *Der schiffsfund von Mahdia im Musée Alaoui zu Tunis*, Bilderheft der Deutsche Arch. Inst. im Rom, 2 (1963).

Lacroix, in *C.R. de l'Académie des Sciences* (25 July 1910), 276ff.

H. Lechat, 'Notes archéologiques', *Revue des études anciennes*, XII (1910), 350; XIII (1911), 140ff.

G. Picard and M. de Frondeville, 'Fouilles à Mahdia', *Bulletin Archéologique* (1955–6), 129ff.
Ph. Tailliez, 'La "galère" de Mahdia', *La Revue Maritime* (May 1949), 573ff.
—— *To Hidden Depths* (Kimber, 1954), 85ff.
—— *Nouvelles plongées sans câble* (Arthaud, 1960), 80ff.
Schulten-Curtius, in *Archäologische Anzeiger* (1909), cols. 207ff.

(c) Albenga

Amphorae were first recovered from this area by fishermen in 1930 and again in 1945–7. The position is fixed by three co-ordinates from the coast: the campanile

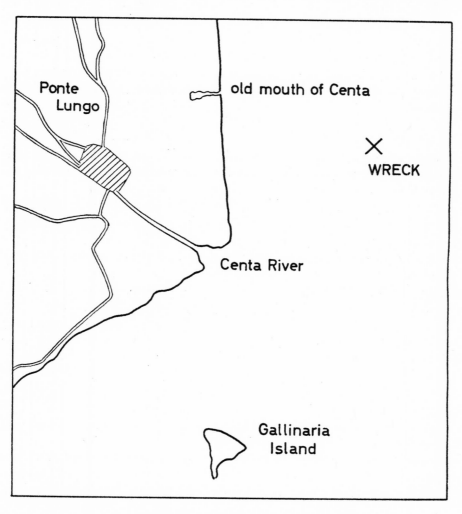

FIG. 11.   Map showing position of Albenga wreck

in the suburb of Bastia and the chimney of the Morandi foundry; the chimney of the Conserva Pisonis factory at Ceriale and the Casa Sasso behind it; the chimney of the Vadino distillery and the Casa Balbi behind it. They give lat. 44° 3′ N. long. 8° 15′ E. of Greenwich. About a mile from the shore, the wreck lies off the old mouth of the Centa (called 'Burrone'), a little east of the town (Fig. 11).

The deposit was identified at a depth of 40 m. In 1950, with the support of S.O.R.I.M.A., the diver Quaglia was persuaded to undertake an investigation with the salvage ship, *Artiglio II*. On 8 February 1950 the *Artiglio II* was directed to the position by Antonio Bignone, the fisherman who had found the original amphorae. Observation with the diving bell confirmed the position of a cargo some 30 m. long by 10 m. wide and about 2 m. high. A few amphorae were hoisted on board by the divers, but to make a fuller examination it was decided, not without misgivings, to take up a larger quantity of amphorae with the grab in order to find out if any of the hull was still present beneath the sand.

Much of the cargo was raised unbroken, as well as other pottery vessels; and on 12 February part of a bronze helmet and some lead piping from the side of the ship were brought up. Further amphorae were collected by divers and raised in a net, but work was discontinued after ten days. From the cargo, 728 amphorae were recovered, of which 110 were intact, and many others were restorable, to an estimated total of 1,200. The divers believed that at least two-thirds of the cargo was still on the bottom, giving a figure in the neighbourhood of 3,000 for the total. Most of the amphorae (Fig. 12), of which there were at least four sub-types, belonged to the wine group of Dressel 1. Several were closed with a pine cone as stopper beneath the clay sealing, but none was stamped; nor were there any marks on the amphorae. From the form, they may be dated to the end of the second or the beginning of the first century B.C. Three small oil amphorae were also recovered and part of another contained some nuts (Fig. 13).

Pottery which could be assigned to use in the galley included the neck and base of an amphora with a ring foot, three Campanian dishes (Fig. 14), bowls of imitation Campanian ware, and red glazed dishes. The cooking-pots (Figs. 15–19) of grey ware included store jars (*olle*) and jugs (*olpi*) of several types and a number of large, coarse jugs (Figs. 20–21).

The metal objects were mostly of lead, and included a horn-like object pierced by three holes; a circular disc with square holes through which cords appeared to have passed; a leaden crucible; and also some piping. What purpose the disc served in the working of the ship has been the subject of much speculation.[1] The most surprising finds have been the fragments of three bronze helmets.

Of the ship itself, pieces of the hull were recovered, including oaken ribs, and planks and other morticed fragments of soft wood. Some had been covered with sheets of lead fixed with copper tacks. A few tile fragments were also found.

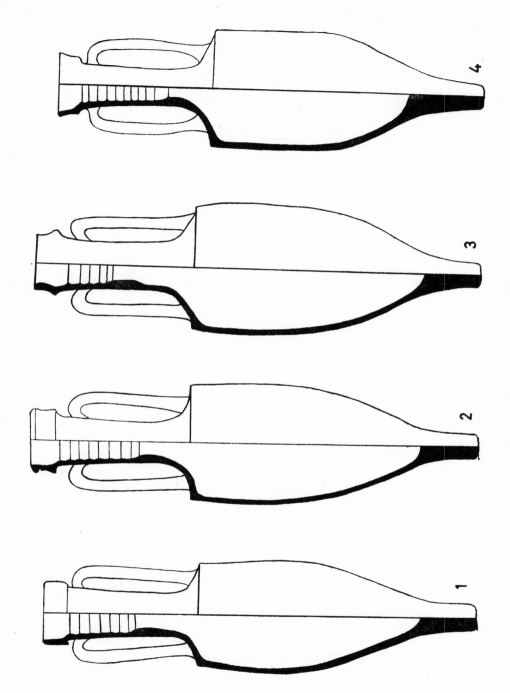

Fig. 12.   Four sub-types of wine amphorae, Dressel 1   Scale 1 : 10

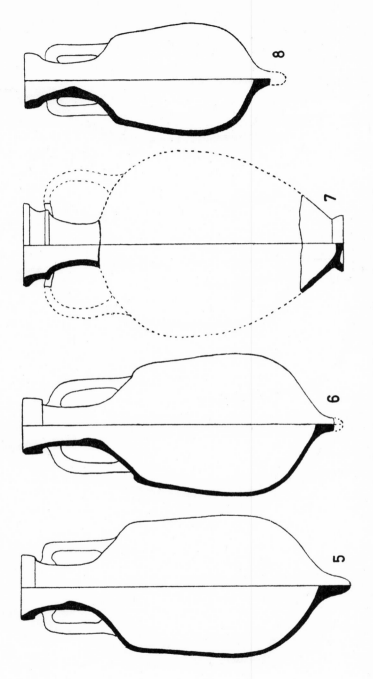

FIG. 13.   Oil amphorae 5, 6, 8; domestic amphora 7   Scale 1 : 10

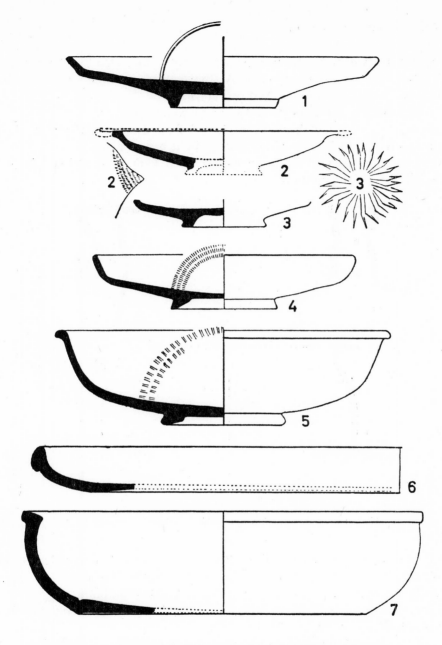

FIG. 14. Campanian dishes 1–3; imitation Campanian 4, 5;
red glazed dishes 6, 7   Scale 1 : 3

The domestic pottery (Figs. 14–21)[2]

1   Campanian A dish similar to type 5[3] but not unlike type 7 of Campanian B. Though the clay is Campanian A, the features relating to Campanian B indicate a date early in the first century B.C.

2–3   Campanian C dishes of form 6 in good-quality pottery.

4   Imitation Campanian dish, reconstructed from fragments; type 7 of Campanian B–C, in ash grey with graces of light brown glaze.

5   Deep bowl, broken in antiquity and covered with incrustations; form 8 in imitation of Campanian B type.

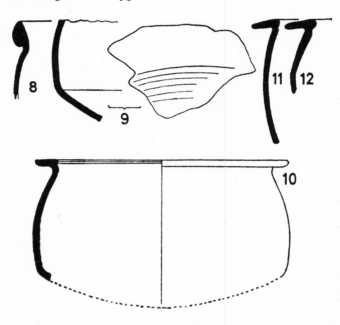

FIG. 15.   Grey ware *Olle* (cooking-pots)   Scale 1 : 3

6   Part of a large dish with interior red glaze which precedes terra-sigillata in the Mediterranean. Types close to dishes from Albintimilium IIC.

7   Flat-based bowls with red glaze, not found at Albintimilium.
Grey ware was found in quantity, broken in antiquity, and comparable with second-century types at Albintimilium.

8–12   Fragments of rims and bodies of *olle* (cooking-pots).

13–34   Fragments of urns with flat bases in red ware; sometimes red inside and grey outside. These types did not occur at Albintimilium, and their source is yet to be found.

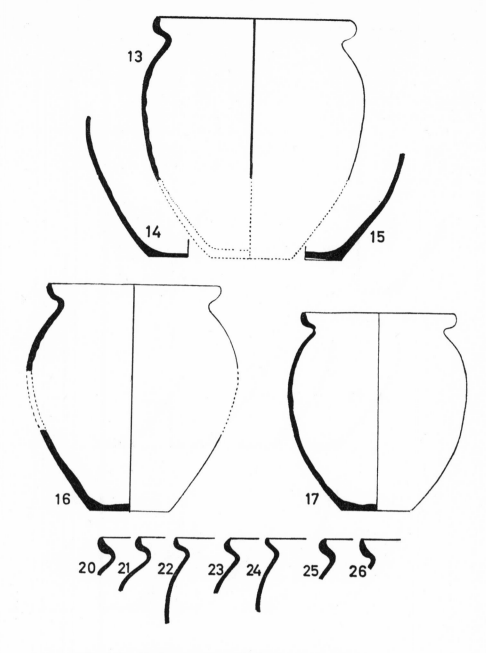

FIG. 16.   Red ware urns with flat bases   Scale 1 : 3

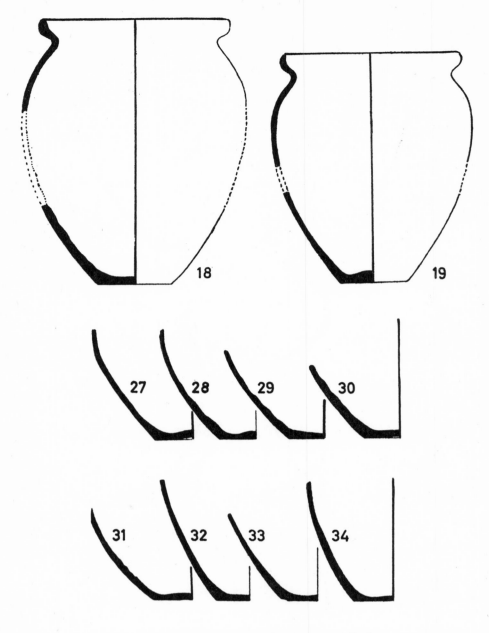

FIG. 17. Red ware urns with flat bases   Scale 1 : 3

Several *olpi* of a type not found stratified at Albintimilium were recovered intact.

35–38 *Olpi* with spherical bodies; in light-coloured clay with brown glaze of Campanian type.

39–44 With high shoulder in reddish clay.

45–46 Others with squat body, in fine clay, unglazed; the interior covered with a bituminous coat similar to the amphorae.

Cooking-ware: large pots with one handle, some lined with an aromatic, bituminous coat. The forms have not yet been studied.

47–49. Rims only, in coarse red clay.

50–55 Jugs with incised lines on outside; reddish clay with white surface similar to amphorae.

56 Amphora.

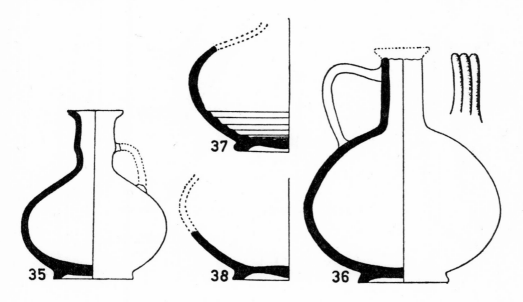

FIG. 18. *Olpi* (jugs) of Campanian type   Scale 1 : 3

A. Pederzini reports on later exploration:[4]

'In 1957, only vague and contradictory information was available, obtained through the divers who, either with diving apparatus or with a bell, had gone down to the sea-bed. There was no survey or photos, nor did anyone know the exact condition of the wreck after the work had been carried out. No one had dived on the wreck since 1950, and no free-diver had ever explored it. There were, therefore, many reasons which made a series of reconnoitring dives attractive. Professor

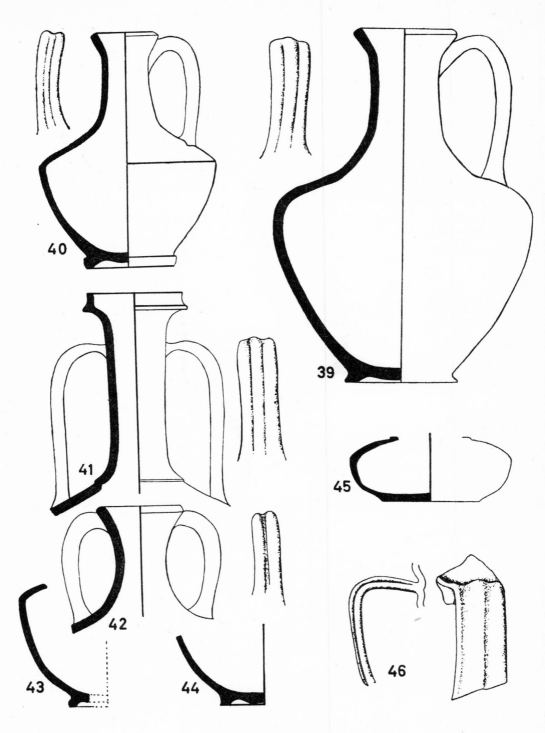

FIG. 19. Plain *olpi* Scale 1 : 3

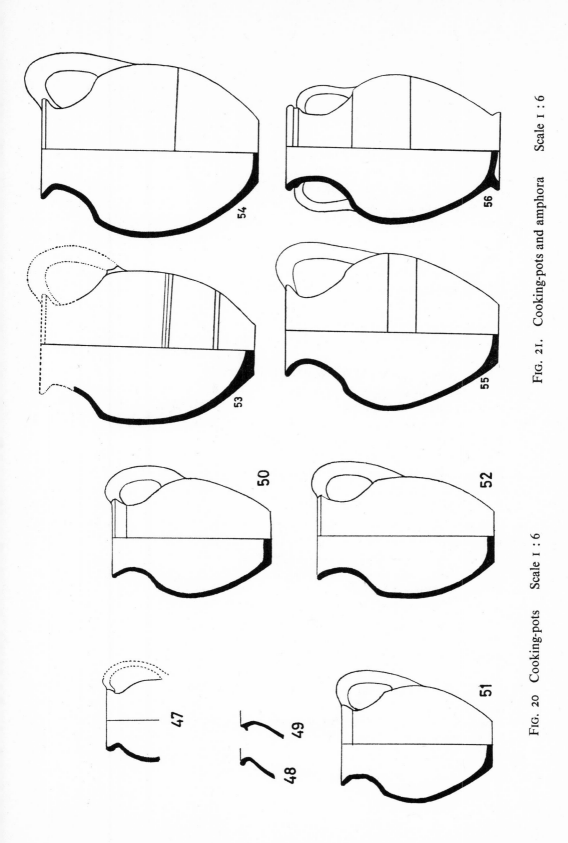

54

56

53

55

50

52

51

47

48 49

Fig. 21. Cooking-pots and amphora   Scale 1 : 6

Fig. 20 Cooking-pots   Scale 1 : 6

Lamboglia, who had directed the first operations with the S.O.R.I.M.A., looked forward to receiving more detailed information and to obtaining an exact survey of the condition of the wreck. In fact, it must be remembered that the Museo Navale Romano at Albenga was inaugurated with the first part of the material recovered, and counted upon further work to enrich it.

'Our first attempt took place on 24 April 1957. A team of four men (Divizia, Ferrandi, Pederzini, Roghi) dived vertically down on the spot where some Albenga fishermen, who accompanied us, assured us that the wreck was to be found. Having reached the sea-bed, which was level and muddy, through very turbid water (maximum visibility, 3 m.) with a rather strong current, the team did not give up the attempt, but started on an exhaustive quest by groping in the water at a depth of 38–40 m. for thirty minutes. One of the divers (Divizia) was ordered to come up again after twenty minutes, as he was equipped with a smaller breathing apparatus than the others. Without having discovered any traces, the three remaining men started to come up in the open sea, which was disturbed by a strong surface current. This current, and the certainty of being carried far from the anchored boat, persuaded them to shorten the last stage of decompression by six to eight minutes at 3m. This caused the writer of this article to be seized with a bout of gaseous embolism about ten minutes after he had climbed back into the boat, followed by nervous symptoms and subsequent paralysis of the lower limbs. A prompt recompression at the Croce Bianca in Savona and further treatment enabled him to recover from this serious condition.

'The second operation was carried out successfully on 23 November 1957 by the writer and Gianni Roghi. This time the dive took place a few metres from the wreck, whose position was indicated by fragments of amphorae scattered on the sea-floor. The wreck was found and explored. The dive was limited to sixteen minutes so as not to run risks on surfacing; in fact, this time too we lost contact with the support-boat and decompression took place in the open sea. On the next day, 24 November, further dives were made (Callegaro, Roghi) to complete the survey. A cable, like Ariadne's thread, was fastened to the boat anchor, a system which was completely successful. The very clear water made it easier to make an exact plan and perspective survey of the whole huge deposit. The dive lasted twenty-five minutes, plus twenty-two for decompression.'

First description of the wreck

It looked like an upheaval of detritus on the sea-floor, with an average length of 30m. and an average width of 10 m. The maximum height from the sea-floor, which consisted of sand and mud and is level and bare, is about 2 m. (Fig. 22). The orientation of the deposit was exactly from south to north, and is therefore parallel to the coast. The longer sides are parallel. From the north end it rises

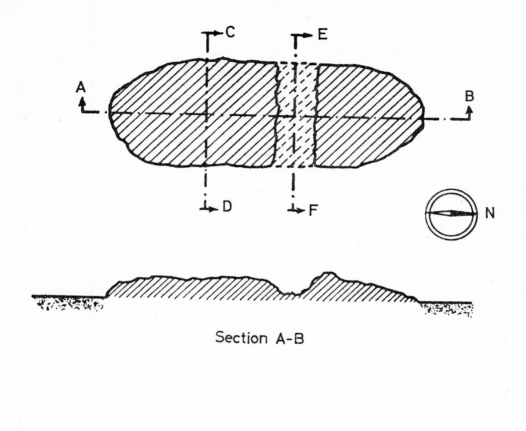

FIG. 22. Plan of the site of the Albenga wreck made by divers in 1957

gently upwards to the maximum height, while at the south end the fall is steeper. The surface of the heap is of hard, compacted detritus, made up of broken amphorae interspersed with a few almost intact ones. There is no evidence of vegetation or of algal incrustation. The wreck is populated by numerous small fish and large lobsters.

At about three-fifths of its length, towards the north, the heap is divided by a deep trench 3–4 m. wide, in which numerous whole or broken amphorae are scattered. Here the work of the grab is visible. The floor of this trench, composed of more or less complete amphorae, is only slightly higher than the sea-floor. The top of the deposit is not a ridge, but a flat and level surface.

From the exploration made by us, we can affirm that the wreck has not, in fact, been mangled by the work of the *Artiglio II*, and particularly by the grab, as has often been said and written by people who have never seen it. It is still impressive and of such vital interest as to invite the continuance of the survey and the work of recovery. This position, as other data, is in contrast to the indications supplied by the divers in 1950.

A further visit to the wreck was made by the *Daino* in June 1959,[5] when the deposit was used as a check on the use of the echo-sounder. 'The first survey of the ship, giving its size and position, was there obtained mechanically by means of the echo-sounder, and it has been possible to observe its close correspondence to the earlier survey made by divers.' (See pp. 152–3 for full report.)

NOTES

The account of the recovery of the Albenga cargo is taken from the reports of Professor Nino Lamboglia in the following journals: 'Diario di scavo a bordo del *Artiglio*', *Rivista Ingauna e Intemiglia*, V (1950), 1ff.; 'Albenga: Anfore romano pescate in mare', *Rivista di Studi Liguri*, I (1934), 39–40; 'La nave romana di Albenga', *Rivista di Studi Liguri*, 18 (1952), 131ff. See also A. Pederzini, 'Primi rilieve e fotografie della nave romana di Albenga', *Atti del II Congresso Internazionale di Archeologia sotto-marina*, Albenga (1958), 124ff.

1 Tea Coco, 'Sulla cosidetta "ruota di manovra" della nave romana di Albenga', *Rivista di Studi Liguri*, 20 (1954), 55.
2 N. Lamboglia, 'La nave romana di Albenga', *Rivista di Studi Liguri*, 18 (1952), 166ff.
3 N. Lamboglia, 'Per una classificazione preliminare della ceramica campana', *Atti del I Congresso Internazionale di Studi Liguri* (Bordighera, 1952).
4 A. Pederzini, 'Catasto archeologico dei fondali dell' Isola Gallinaria ed esplorazione del relitto della nave romana di Albenga', *Bollettino e Atti* (Centro Italiano Ricercatori Subacquei, 1957), 9ff.
5 N. Lamboglia, 'La prima campagna sottomarina del *Daino* nelle acque Liguri', *Rivista Ingauna e Intemiglia*, XIV (1959), 126.

(d) Grand Congloué

The wreck at Grand Congloué seems to have been discovered by divers working on the construction of the great Marseilles sewer, whose outlet is at Cortion between Marseilles and Cassis, nearly opposite the little island of Grand Congloué. However, little importance was attached to the discovery of these 'old pots', well known to fishermen, who had often cast their nets over these veritable traps for fish and lobsters and who were hardly anxious to point out the location to divers with their apparatus, for reasons which are apparent.

In 1951, if my memory serves me aright, a diver, M. Cristianini, suffered a very serious accident through not using decompression tables correctly. He owes his life to the G.E.R.S. of the Marine Nationale, and, in gratitude for the devoted and effective care which he received, he handed over to Commandant Cousteau and Frédéric Dumas information regarding the site of the wreck. Cousteau, on his return from the Red Sea with the *Calypso* in 1952, had several months of freedom ahead, and decided to spend them in organizing the systematic investigation of an ancient wreck. With this end in view, he examined a number of wrecks with his friend Dumas and other divers of his team. For several reasons, the wreck at Grand Congloué appeared the most interesting. It was the only one which contained an important cargo of pottery, the others having only a few vessels, comprising the domestic crockery of the ship, apart from the regular load of amphorae. Furthermore, it appeared from its size to be the most important. And, lastly, it was situated at the base of the cliff of a small island, where it was possible to install a land base and a permanent derrick.

Commandant Cousteau quickly realized that this wreck was going to need many more men and more time and resources than he had at first thought. He therefore approached the late M. Borelli, President of the Fédération Française, to ask if some well-disposed divers would generously come to help him in his task. His appeal was answered, and divers came from every region of France to unite their efforts with his in order to carry through successfully this overwhelming task. It was literally overwhelming because of the 45 m. of water over their heads, and figuratively because of the many difficulties inherent in any undertaking carried out by new methods on a site that was enchanting in good weather, but, according to the divers, was very bad underfoot if there was the least swell.

The wreck took the form of an enormous tumulus about 40 m. long and from 10 to 12 m. wide, whose depth varied between 38 and 45 m. From the tumulus protruded the necks of amphorae and broken pottery. The first important underwater archaeological excavation was under way. It was soon realized that it would be necessary to make use of mechanical means to extract the mud and sand which had invaded and covered up the wreck. A 120-mm. air-lift was therefore installed on board, supplied by the Junkers 35-h.p. compressor of the *Calypso*, giving a capacity of 130 cu. m. per hour. But an almost dead calm was necessary for the air-lift to work from the ship, so it was decided to mount the air-lift on a large derrick whose base rested at the foot of the cliff, and which was held by steel cables attached at the top of the cliff (Pl. 7). The flexible hose was hooked on to the 27-m. derrick, and then led vertically down to the wreck. At the point where it emerged from the water, it was parallel to the derrick, and was then led away to discharge at some distance from the site, where, after filtering, the mud was returned to the sea.

A platform was next constructed on a ledge of rock, on which was installed a large, low-pressure compressor powered by a diesel engine which supplied the air-lift with air at 9 kg. per square centimetre.

The *Calypso*, however, was called away to other jobs, and so, after many months of work, it was decided to establish a base on the island. This base would be supplied by a new ship, the *Espadon*, a substantial fishing boat 18 m. long, which was purchased when the Office Français de la Recherche Sous-Marine was set up to relieve the *Calypso*. The *Espadon* also undertook to carry back to Marseilles the archaeological finds from the wreck. Thus even in bad weather the men stationed on the island could go down to the wreck. An Army hut, which had been erected on a site previously levelled by blasting, was placed at our disposal by the M.R.V. It was in two parts, one for use as a common-room and kitchen, and one as a dormitory, in which eight beds were installed. A generating set supplied electricity, there was a refrigerator and an oil-stove—in fact, it was quite reasonably comfortable.

The outstanding feature of this first excavation was, I think, the extraordinary amount of help received on all sides, without which we could never have achieved the results we did. This applies particularly to the Chamber of Commerce in Marseilles and their workshops, on whom we made urgent demands at all hours for welding equipment, cables, hose, and everything else we needed. Next it was necessary to transport this material, and M. Juniet, chief engineer in charge of lights and buoys, was often called upon. The captains and crews of his ships came cheerfully on Sundays and even at night to help us when we had a breakdown. Even the Army made its contribution. The 7th Regiment of Engineers from Avignon lent us winches and built platforms for us. The General Officer Commanding at Marseilles actually lifted the embargo on war supplies (and we were civilians!), which were turned to peaceful ends, for it was two rifle shots fired into the water that gave the signal to the divers to come up. Finally, private industry made its contribution in the form of paint, hardware, food, drink, wood, oil-stoves, etc.

But let us return to the work of our divers. They were equipped either with a triple-bottle set, or with a *narghile* (an air-hose used in place of bottles) supplied with air by a compressor on the shore of the island. The permitted duration of the dives was eighteen minutes for the first, fifteen minutes for the second, and twelve minutes for the third. In a series of several thousand dives we had no serious accidents due to decompression, and only a few slight incidents (aching shoulders and headaches), nearly always because the divers were cold and did not strictly follow the decompression routine. In view of the fact that we were working at the limits of the decompression tables, we had to obey absolutely strictly the rules which apply to all divers, but which were specially necessary here where the divers were making two or even three dives per day. Some of them were doing this throughout the whole year.

On 6 November 1953 we mourned the death of one of our comrades, Jean-

Pierre Servanti. He died, not while working on the wreck itself, but while trying to recover an anchor by which the *Calypso* had been made fast and which we had lost. The chain had in fact been broken, and the mooring buoy had gone adrift. It was, however, caught by the loose end of the chain. What happened we do not know exactly. We imagine that, wanting to recover the mooring quickly, he swam too fast and suffocated. He was at a depth of about 65 m. We brought him up unconscious a quarter of an hour later and, in spite of all our efforts, we did not succeed in reviving him.

The divers used different methods of protecting themselves against the cold. In winter the Tarzan type of soft rubber suit allowed of working in water of a temperature as low as 8°C. The divers were able to get warm on the island with the help of Mazda infra-red lamps. Before going down, they often spent two or three minutes under the lamps, and a similar period when they came up. This proved an excellent practice, because the divers got warm quickly and didn't shiver for hours on end.

The objects released by the air-lift were placed in baskets of metal mesh, which were raised to the surface when full by the winches of the *Calypso* or the *Espadon*. But in some places enormous blocks had fallen on to the wreck. It was out of the question to raise a block weighing 6 to 8 tons with the derrick on our boat. After trying in vain to split it up with a 600-g. 'plastic' charge, which only resulted in breaking one or two amphorae and had no effect on the rock, we turned our attention to drilled charges. This was the answer. We placed a charge of 2·5 kg., and the block separated cleanly into four or five pieces, causing absolutely no damage to the wreck, except for a few broken amphorae.

The Galeazzi jet was also used. This jet has the advantage of not impeding the diver, because some of the water ejected is diverted backwards, thus carrying away the mud released by the jet. The diver therefore works in clear water, which is not the case with an ordinary jet. This method is particularly appropriate to certain kinds of work—for example, on heaps of pottery. It is actually a very delicate business to work with an air-lift on a fragile deposit; in heaps of pottery, for instance, some pieces may be too violently dislodged and broken. Work with a jet can be much more delicately controlled, but its output is very low. It would perhaps be useful in some cases to use an ordinary high-powered jet. It would be possible to make fast this jet to a suitable weight and thus to create a current of water to carry away the sand and mud. This method was not tried at Grand Congloué, but I had occasion to use it subsequently, and I was able to establish that it gives very good results, especially if the deposit is on a very steep slope.

Little by little, as it became necessary, we introduced, besides the 1,500-kg. compressor, generating sets for lighting, for radio communication, and for underwater filming, welding and cutting equipment, three winches, ranging from 1 to 3 tons, and water tanks to supply our hut. The mechanical equipment was in fact a veritable factory. We also established underwater telephones, allowing us to give and receive orders from the surface; this was most useful for some operations, especially hoisting and bringing up lumps of rock. The air-lifts were lowered by tackle, and the diver, wherever he might be, had to signal to the winch-man whether to raise or lower them. It was thus possible to lower the hoses facing one another, so that they could be coupled together.

When we had to work where there was a great deal of pottery, we could not use the large air-lift on piles of dishes and bowls (Pl. 7). In these circumstances, the nozzles of the hose were extended by a reducing piece and a tube of only 40-mm. cross-section was used. In addition, a grill was attached to prevent too violent a suction. With this small nozzle, we could not suck up stones or debris, but for working in mud alone it was a very useful device. When work on the heap of pottery was finished, the air was cut off, the attachment taken off, and work resumed with the ordinary hose.

M. Benoit, Director of the Twelfth Archaeological Department of France, has already done a great deal of work on the results of this excavation. I will therefore speak only of the quantities of the material, since I am not competent to draw conclusions about the historical or archaeological interest of the undertaking. We brought up, intact or broken, amphorae by the thousand, and, also by the thousand, pieces of black pottery, most of it in a perfect state of preservation. I believe that pieces representing 137 different forms were brought up, and that this is the finest collection of Campanian pottery of the period; besides, there were lead anchor stocks and many other lead objects whose use we could not always establish.

The excavation is not finished. Circumstances obliged Commandant Cousteau to give it up, and I am sure that he made the decision regretfully—as regretfully as the divers who left the bare rock where we had spent such arduous as well as such enjoyable moments.

As the excavations are still in progress, it is only possible to give interim notes on the finds and the date:[1]

'The layers of amphorae of several types are mixed, and in addition that part of the cargo against the rock was covered by large blocks of stone fallen from the cliff in ancient times.

'The position of the pottery and amphorae, in relation to the few much-corroded and fragmentary pieces of wood from the boat, gives little indication of the method of loading (as it lies at an angle of 45°), except that the Sestius amphorae were for the most part above the Graeco-Italic. A more scientific result may be derived from a calculation of the approximate capacity of the ship, based on the size of the keel and ribs which were brought up in 1957 [Fig. 23] and taking also into account the size of cargo attributed to merchant ships of the hellenistic and Roman periods.

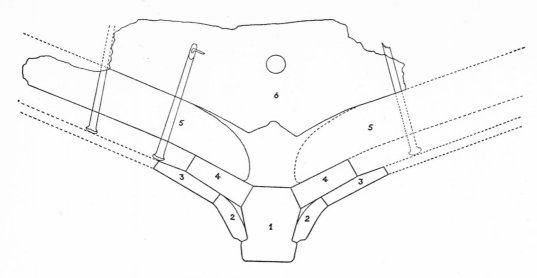

FIG. 23. Grand Congloué wreck; diagram of keel

'As far as can be ascertained at present, the deposit can be arranged in two groups: the first cargo from two sources, Greek and Campanian, is fairly securely dated.

'*Group I*
(*a*) *Rhodian and Knidian amphorae* (I–II, Fig. 24); dated by Rhodian stamps 220–180 B.C., after V. Grace; *Kleitomarchos* and *Aratophanes* eponyms, and *Aristion, Agathocles, Damocrates*, manufacturers.
(*b*) *Relief decorated bowls*, second-first century B.C., from the east Mediterranean.
(*c*) *Campanian pottery*, second century B.C., from the Naples-Ischia region, included lamps and a guttus (Figs. 25–6). More than 5,000 pieces in twenty-two forms and seven sizes and also two goblets with inscriptions are recorded (Pl. 8).
(*d*) *Graeco-Italic amphorae* (III, Fig. 24). These can be dated 180–150 B.C.
       A Punic amphora VI found with the *Sestius* amphorae is of a type known in France and Spain as well as at Carthage and in south Italy (Fig. 28).
'*Group II*
Italic amphorae (IV, Figs. 27–8) all with *Sestius* stamps. These cannot be dated except by comparison with Dressel 1 and by the epigraphy; they are classed in Benoit's Republican II series. Much has been written as to the source of the amphorae of the house of *Sestius*, whether Delian, Campanian, or Etruscan, the latter of considerably later date than the first group of pottery. Until the full report is published there is no evidence to suggest that this latter group does not belong to the rest of the cargo. Stoppers of lime plaster (Pl. 8) were stamped with the merchant's name round the edges, L.TITI.C.F. A black

71

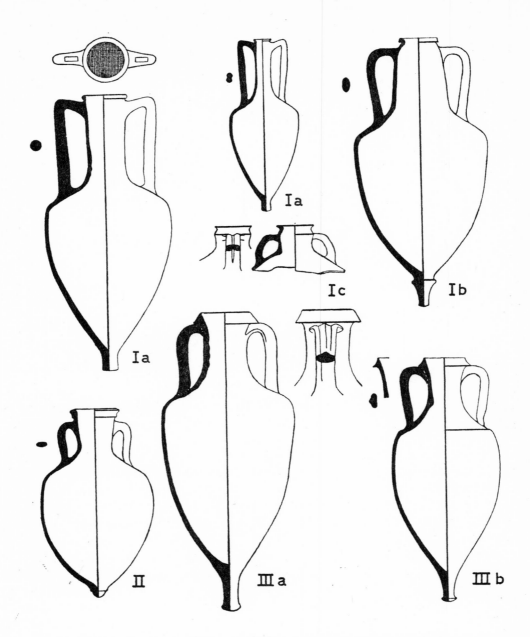

FIG. 24. Amphora types: Ia large and small Rhodian; Ib Knidian;
Ic unknown type; II Greek; IIIa-b Graeco-Italic, large and small
Scale 1 : 10 (after *Gallia* XII)

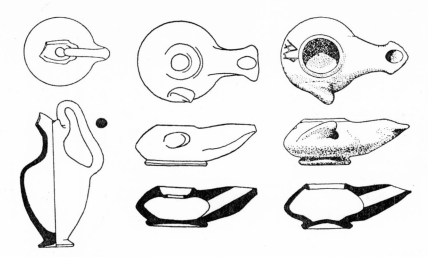

FIG. 25. Campanian *oenochoe* and lamps   Scale 1 : 3 (after *Gallia* XII)

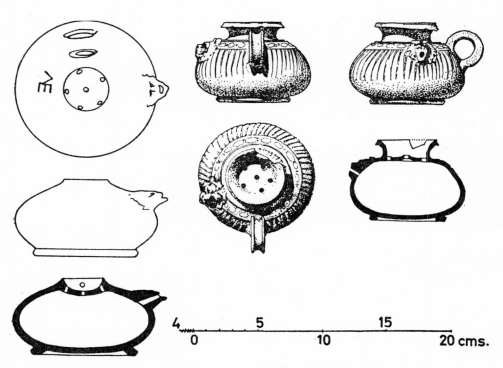

FIG. 26. Campanian *guttii*   Scale 1 : 3 (after *Gallia* XII)

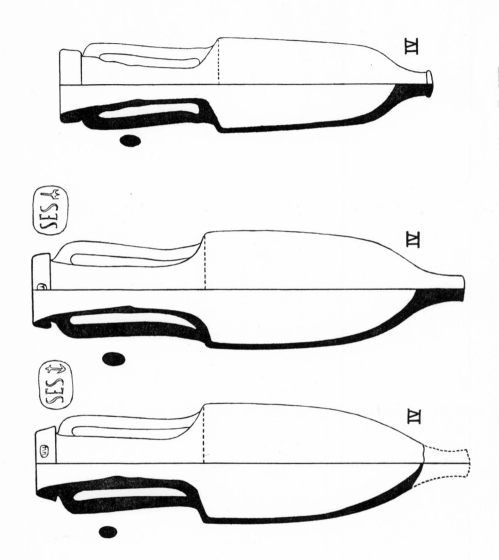

Fig. 27. Amphora types: IV Roman of SES   Scale 1 : 10 (after *Gallia* XII)

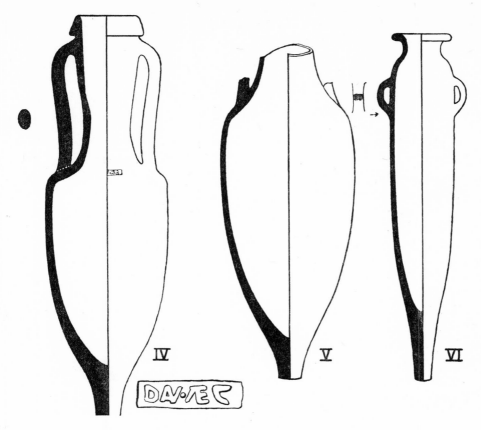

FIG. 28. Amphora types: IV Roman of DAV.ATEC;
V Roman with fusiform body; VI Punic Scale 1 : 10 (after *Gallia* XII)

lining to the amphorae was "mastic", used for making the amphorae water-tight. A large and a small lead anchor stock have been recovered, one from a ledge above the wreck.'

NOTES

This report appeared in *Le Plongeur et l'Archéologue* under the title 'Les fouilles sous-marine au Grand Congloué'. Other articles on the subject are: J.-Y. Cousteau, 'Fish Men discover 2,200-year-old Greek Ship', *National Geographic Magazine*, CV (1954), 1ff. F. Benoit, 'Amphores et céramique de l'épave de Marseille', *Gallia*, XII (1954), 35ff.; 'Typologie et épigraphie amphorique: les marques de Sestius', *Rivista di Studi Liguri*, 23 (1957), 247; 'Additional Finds', *Gallia*, XIV (1958), 28; 'Archéologie sous-marine: l'épave du Grand Congloué', *Gallia*, supp. XIV (1961); 'Synchronismes des amphores rhodienne et de la céramique hellénistique de l'épave du Grand Congloué', *Rhodania*, 30–1 (1954–5), 9. Maria Pilar G. Serrano, 'Anforas romanas con la marca *Sestius*', *Archivo Español de Arqueologia*, XXXIII (1960), 113. E. Thevenot, 'La marque

de l'amphore *Sesti*', *Revue Archéologique de l'Est*, V (1954), 234. E. L. Will, 'Les amphores de Sestius', *Revue Archéologique de l'Est*, VII (1956), 224.

1   *Rivista di Studi Liguri*, 23 (1957), 248ff.; but see now *Gallia*, supp. XIV (1961).

(e) Titan

At Toulon in the spring of 1957 I received the news that the Navy had decided to
found a school of diving of which I was to be in command. I had also received the
department's approval for two diving projects, which had for long been near my
heart. One concerned a film,[1] and the other a wreck. Dr. Piroux of the Club de la
Mer at Antibes had discovered the latter by chance in the preceding summer while
chasing a merou. He had taken the precaution, as is the rule among discoverers
of wrecks, of having an affidavit drawn up in due form by a lawyer, and had also
notified M. Fernand Benoit, Director of Antiquities for Provence. He refused
firmly to disclose its location, a very wise precaution considering the publicity
which was given to it.[2] But his diving colleagues considered this prudent silence
inimical. One of them, Charvoz, who was cared for by G.E.R.S. following an
accident, had suggested he should take us to the place. But, wishing to maintain a
correct official position, I had asked the approval of Fernand Benoit and invited
him for the visit by G.E.R.S.
    Early in the morning of 8 October, at Lavandou, our passengers embarked on
the *Elie Monnier*, and we steered for the eastern point of Île du Levant. The sea
was calm, the coast hidden by mist, and Charvoz had difficulty in finding his landmarks with the binoculars. After many circuits on the sea, we were able to throw
the marker-buoy overboard and moor alongside it. We lay beneath the high cliffs
of the island which are dominated by the lighthouse and the old semaphore of
Titan. Nearby, some 120 m. to the west, the sea, calm everywhere else, broke
gently over the Esquillade, a turret with red and black bands built on the reefs
just beneath the surface.[3] When the divers were ready, the coxswain gave the
depth at 27 m. but the strength of the current at this point was such that we had to
take to the water from a dinghy, well above the buoy. We followed a narrow,
sinuous river of sand, which rapidly widened. Through a gully, we penetrated
into a circle of sand, bounded by a rocky talus some 5 or 6 m. high, which broke
the force of the current. From the centre emerged a heap of amphorae, about 30 m.
long by 12 m. wide and 2 m. high (Pl. 9). One after the other, four amphorae chosen
from the top of the deposit were fastened to lines and heaved on board the *Elie
Monnier*. Fernand Benoit identified them at once; they were amphorae of Dressel
type 6/14 of the time of Augustus, first century B.C.: they had no stamps and their
funnel mouths differed from the typical cylindrical types with straight necks of
Dressel 1.

Never had a wreck, ancient or otherwise, fired me with such curiosity and urgency. No other seemed to me to present such propitious conditions for recovery. A depth of 27 m. was sufficient to keep away the tyro, but diving could take place there with reasonable ease and almost complete safety.

By a wonderful chance, the wreck had come to rest in a rocky basin where one could be certain that the whole ship, down to the last nail, and all the cargo would be found; whereas more often, along sloping and flat bottoms, wrecks break up and in the course of centuries become dispersed.

Before making a proposal to the archaeologists or asking the assistance of the Navy, I had to consider and study closely the various aspects of the problem, to complete the examination of the wreck, and to try out some experiments on the site.

Preliminary observations

On 19 October, we again set out for Titan to make plans, take photographs, and to try out the air-lift. Agnès, our student draughtsman, assumed the function of underwater surveyor, and prepared in a few hours the plan and section of the basin and the wreck. For my part, I took vertical photographs. Not being able to get the whole wreck into one frame, I took them at regular intervals at exactly 10 m. from the bottom, which gave, when developed, a complete map of the wreck right up to the edges of the basin.[4] These, with the plans prepared by Agnès, were excellent records from which to work.

I also tested the efficiency of our air-lift, a wonderful tool which we had invented at G.E.R.S. and perfected in 1946, and which was now an indispensable adjunct of underwater archaeology.[5] In this case we wished to find out if it was possible to dig a trench with it from the rim of the rocky basin to the edge of the heap of amphorae. In two hours the trench was cut and Quartermaster Roussel, in charge of the air-lift, had in addition uncovered between points 4 and 5 a lead stock of classic Roman type, irrefutable proof of the presence of a ship.

The experiment was conclusive, but it demonstrated that the narrow after-deck of the *Elie Monnier* was not a suitable position for the air-lift, and that it was not possible to keep the pipe immediately over the area of work because of the currents.

Some kind of platform had to be found on which to install all the equipment. My choice fell on a type of lighter of 50 tons with a flat bottom, 26 m. long by 6 m. wide, which was unsinkable, as it was fitted with buoyancy tanks. The pipe of the air-lift, made up of sections of rubber tube, could be put into the water or raised by derrick. It rested in a gutter along the length of the lighter and disgorged at the other end through a system of screens and baffles, which enabled the material to be filtered and sorted.

At the end of March, Lighter 26 was ready. After it had been towed to the wreck, we tried out all the equipment, and returned to Toulon full of enthusiasm and confidence in its possibilities.

After these trials and experiences, I had sampled the rude problems which the sea posed for a floating workshop anchored in the open. I understood that the recovery could not be properly conducted unless it was firmly directed to the end; but I also knew that the naval divers, if their assistance was granted, would carry out this task with pride and enthusiasm, and without loss of discipline. Finally, I considered that the Naval Museum at Toulon, in the fine setting of the Tour Royale, would be in a position to receive and exhibit the reconstructed remains of the wreck.

Administrative negotiations with the Beaux Arts and the Navy were lengthy, and in the spring of 1955 I had to adjourn the expedition, having been appointed to the command of the Rhine Flotilla in the north.

I moved to the shores of the Rhine, where occasional news of Titan reached me through Fernand Benoit. The wreck had on several occasions been visited by divers.[6] But from a distance I told myself that these exploiters of amphorae could only take the easiest, and would not have reached the bottom: the Titan wreck did not seem to be lost to archaeology. In April 1957 I returned to the Mediterranean and resumed my project.

The authorizations were taken up once more and the equipment, including the lighter, was again lent by the Arsenal staff.

The excavation

It only remained for me to undertake the practical organization of the work and the team, and to put the principal director in the picture. I had asked for the assistance of Chief Petty Officer Jean Pinard, one of our first divers of G.E.R.S. and now serving on board *Béarn*. He had collected an excellent team of diving instructors: Petty Officers Treville and Moran, and Quartermasters Guillerme and Guillemot. All had been down to the Titan wreck, and the prospect of its recovery thrilled them. They worked furiously at the equipment of Lighter 26 in order that all might be ready in June.

I had requested a Service boat to ensure the liaison between Toulon and the Île du Levant, some twenty-seven miles off, but it was also necessary to establish our headquarters on the spot. The Navy is the principal owner of the island, and for the last ten years has used it as an experimental station of C.E.R.E.S. (Centre d'Essais et de Recherches des Engins Spéciaux). At the desired time this unit would supply the camp (tents and camp-beds), and food could be arranged by direct contact with the lighthouse-keepers.

The staff

To use Lighter 26 to the full, a permanent team of a dozen divers was required, not counting the mechanics and seamen needed to ensure the working of the surface machinery. Volunteer divers were not lacking, but for Service reasons it was necessary to foresee and organize frequent reliefs and continually put fresh divers in the picture. Service frogmen requested permission to spend their leave on Titan. So, around a permanent nucleus of divers, those newly arrived could be integrated painlessly, and the frequent changes would make no difference.

Master-Gunner Auger, Petty Officer Deguerres, Quartermasters Schaufelberger, Cathelineau, and Tonetti were remarkable divers—indefatigable, and accustomed to hard knocks and to working as a team.

I had obtained, for a few weeks at least, the assistance of Lieutenant de Clarens, also a Service diver, who was methodical and active, devoted to diving and archaeology. He was better qualified than any to ensure a good start to the work at Titan. Several officers, excellent divers, came by turns to take part in the operation; and the officer in charge of equipment, Warrant Officer Gouel, formerly of G.E.R.S., a wonderful diver and organizer, directed the towing out of the lighter and mooring at the beginning.

Two young probationers from the École de Santé Navale, Lapèze and Lamblin, and a sick-berth attendant and diver, Garmyn,[7] were in charge of the medical care of the divers. Finally, Ordinary Seaman Guy Delas, a champion spear-fisher, dealt with the various clerical duties.

Many diving friends belonging to the Mediterranean and Atlantic clubs came to see our work and to visit the wreck: Jean Piroux, who discovered it; Jean Pierre Charvoz; Dr. Delonca, President of the St. Raphael Club; Yves Girault; and George Beuchat and his son. From the start, three volunteer divers became so closely associated with the work that they formed part of the team. Paul Georgeot, Director of the Natural History Museum in Toulon, was enthralled by the wreck, Prince and Princess Napoléon, the latter a former pupil of Fernand Benoit, were the first to arrive and the last to leave the pontoon.

On 9 July, at four in the morning, Lighter 26 left Toulon, towed by the *Pachyderm*. The sea was high, the crossing was rough, and mooring a tough battle. At midday the job was done, and the team landed on the island, completely exhausted. The storm lasted eight days, during which we could do nothing but organize the camp. Every morning and evening a party went to check the moorings of the lighter. When in the end the wind and the sea died down, and we could see our way on board the raft, it was to find a real jumble of equipment. It took another eight days to put it in order, but we were proud of our floating island and knew what precautions to take.

Organization of work

I had made use of the bad weather to explain to the divers the general problem of underwater archaeology, and the necessity of conducting the excavations methodically and with great care throughout.

I had a line, graduated legibly from 0–30 m., permanently stretched along the edge of the site parallel to the axis of the basin, which was approximately magnetic north. This line was marked on a plan at 1 : 25 kept by the supervisor on the pontoon, on which the contours of the rocky basin, the limit of the work, were also reproduced.

If a diver, in the course of work with the air-lift or while exploring, discovered an object of interest he was instructed:

1. To leave the object in position.
2. To measure, with the aid of a line attached to the base-line, the distance at right angles from it.[8]
3. To report it to the supervisor on the surface, who would mark it on the plan and decide what was to be done after seeing it *in situ*.

A try-out in the handling of the air-lift enabled us to improve the filtering system by placing three screens across the sorting channel in the stream of water.

Every night at dinner reports were made on the day's work, and plans for the next day were prepared. Lieutenant de Clarens and a seaman, Alemany, were past-masters in reconstructing the pots from the debris brought up by the air-lift, caught in the nets and sorted by colour; they spent all their evenings at it.[9]

Each day, the plan of work having been prepared the night before, each one knew what he had to do, and in what part of the wreck and with whom he had to work. After the more or less lengthy operation of starting the compressor to fill the bottles, the divers went down in teams of two or three, being checked off at the ladder by the secretary, who kept a note of the time. The discipline for diving times and the routine was strict.[10]

The plan was prepared on the surface from the clear reports of the position made by the returning teams. I dived with one or other of the teams, either to see how the work was going on or to inspect a newly discovered object, and to film and photograph the site. There were two jobs to be undertaken: firstly, the clearance and raising of the cargo of amphorae and of the objects on board, and, secondly, the cleaning and raising of the hull.

We began by bringing up a batch of twenty amphorae, in order to estimate the time it would take. Having made the experiment, it seemed wiser to leave the amphorae on the bottom, but stacked on either side of the deposit along the walls of the basin. They could be raised later with basket and derrick to a deep barge specially prepared for their transport.

The work of clearing the amphorae lasted till the end of July. The air-lift having dug into the sand, the divers then removed the amphorae and arranged them in hundreds round the edge of the site. They had a tough, navvying job to which no one could see an end and which had to be undertaken with great care.

As well as the amphorae, the air-lift exposed bits of wood, objects of daily use, and in some places, under the amphorae, even touched on the ribs. But before they could be explored, some 500 amphorae had to be brought up. We calculated that to raise them one by one by hand would take eight days; with the basket and derrick, the time could be reduced to four days. Made with cross-bars, the basket looked like an immense bottle-container. It raised sixteen amphorae at a time, all filled with sand and weighing about 50 kg.

On 31 July raising began. The first load from the basket was a wonderful spectacle, for these amphorae, streaming with colour, water, life, and light, thrilled the assistants. While the basket went up and down ceaselessly, bringing up sometimes a full load of amphorae, sometimes fragments of pottery, the washing of the amphorae proceeded on deck. The workers found an easy method: they laid them on their sides with the point slightly raised, and each in turn was hosed through the neck with a fire-hose. A few still had their stoppers in position,[11] but all without exception were filled with sand.

In each of those which retained its stopper, we observed a brownish deposit of sand mixed with debris. A careful study revealed the presence, without possible doubt, of bones, scales, and vertebrae of fish of various sizes. This sand tainted the fingers slightly, and even, if one is to believe some of the divers, smelt of olive oil.[12]

Contrary to the amphorae from Anthéor and Grand Congloué, none of those from Titan was stamped; none was exactly alike, and it seems that they have not been made in a mould, but formed by the hand of the potter.

M. Fernand Benoit[13] has distinguished the two following types: (Fig. 29).

(a) Dressel type 12, 48 of Pelichet (time of Augustus); tapered amphora, of which the neck joins the body at an angle at the point of attachment of the handle, prolonging the general line of the body. Handles, angular or rounded, form an oval volute, sometimes with a central ridge widening out at the angle. The everted mouth is marked by a ridge. A massive foot prolongs the body. Several variants of the same type are distinguished by the width of the neck, often shorter and wider; height 1·10 m., diameter of body 0·19–0·28 m. (Borély Nos. 385–6726).

Several of the amphorae of this type have retained their terracotta stoppers (diameter approximately 112 mm.), with knobs, sometimes pierced, but without stamps.

(b) Ovoid amphora with double handles, Dressel type 10, resembling in shape the amphora of pickled fish from Augst in Switzerland. In another article,[14] M. Benoit states that this amphora, found in 1955, is preserved at the C.A.S.M. of Cannes. In 1957 another of Dressel type I B[15] with horizontal shoulders was found

F

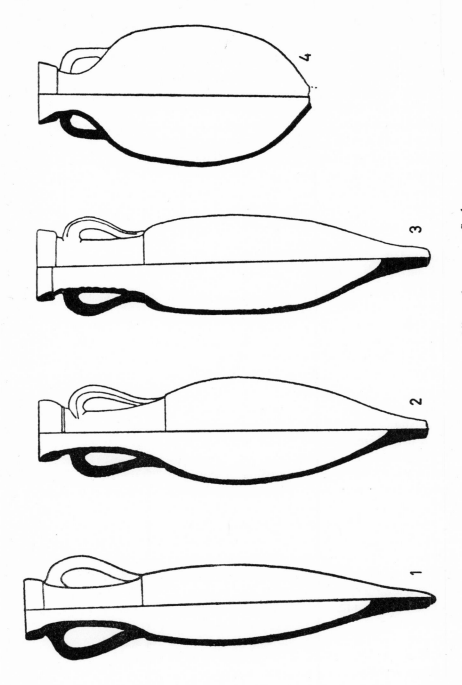

Fig. 29.   Wine amphorae 1–3; Oil amphora 4   Scale 1 : 10

with part of the neck missing. All the others are of the same type, but of five different shapes, some being taller and narrower (1–1·10 m.)

It is rather difficult to estimate the number of amphorae which had been taken from the site before our excavation commenced, perhaps between 500 and 1,000. Did any of these bear stamps? In this case only would they have furnished more information.

Throughout the excavation the air-lift revealed a certain number of objects which did not form part of the cargo, but were ship's utensils. On several occasions, we found fragments of tiles (Fig. 30) with quarter-round moulded edges,[16] similar to those found on the wrecks of Mahdia, Anthéor, and Congloué. The generally accepted theory is that these formed the roof of the cabin.[17]

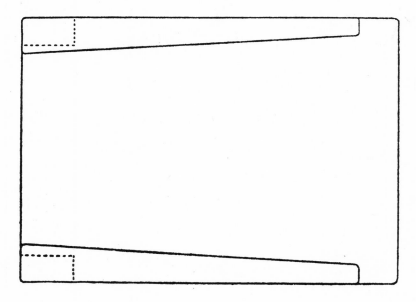

FIG. 30.   Roof tile   Scale 1 : 6

A corn-mill, very similar to the one we found at Mahdia in 1947, was found at point 22D.

Several times we found a rather heterogeneous group of pottery:[18] sundry pieces of Campanian B, with pinkish-grey body and mat black glaze which included:

Pyxides (Lamboglia forms 2 and 3) (Fig. 31.7, 9).
A handleless bowl with incurved sides, derived from a skyphos (Lamboglia form 1).

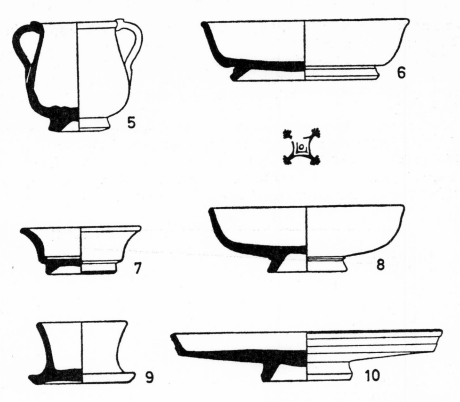

FIG. 31. Campanian B pottery: 5 two-handled pot; 6 bowl with everted rim;
7, 9 pyxides; 8 bowl with palmette decoration; 10 dish with incised circles
Scale 1 : 3

A plate with vertical sides and a flat bottom (Lamboglia form 5), prototype of the
Aretine dish (Dragendorf 17), decorated with incised concentric circles (Fig.
31.10).
A small pot with two handles (Lamboglia form 13) (Fig. 31.5).
Lastly, two terracotta lamps, both with conical bodies, lugs on the sides, and a
ring handle. A complete one of pink clay with red-brown slip belonged to
Dressel type 3; the other, of which the handle was found separately, was of
red clay with red glaze; the body was taller and the spout, almost triangular,
heralds the classic form of the Augustan period[19] (Fig. 32).
Plain *olpi* or jugs, five in all; four were found together on 26 July and the other on
12 August.
There were also metal objects: two semi-oncial *aes*, the metal much corroded.
One illegible, was brought up by the air-lift at the same time as a thin leaf of
finely ribbed yellow metal; it weighed 9·7 gm.; the other, which has supplied

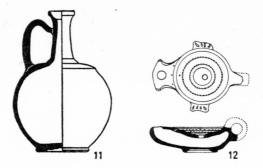

FIG. 32.   Coarse ware *olpe* 11; lamp 12
Scale 1 : 3

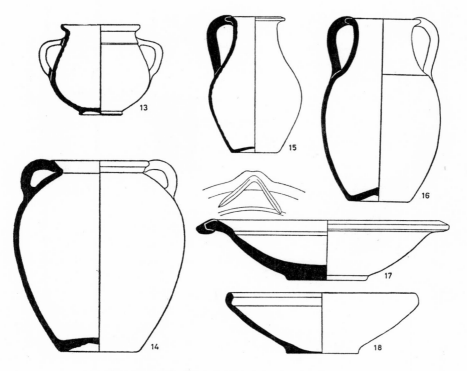

FIG. 33.   Cooking pottery   Scale 1 : 6

valuable information, was found in a hole where the trenail was missing: it weighed 11·8 gm.;[20] maximum diameter 0·029 m. The prow of a ship to the left was visible on the reverse.

Part of a dish with flat rim, imitating a Campanian type (Lamboglia form 6);

small round holes in the rim, perhaps for fixing the lid; diameter 0·33 m, height 0·41 m. (Fig. 34.22).

A *cyathus*, or ladle with long handle and spatulate end, length with handle 0·35 m.; height 0·070 m.[21]

A small bronze spoon; length 0·125 m. (Fig. 34.21).

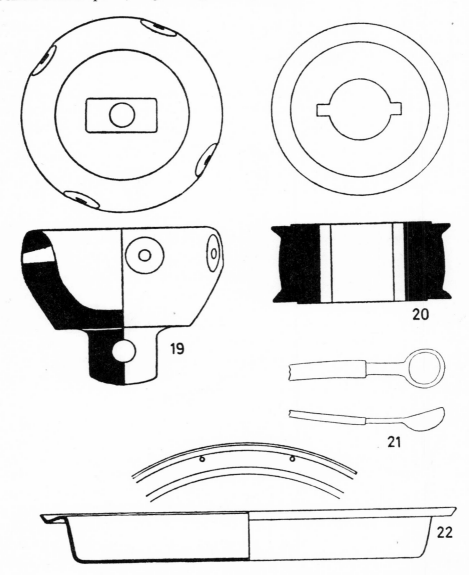

FIG. 34. Hollow lead object with four holes for cords 19;
wooden pulley block 20; bronze ladle 21; bronze dish 22
Scale 1 : 3

Fish-hooks, identical with those from Lake Nemi and Grand Congloué, were
found in a ball of tangled line completely covered with concretion.
We also found strips of lead, one piece in the shape of a horseshoe with holes at
either end, of unknown use.

At the beginning, on 16 July, de Clarens had found in the top of the sand a
piece of wood, 1·50 m. long, curiously eaten away. All the fibres of the wood were
still visible but the piece was very brittle. This isolated fragment, found to the
south of the site, seemed to us to belong to the after-part of the keel near the
stern.[22]

In many places under the amphorae wood had appeared, but before we could
deal with it we had to clear the site of all sorts of debris with which it was covered.
We had to suck up many metres of sand mixed with calcareous concretions, pale
mauve *pralines*, and innumerable skeletons and fossils, which were the delight
of Georgeot.

On 1 August, abeam of point 2 at the north part of the site, a piece of wood
emerged; it was almost as warped and eaten by teredos as the former piece. It
measured 1·65 m. long, and we thought it might be a piece of the poop. Suddenly,
on 3 August, the air-lift uncovered, between points 11 and 17, seven ribs very
close together, partly resting on lumps of rock. The planking was still in place,
but this wood was so fragile that at one point the head of the air-lift cut through
it.[23] The ribs were so friable that even the pressure of a finger left its mark. To raise
them from the water already posed an embarrassing problem, and even in position
they required the greatest care.[24]

During the work of clearance, miscellaneous objects continued to be found.
We uncovered another group of amphorae containing the usual scales and bones
of fish. In one I found a handful of almonds which in shape and colour were
almost unchanged. Two finely worked platters of wood, caught between two ribs,
disintegrated into dust as the divers touched them.

Days passed, and we worked to reach the bottom. The lead line showed 29 m.
instead of 27 m., as at the beginning, and we had to adjust the dives to allow for
this. The hull was now completely clear—at least, what was left of it. It was a
strange sight, like the giant backbone of a fish or a ladder with very close rungs,
between which the divers busily finished removing the sand. I pondered about this
method of construction of keel, ribs, floor timbers, and planks, this vertebral
column with its ribs imitating the upper vertebrates, which had been in use more
than a thousand years ago (Pl. 9).

The ribs were very close together, about 15 cm. apart, inserted here and there
in the keel for a distance of 1 to 2 m. The backbone arrangement of these remains,
surprising at first sight, is, after all, logical. The Roman merchant ships (*naves
onerariae*) had a very flat bottom. From all accounts, except for the pointed ends,

they must have resembled our lighter in shape and dimensions. Judging from the two pieces initially raised, thought to be part of the stern and stem, the ship was not more than 25 m. long.[25]

I filmed the wreck constantly, as a whole and in detail, for it was necessary to have an indisputable record of the backbone. Certainly we would attempt to raise it, but the wood appeared so fragile that I had grave doubts—as much for the success of the operation as for its ultimate preservation on land. Georgeot and I examined carefully *in situ* the assembly of the keel, ribs, and planks. It would later be drawn at the Tour Royale and reconstructed by Charles Lagrand from my directions and those of the naval architect, Mauric (Fig. 35).

The hull planks, freed from their lead sheathing, are of carvel construction and of lighter wood, which might be pine. They are joined, without any caulking, by excellent mortices.[26]

The keel of the Titan wreck, for the middle section at least, is doubled by a keelson. They were joined together at varying distances by vertical pieces of wood, thick trenails, which passed through the ribs to ensure the rigidity of the hull throughout its length. The ribs perpendicular to the axis are in one piece, like 'Caesar's Galley'; the thickest part, the floor timber, is inserted into slots made in the lower side of the keelson. A repair on one side of the hull shows the insertion of an extra piece between two ribs.

But this very fragile wood had to be raised from the bottom, to which it still adhered strongly, and we were much bothered.[27] But time pressed, and we resorted to a crude solution, which consisted of sawing the keel into two pieces 8 m. long, and one by one detaching the ribs and the planks still in position, after having drawn a plan of them. To bring up each piece, at the base we prepared a lot of frames and planks sawn to the requisite length: the divers attached them to each rib and half-keel so that they could be raised in the water and brought to the surface without risk of breaking.

The big job was the raising of the two parts of the keel. The frames, ballasted at first, were fastened by goose-feet to the cable of the derrick, guided to the bottom on to the half-keel and lashed up by four divers. The cable was slowly tightened and each piece was detached from the bottom, raising a black eddy in its wake. It was stopped at the surface to adjust each support, so that the ancient wood rested squarely in its cradle. Then it was deposited in the bottom of a barge brought from Toulon and specially prepared to transport the wood. We worked for two whole days at this delicate piece of salvage. On 9 September the barge was towed back to Toulon with 2 to 3 tons of ancient wood in its hold. A similar task of stretcher-bearing would have to be repeated this time, for some 400 m., from the quay to the Tour Royale.

Before leaving the site, which had the appearance of a robbed cemetery, the air-lift was put to work for the last time. It uncovered a sort of leaden bell with

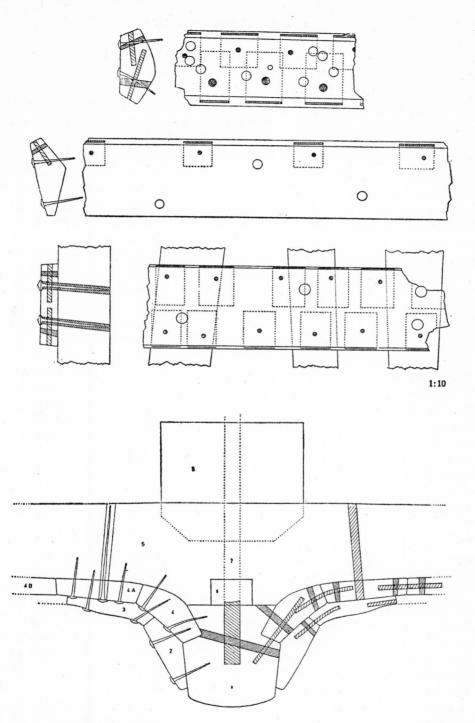

1:10

1:10

FIG. 35.   Titan wreck; diagram of hull and keel

four holes and having a suspension ring, some nails, and debris of tiles and a wooden disc, which disintegrated like its predecessors.

We returned to Toulon, where several problems had to be resolved, notably those concerning the preservation of wood. The latter appeared to me practically insoluble. I had consulted a number of archaeologists, abroad as well as in France, without success,[28] and it was a problem which had been considered at the second congress at Albenga. Since then Professor Brouardel had experimented, it seems with some success, with a new process of treatment, and had constructed a tank for its application at the Oceanographic Institute at Monaco, but no more than several cubic decimetres of wood could be treated. If this apparatus had been in existence at the time of raising of Titan we could at least have used it to preserve the shape of some of the pieces which have now disintegrated.

As to the several tons of wood of the wreck, we had to be satisfied, on the direction of Fernand Benoit, with wrapping them in cloths, resting them on a bed of shavings, and placing them in cases. In that way he believed by slow drying the fibres would be saved.[29]

Dating

According to Fernand Benoit, the whole group of material, the pottery (Campanian B), the amphorae and the lamps (Dressel 3 of Republican times), and the coins, from the point of view of the ship, are of a period sufficiently close to that of 'Caesar's Galley' to permit of a theory. These various objects can be dated in the first century, at the time of Caesar, more particularly to the time of the Gallic Wars. The cargo of pickled fish suggested to Fernand Benoit that the ship was destined for supplying Caesar's army during the siege of Marseilles (51–49 B.C.).

Conclusion

On an ancient wreck, after having planned the cargo, it is then necessary to take care of the objects on board and, at the end, the hull and the equipment. That was the way I felt compelled to organize the work on Titan.

What distinguishes the remains of a wreck is first that we have an assemblage of objects which we are certain were collected and in use at one time at a fixed date, when it sank; they constitute a slice of time. Further, they have suffered no alteration or destruction by human agency since the time of the wreck. These two characteristics, rarely encountered on land, confer a particular importance on underwater excavation within the general framework of archaeology, and a documentary value, which enhance all the aspirations of discovery. They cannot fail to become more noticeable as the techniques of underwater investigation progress.

But for the present, it must be said, underwater archaeology is still in the early stages. It must find its feet through the experience gained on the first sites. Titan is one of them, and if I have devoted considerable space to it, it is neither a vanity of the author nor to present a model method. We have tried sincerely, to the best of our ability, but I know many mistakes were made and we had to leave the site before we had completed our task; and after the excavation I found myself with problems which were none of my making and which none knew how to solve.

If we had been assisted from the beginning by an archaeologist, he would surely have noted with much greater accuracy the position of each object; by personal inspection he would have drawn more information from the slightest indications.

But I can at least show that the beginning and conducting of an underwater archaeological site is definitely a difficult task which demands from the participants, at all levels, faith, persistence, and courage. It cannot be undertaken by casual methods, but, on the contrary, necessitates, over a long period, the preparation of the appropriate marine appliances and of specialized equipment.

Underwater excavation is a problem for sailors and divers rather than the archaeologist. How difficult it is, in this century of specialization, to be all three at once! The archaeologist in particular must realize that he cannot accomplish this task without the help of the other two.

It is for the leader of the excavation to co-ordinate these three tasks. Sailors, divers, and archaeologists will ease his position if they work as a team and neither permit any activity on a wreck nor bring up any object for which the information obtained from its position on the site has not been recorded.

NOTES

The account of this excavation appeared as 'Travaux de l'été 1958 sur l'épave du "Titan" a l'Île du Levant (Toulon)', in *Atti dell' II Congresso Internazionale di Archeologia Sottomarina* (Albenga, 1958), 175ff.

1 The film *Mars and Neptune* had been taken in the sea off the Îles d'Or.
2 Some excellent photos, taken by Rebikoff, had appeared in *Pointe de Vue—Images du Monde* of 5 November 1953.
3 The level of the Mediterranean, we now know with certainty, has not changed greatly in the course of history; the same reefs, it seems, were there at the time when Julius Caesar was suppressing the Gauls.
4 This is the first time, I believe, that the technique of photographic air-cover has been applied to submarine geography, which is particularly helpful for numbering amphorae visible on the surface.
5 The air-lift consists of a pipe with a flexible end, 10–20 cm. in diameter, and a conical metal head fitted with handles. A thinner pipe, fed by a low-pressure compressor, runs parallel to the main pipe and leads into the head of the air-lift on the bottom; the operator keeps the head firmly in contact with the floor. The air passed into the pipe establishes a strong vacuum: the head sucks up sand, mud, sherds, and all objects smaller than its diameter.

6 Two of them had been arrested on this account and sentenced after a long trial.
7 They were trained by the Chief Medical Officer, Pierre Cabarrou, and were in charge of the one-man decompression chamber, in the case of an accident.
8 5.D.7., for instance, indicated an object 5 m. to the right of the base line at 7 m. along it.
9 The interesting fragments were submitted to M. Fernand Benoit for identification, or sent to the Endoume Laboratory at Marseilles, or to the Musée Borély for analysis, cleaning, and reconstruction.
10 The length of the dives was fixed at twenty-eight minutes: the first without decompression stop, the second with stops depending on the interval between dives. Active work carried out on the bottom added to the fatigue of the divers, so that only two dives per day per man could be made, instead of three, as I had anticipated. For decompression stops, the amount of nitrogen remaining dispersed in the body from the first dive had to be taken into account.
11 Thin discs of pottery which had, perhaps, been sealed in position by plaster, though no trace of the latter now remained.
12 The analysis of this debris at the Endoume Laboratory at Marseilles showed that for the most part it consisted of *pelamides*, a variety of tunny still caught in the Mediterranean. See F. Benoit, 'Épaves de la Côte de Provence', *Gallia*, XIV (1956), 29.
13 F. Benoit, *Gallia*, XIV (1956), 29; types of amphorae, Fig. I, 11–13.
14 Ibid., XVI (1958), 5.
15 Ibid., 6, note 5.
16 Characteristics of the Republican period: F. Benoit, *Gallia*, XVI (1958), 8.
17 N. Lamboglia, 'La nave romana di Albenga', *Rivista di Studi Liguri*, XVIII, 8.
18 The descriptions and references are those of F. Benoit's article, 'Nouvelles épaves de Provence', in *Gallia*, XVI (1958), 5.
19 Both of the Republican period, one rather late; they furnish some precision for the date: *Gallia*, XVI (1958) 9, Figs. 4–5.
20 'It is later than the monetary reforms of 89 which had fixed the weight of the aes at 13·50 gm.', F. Benoit, *Gallia*, XVI (1958), 6.
21 Covered with calcareous concretion, which had destroyed the wall of the vessel, it was reconstructed by Mme Gil Faure at the Musée Borély from a cast of the concretion.
22 Two years previously, at the other end of the site, we had uncovered an anchor stock which normally would be found at the bow.
23 The hole gaped and intrigued us, for it might have led into another deck or hold, containing different goods.
24 Our air-lift was too heavy, and we replaced it with another of only 10 cm. diameter, and with a proportionately reduced head.
25 This reduced tonnage must have been common in antiquity for several reasons: ease of handling, shallow draught, and anxiety of the shipowners to spread the costs because of piracy or shipwreck.
26 'The construction', writes F. Benoit, 'differs from that of Grand Congloué, of which a small part of the hull has been raised, and from that of the Mahdia wreck. But it recalls "Caesar's Galley", a flat-bottomed boat without lead sheathing, found in the mud at Marseilles in 1864, during the construction of a building at a point corresponding to the bottom of the harbour in Roman times,' *Gallia*, XVI (1958), 11.

27   In calm water at a depth of 5 to 6 m., we could have constructed a coffer-dam round the wreck and worked in the dry. This was not possible here. The other solution would have been to build a full-scale model in wood and to bring the whole lot up lashed to the copy. But to make a copy of this size on the island and manipulate it proved impossible.

28   Methods are known for the preservation of wood of ancient ships found in fresh water: by soaking and exchanging the water for alcohol and xylol from time to time, followed by warming and stiffening with paraffin wax. None is entirely satisfactory, nor applicable for sea use.

29   Two years later I measured a piece of this wood and found a shrinkage at the surface, but the texture and grain of the heart were sound. This wood could be sawn and gave off an odour of musk and cedar.

(f) Dramont 'A'

The wreck[1] was discovered by M. Claude Santamaria in 1956 and explored by the St. Raphael diving group. M. Santamaria writes:

'The wreck lies near a reef about 1 km. south of Cape Dramont. Without doubt, the merchant ship, disabled either by a gale from the east or by the mistral, was driven ashore, having struck the reef, which is barely covered by 2 m. of water. The currents and the natural slope of the bottom have certainly drawn her away from the rock, for she lies 80 m. from it; this may explain why she was not found previously, for divers usually search nearer the reef. After descending some 35 m., the diver finds himself before a slightly oval tumulus of broken amphorae, measuring 22 m. by 9 m. The pile of amphorae, buried some 2·5 m. in the half-mud, half-shell sand of the bottom, lies at an angle of about 30 degrees. Apart from the depth, the chief obstacle was how to attack the crust of concretion and amphorae, and remove the compacted mud which covered everything.

'Nevertheless, two factors gave us renewed hope. First, the existence of a destructive current from the east, which, bit by bit, denuded the site; and also the feeling that we had here a wreck relatively little buried compared to the other archaeological sites off the coast.

'So we went to work, first with my little boat of 5 tons (the *Marie Claude*), later with another boat, and we soon obtained tangible results. The appearance of the deposit made us believe that we had a "cargo" as important as that of Albenga (which Lamboglia estimated as from 2,000 to 3,000 amphorae).

'The almost complete complement was made up of Italic wine amphorae, Dressel type 1 [Lamboglia type IB] (Fig. 36.1, 2). The amphorae of the Dramont A wreck are characterized by high, vertical handles and conical necks; the shoulder meets the body at a sharp angle and the foot is high and cylindrical. The height of these amphorae varies from 118 to 122 cm.; they contained 26 litres, and therefore represented the exact amphora measure, or quadrantal.

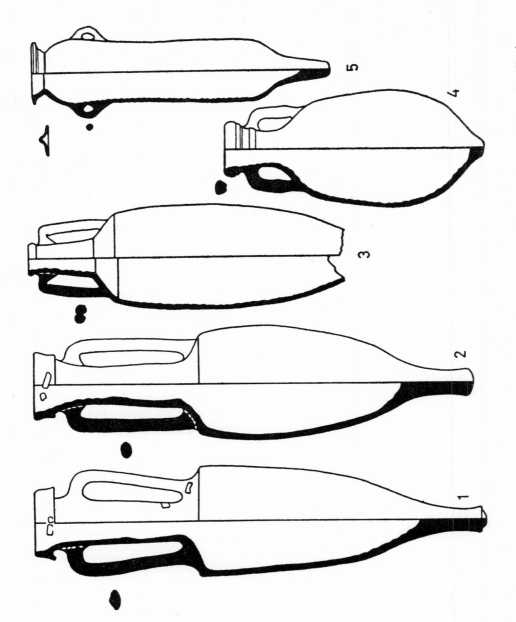

FIG. 36. Wine amphorae: 1, 2 of *Pilip(us)* and *Heraclius*; 3, with double handles and roll rim; 4, oil amphora; 5 Punic amphora with lid   Scale 1 : 10 (after *Gallia* XVI)

'The slight variations in type are evidence of hand-work: vertical or everted lips, and high or low feet. Others have a hemispherical terminal knob, and handles nearer to or further from the neck.

'The great importance of the Dramont wreck, in my opinion, lies in the multiplicity of marks stamped on the few amphorae brought up. In fact, our incomplete excavation has produced ten stamps [see below. p. 99].

'Summary though it is, the excavation that we have undertaken also yielded amphorae of quite different types, mixed with the wine amphorae.

'First of all, at one end of the deposit (which the divers soon referred to familiarly as the "cabin"), we brought up other amphorae and some pieces of domestic pottery. There, lying side by side, were: (1) An oil amphora, short (70 cm.) and fat. The lip is rounded and the neck very short. It does not appear in the Dressel classification and has been placed by Dr. Lamboglia in his type 2 of the Albenga wreck [Fig. 36.4]. (2) A "Punic" amphora, containing olives and an olive branch [Fig. 36.5]. This amphora is much taller than the former (90 cm.) and is completely cylindrical, with a long, conical foot (20 cm.), everted lip and small loop handles on the shoulder; it was closed by a pottery stopper with knob [Fig. 36.5]. (3) Several pieces of domestic pottery, notably an *olpe* with one handle [Fig. 38.10], and a small amphora with flat base and high, vertical rim [Fig. 37.6]. From one side of the deposit were brought up: a small complete amphora, 50 cm. high, besides several fragments of similar type [Fig. 37.8]; a small amphora with angular shoulder and flat base, h. 60 cm.; there were two ridges below the rim and the handles had a flat section [Fig. 37.9].

'The excavations were very brief, for our means were negligible compared to those available at Albenga, Grand Congloué, and even for Titan. But further campaigns may yield more conclusive results and the study of this wreck may perhaps reveal that the cargo was destined to supply the nearby port of Fréjus (Forum Julii).

'There was one curious discovery concerning the equipment of the ship: during the first season, the divers noticed the presence of two lead pipes, some 6 cm. in diameter, in the forward and after thirds of the wreck. These, curiously enough, lay on top of the deposit and followed the slope of the tumulus, descending deep into the mud (one was uncovered for more than 1 m.). The fact that these lead pipes were found on top of the amphorae seems to indicate that they were either on or immediately under the deck of the ship. If, as may be supposed, these pipes belonged to the pump intended for drawing water from the bilge, then the position is, to say the least of it, curious. Once again it seems that the discussion concerning the equipment of ancient ships is open, and it is to be hoped that the Dramont or another will give the much-sought-after solution.'

Unfortunately, the site was looted and dynamited during 1957, but in August 1959 an organized excavation was undertaken, with funds from C.N.R.S., at the request of M. Benoit.

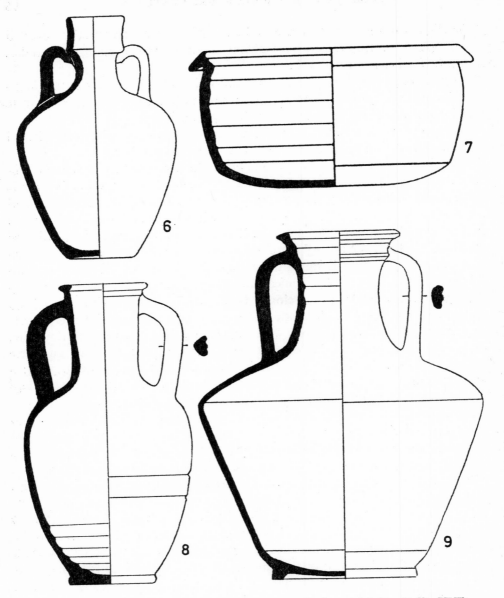

FIG. 37. Domestic amphorae and basin   Scale 1 : 6 (after *Gallia* XVI)

The work was carried out from the *Espadon* of Commandant Cousteau under the direction of M. Frédéric Dumas of G.E.R.S. and M. Sivirine of O.F.R.S. M. Dumas[2] comments:

'One of the reasons which governed the choice of the Dramont wreck was probably the magnificent aspect of her appearance when she was first found.

96

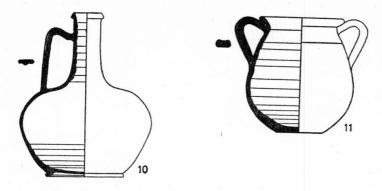

FIG. 38. Domestic *olpe* and two-handled pot   Scale 1 : 6
(after *Gallia* XVI)

Few wrecks are as fine, and many are hardly visible. Often they are mixed with rock and merged with it. The Dramont wreck, sunk in 35 m. of water some 50 m. from the reef on which she struck, was like a real stone boat on a gently sloping plain of sand. The wine amphorae which constituted her load formed a mound 20 m. long by 7 to 8 m. wide, and 2 m. high, on which centuries of marine organisms had spread a roof of calcareous concretion, making a deck of stone covered with flowers for this dead ship.

'In places there were cracks and holes where one could see amphorae, all leaning the same way, stacked one upon another. Many fish inhabited this submarine palace.

'On 8 August 1959, when Alinat and I reconnoitred for a plan of work, the crust of concretion had for the most part disappeared and several hundred amphorae were missing, leaving a few depressing sherds. The wreck, like so many on our coast, had been looted. . . .

'To save some of the cargo . . . Dr. Delonca had worked on the wreck, recovering the amphorae and sherds . . . so from the aspect of this wreck it seemed that the hull was still in fairly good order underneath, an opinion which our work confirmed.

'An ancient wreck is no longer a ship containing amphorae; it is a pile of amphorae entirely buried in the sand, on a flattened hull. After having cleared everything, some sound timber is found, hard wood being darker than soft. In places the marks of carpenters' tools can be seen: the fresh aspect of the wood is misleading, for it is a soft material which is very fragile when it has to be removed and brought on shore, where it shrinks very much. So far no satisfactory method of preserving it has been found. . . .

'So we confined ourselves to cutting a section across the hull, measuring and photographing it, and, after having sawn them out, bringing up various pieces of the hull, keel, garboards, keelson, planks . . . and specimens of their joints.

'The first task was to remove all the amphorae. Those more or less broken were piled around the wreck some 3 m. from her visible limits; the few whole amphorae were brought to the surface. . . .

'Having cleaned up the wreck, we opened a trench across it near the centre. One diver sucked up the sand; another freed the material which appeared on the floor. While the mud remaining on the surface was carried away very slowly by the current, all the shells, the concretions, and some sand fell back about the diver.

'The excavation [Pl. 10] showed us that the orderly appearance of the stacking of amphorae was an illusion, and only in a few places corresponded to the upper layers. Beneath the sand the amphorae were in disorder, and many were broken. On the whole, the load leaned in one direction. About 1 m. below the sand the air-lift struck wood, but this wood was easily disintegrated if care was not taken. We patiently cleared a section some 7 m. by 1 m. There was an internal planking of soft wood which almost everywhere the weight of the cargo had broken down between the ribs; the latter were some 7 cm. thick and 12–16 cm. wide and rather close together, the spaces being no larger than the ribs themselves. Finally, we found a double skin dowelled to the ribs—that is to say, two layers of planks 30–35 mm. thick, making a hull thickness of 7 cm.

'In order to get a cleaner section and examine the hull better, it was necessary to saw through it with a compass saw, removing a strip some 50 cm. wide. After some difficulties and anxieties, we were able to find the keel, riddled with worm, flanked by the garboards.*

'By degrees, as the trench progressed, the undamaged amphorae were taken up. Some kitchen pottery, part of a helmet, and some food were recovered.

'The meagre results of this excavation had a satisfactory end, for a good section of the keel was recovered, but it was annoying not to be able to continue to search for the two ends of the keel.'

M. Benoit writes:[3]

'It appears that the bottom of the ship was composed of a keel and keelson: but the slots in the keelson seem to indicate that the ribs were alternately formed by half-timbers (Grand Congloué type) and whole timbers (Île du Levant type), running from port to starboard: this arrangement gives a third type of ribbing intermediate between the other two.

'The assembling of the planks with tenon and mortice is identical with the

---

* Although the phrase 'and above, a large, massive and well-preserved keelson' appears in the *F.F.E.S.M. Bulletin*, October 1959, I never mentioned a keelson on that wreck; there was nothing like it in our trench. The big timber we recovered on the axis of the ship, outside the trench, was unknown to me at that time (F. Dumas).

other wrecks. There was no lead sheathing, but lead rigging fittings, pipes, pyramidal net-sinkers, and a thick, folded sheet of lead (for an oar?) were found.

'Other objects from the second expedition included Campanian C pottery, a lamp with thumb-piece and ring handle of the time of Augustus (Dressel 2), a two-handled jar with a flat base, an oil amphora, and a much-corroded *aes*, which may belong to the coin type with the prow of a galley of late Republican times.

'About 180 amphorae of Dressel type 1B were brought up, some with new stamps: *Heraclid(es)* with two counter-marks, no doubt the name of the exporter; *S* followed by an anchor, already known, and three examples of *Fab(ius)*; also some uncommon plaster stoppers, incomplete, and stamped *Sex*.'

M. Benoit describes the finds from the first campaign:[4]

'These amphorae (Fig. 36) belong to several types, of which the synchronism poses an enigma. The most numerous group, of which some twenty fragments have been brought up, belonged to the most recent and largest (1·15–1·26 m.) form of Dressel 1, which is distinguished by the letter B from the traditionally earlier group (Dressel 1A) whose height does not exceed 1 m. The cylindrical amphora with a massive foot rejoining the ogive of the handle is remarkable for the profile of the lip—vertical or slightly oblique, sometimes concave in the widest examples, which reach a depth of 6–8 cm.

'Two varieties can be distinguished in this group: the tallest amphora, 1·20–1.26m., having a lip measuring 8 cm., has no mark: this seems to be reserved for a rather shorter variety of 1·15–1·18 m. Some ten of the latter do in fact bear double marks stamped on lip and shoulder, near the base of the handle, and in one case at the base of the neck, sometimes followed by a counter-mark on the lip. These marks are different, as are those of the La Ciotat wreck.

'The names inscribed in a rectangular stamp (3 cm. by 1·6 cm. approx.) (Fig 39) belong to the *Gentilicai* known in Campania, of which several are also found in the Narbonnaise: *Bac(chius)*, *Dam(a)*, *Evta(clus)*, *Onel(lus)*, *Heracli(us)*, *Pilip(us)*, *Herm(aores)*, *Moc(conus?)*.

'Several other types of contemporary amphorae have been brought up from this wreck: (1) a fat-bellied oil amphora with a moulded neck and a quarter-round lip; (2) an ovoid amphora less than 1 m. high, with a short, conical neck, rounded lip, and angular double handles, a late type from Cos; and (3) an amphora of the so-called Punic type, with its pottery stopper, which still contained olives and in the middle of which were pieces of twig. This type of amphora, descendant of the Phoenician or Punic amphora, which could not have been made anywhere else than in south Italy, is now known by the typological evolution which V. Grace has traced through the material from the Agora excavations. The oldest example in Provence has been found in the excavations of the *oppidum* of Rennes

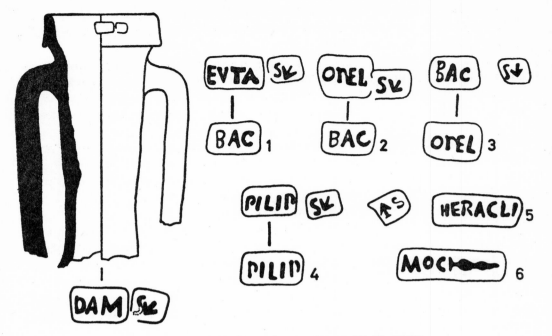

FIG. 39. Stamps from the amphorae (*Gallia* XVI)

of third to second centuries B.C. [Musée Borély, 11,719]: it measures 87 cm. high and 22 cm. in diameter: the cylindrical body, with two small handles at the top of the shoulder and short neck ending in a straight flange, can be compared to the Agora amphora SS.14,069, dated to 200 B.C. by V. Grace.

'These may also be related to the amphorae with straight necks, used as drain-pipes, found in the excavations of Ruscino, near Perpignan, which have an Ibero-Punic origin going back to the third and second centuries B.C.

'Amphorae coming from underwater excavations, in spite of their relation to these types, are of later date. The amphorae from Fos found recently in the Bay of St. Gervais can be compared to the amphorae S.14,069 and P. 6,762 of the Agora, with straight and bevelled necks, dated to 200 B.C. and the second half of second century B.C., but they cannot be older than the founding of the port of Fos by Marius (104 B.C.). The Dramont amphorae with the moulded neck is related to Agora SS.6,598 and 6,815 of the end of the second century B.C. Its association with the Italic amphora, Dressel 1, and the amphora with double handles, Dressel 5, inclines one to lower the date to the end of the first century B.C. following the typological evolution which can be defined by the wrecks of Albenga, Genoa-Pegli, and La Maddalena in Sardinia.

'The source of the amphorae sets another problem. If the type is related to that

100

of the Punic amphorae of Cintas dated by the necropolis of the fourth to second centuries B.C. and to which belong the examples from Ruscino, the manufacture of this amphora can only be Italian. This is what we supposed for the examples of so-called Punic type, with a body of medium size, found with the amphorae of Sestius from Grand Congloué; the date for the incomplete specimen of the Agora P.8,946, at the beginning of the first century B.C., would appear, on the other hand, to be too low.'

Special underwater apparatus used on the Dramont wreck (A. Sivirine)

This note appeared in *Le Plongeur et L'Archéologue* as 'Particularités du travail sous-marin sur l'épave du Dramont' (Fig. 40).

'The limited time available for the *Espadon* to carry out the work on the wreck of the Dramont, near St. Raphael, made it necessary to use better techniques than in an ordinary investigation. The working depth of from 32 to 39 m. emphasized this necessity.

'The preliminary work had to be done as quickly as possible, with the help of an air-lift, the "Pointe Bic", that was very light and easily handled, but unfortunately was not very effective; it had a diameter of 10 cm. and a length of about 4 m.

'For the transverse section, a larger air-lift was necessary. We therefore installed the old hose of the Grand Congloué, which was made up of components 5 m. long and 120 mm. in diameter. This hose, which comprised five components, weighed about 400 kg., and had to be supported at its upper end. Since we were 1 km. offshore, in an area where the sea was never calm, there would have been constant repercussion between the fixed float and the working end of the air-lift.

'Under these conditions, work of any precision would have been impossible, and there would have been more material damaged than was recovered. The solution of the problem, already tried out on a small scale at Mahdia, was to suspend the hose from a float, submerged in calmer water about 6–7 m. down.

'The balance of weights was established as follows:

		kg.
Weight of hose .	. . . . .	400
Weight of anchors (pig iron)	. . . .	400
		800
Steel buoyancy floats	. . . . .	700
Difference.	. . . . . .	100

'This allowed the hose to remain stable while permitting it to move easily from one side to the other of the working area by attaching an inflatable bag capable of lifting about 100 kg. to the anchors. The assemblage, therefore, having a positive buoyancy, it was possible to move the contrivance from one side of the site to the other.

'It should be noted that in order to make the bottom end lighter, a float weighing about 10 kg. was permanently hooked to it.

'If the section through the cargo could be made relatively easily with the help of the air-lift, it was by no means as easy when it came to the wood, which was inevitably drawn in by the nozzle whenever we approached too near. The logical solution was to scoop up, so to speak, the sand with our hands and let the air-lift take it away as suspended mud. Girault's picture showing Manganelli at work illustrates this method [Pl. 10].

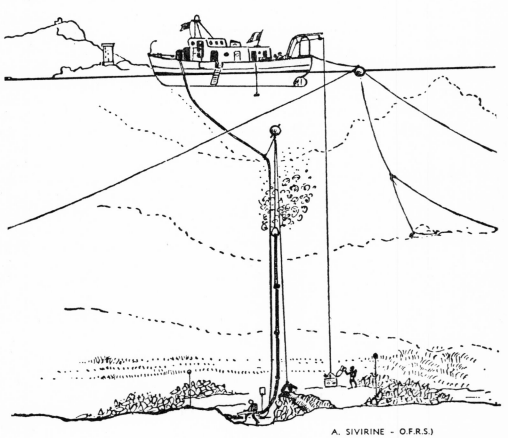

A. SIVIRINE - O.F.R.S.)

FIG. 40.   Dramont wreck: air-lift in action. The *Espadon* was equipped for under-water search with high- and low-pressure compressors and a derrick

'It must further be noted that all the larger finds, including shells and sherds of amphorae, fell back under their own weight. It seems necessary, in any future operation, to install at the top of the extractor an angle-piece of large cross-section, so that the debris is thrown out of the working area.'

NOTES

1 C. Santamaria, 'Travaux et découvertes sur l'épave "A" du Dramont à Saint Raphael (Var)', *Atti dell' II Congresso Internazionale* (Albenga, 1958), 167ff.
2 F. Dumas, 'Le Dramont: troisième chantier français d'archéologie sous-marine', *Bull. Études et Sports Sous-marins*, 6 (1959), 15.
3 F. Benoit, 'Nouvelles épaves de Provence II', *Gallia*, XVIII (1960), 51ff.
4 F. Benoit. 'Nouvelles épaves de Provence I', *Gallia* XVI (1958), 17ff.

(g) Spargi

The Roman ship lies sunk on the Secca Corsara (a shoal) between the northern coast of Sardinia and the island of Spargi (Archipelago of La Maddalena), at a depth of 17–18 m. (Fig. 41). The sea-bed is sandy and covered with *poseidonia*

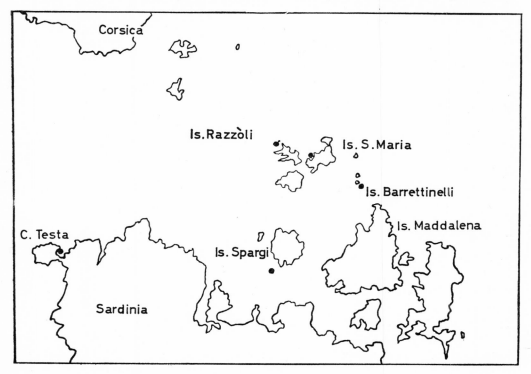

FIG. 41. Map of archipelago of Maddalena.
Black spots indicate archaeological deposits

weed, but at a few metres to the west of the wreck rises a massive submerged reef, made up of huge granite blocks. The largest of these is the nearest to the field of amphorae (some 3–4 m.), and rises up sheer from the sea-bed to 7 m. below the surface.

On the Secca Corsara the main current is from west to east, and it sometimes becomes very strong. Corresponding to the surface current, an anticyclonic bottom current flows in the opposite direction; at a depth of about 8 m. there is a neutral band of still water. The surface current generally follows the direction of wind and waves, but its intensity is relatively independent of them. The intensity of the bottom current is always much less than the surface one, and it is most apparent at 3–5 m. above the sea-bed.

During the work the water was generally clear, with an average visibility of about 14 m.; its normal clarity is much greater in a good season (up to a maximum of about 30 m.). During the first two weeks' work, showers and water from the estuary of a large torrent on the Sardinian coast made the surrounding sea turbid, which increased the difficulties of the photographic survey.

Underwater work began on 23 April and ended on 23 May 1958, with seventeen days' effective work and a total of 115 hours, 19 minutes' diving. As a working rule the free-divers made two dives a day, with a rest of from two to three hours in between; exceptionally, three dives were made.

The boats used were the motor fishing craft *Medusa*, of 28 tons, from Maddalena, 17 m. long and of 4 m. beam, with a powered capstan and derrick, accompanied by two rowing boats and a motor-launch. A pontoon and a deep-sea tug, the *Albenga* of the Italian Navy, laid down the floats and mooring buoys.

The free-divers who collaborated, all of them civilians and amateurs, were: Mino Callegaro, Ranzo Ferrandi, Giorgio Fontana, Alberto Laviano, Giovanni Maestrale, Duilio Marcante, Alessandro Pederzini, Nino Pontiroli, and Raoul Vernetti. The underwater cameraman was Masino Maunza. The organization and technical direction of the operation were undertaken by the writer.

EQUIPMENT

Diving apparatus

In general, use was made of large-capacity aqualungs (about 5,000 litres) of our own make, with Mistral regulators. Tricheco and Aga apparatus was also used. The cameraman was equipped with a Pirelli oxygen aqualung.

The free-divers were equipped with Pirelli diving suits of cellular stretched rubber, Pinocchio masks, and Pirelli fins and leather gloves expressly made by the A. Motta Company for handling the amphorae.

Air-refilling

The refilling of aqualungs was carried out with an MA1 Radaelli motor compressor, with a capacity of 170 litres a minute.

Photography

Two Rolleimarin cameras and a Robot with a waterproof case of our own make were used. With the Rolleimarin cameras, about 300 underwater photos were taken, in colour and black and white; the coloured ones with flash (clear bulb, Ektachrome daylight film, and occasional use of filters). With the Robot camera about 200 photos in black and white were taken. For the photos in black and white we chose Ilford films FP3 (19 Din), and sometimes HP3 (24 Din).

The underwater filming was done with an Arriflex 35-mm. camera, using Eastman colour film without artificial light. A 300-m. documentary has been made from the filmed material.

Gridding the archaeological part of the sea-bed

Two grids of yellow canvas tape, 6 m. by 10 m. each, were made with squares of 2 m. by 2 m.; these, in their turn, were divided internally into squares by black lines at right angles to the tapes. At the intersection of the lines, white-painted metal tags were fastened, each with a black letter indicating the square.

The letters of the first grid ran from A to Q, and of the second from AA to QQ (Fig. 42). The grids were stretched over the deposit of amphorae so as to cover it entirely with a wide margin. We drove in twenty-two wooden stakes, to which we fastened the grid lines with cords, with their long sides parallel. For knocking in the stakes a mallet of 5 kg. was used.

When we took away the grid to recover the amphorae, wooden stakes were also stuck in the places where the tags had been. A tag with the corresponding letter was attached to each of these stakes. The angles of the squares were marked with iron stakes.

For the sectors outside the grid, covering the excavation of the wreck, the gridding of the sea-bed was marked out in squares equal in size to those of the grid, with more stakes embedded in cement bases, proceeding outwards as in a game of dominoes.

Surveying instruments

For measuring we used flexible metal measuring rods, tape-measures, 2–m. rods, large triangles, plastic and ordinary slate boards with white, yellow, and red 'Caran d'Ache' chalks.

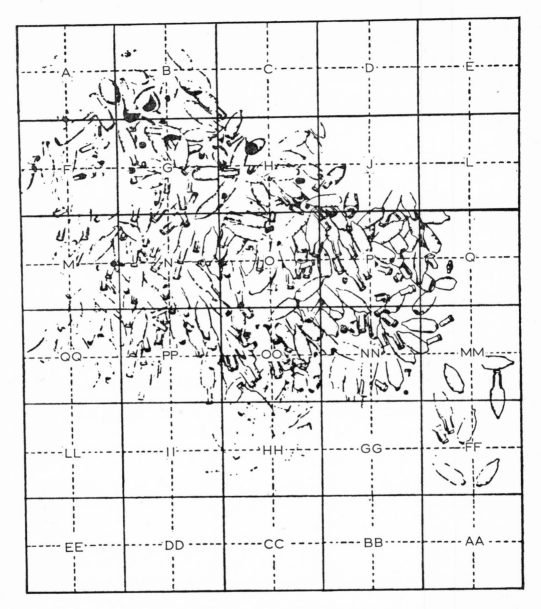

FIG. 42. Layout of grid over the deposit. The draughtsman, following the photographic overlay, has begun to draw out the plan of the first layer of amphorae

For numbering the amphorae on the sea-bed we used at first photos, 12 cm. by 24 cm., nailed on to wooden boards, on which the amphorae were numbered with indelible ink. The free-divers took these boards down to the sea-bed and, following their markings, numbered the actual amphorae by means of round metal plaques with serial numbers, strung on wire. These plaques were tied either to the handles or to the foot of the amphorae, according to their state of preservation.

Sundry tools

We tried to clear the very thick coat of seaweed with a common rake, then with a sickle, but with no useful result. Even digging in the sand with a spade was of no use. We had good results, on the other hand, with a tool which we called a 'hand': the sharp edges of the three large fingers of the iron hand cut the roots of the *Poseidonia* weed and dug firmly into the earth. Communication with the surface was sometimes carried out with the Galeazzi throat microphone. It was dispensed with, however, in shallow-water work, where the free-diver was in a position to surface at will and to communicate directly.

We also made use of a floodlight with a Cressi battery.

Recovery equipment

The amphorae were recovered in two wire cages, hoisted by means of the motor derrick. The cages at first had eight partitions, which were afterwards reduced to four, since the weight of eight at one time proved too much for the derrick. The amphorae, full of mud, weighed, in fact, about 40 kg. each. The bottoms were of pierced sheet iron, on which was a wooden frame in which it was possible to insert the feet of the amphorae, to prevent them from slipping.

The sherds and other minor objects were placed in a perforated half petrol can, which was hoisted by hand.

Air-lift

We made an air-lift of plastic material (Gresintex, stiff polyvinyl chloride), with segments of 3 m. each fitted together with flanges. Between every two segments there were joints of rubberized canvas, and the segments were so adjusted as to prevent the inner side of the joints being sucked inwards, and the regular flow impeded. In this way the pipe was made sufficiently flexible: in spite of its length of 20 m., it could be easily moved by the operator, and it withstood even a rough sea quite well. The internal diameter of the pipes was 122 mm.

The sucking head of steel, with handles and a tap, was screened by two strong nozzle-pieces, with which the operator was enabled even to dig into the bed.

It was found perfectly easy to regulate the air-flow. The hose-section was 25 mm.

The top of the air-lift was made of flexible armoured rubber hose, 2 m. long. It discharged directly on board, into a sieve. On the days when the pipeline was broken by mishandling, we kept on working with a length of only 9 m., discharging into water; the suction was just as good. When repairs had been made, we no longer attached an armoured rubber hose, and discharge took place at surface level without filtering. The air-lift was supported from on board by means of a rope, so that it could work in a vertical position.

The air-feed was obtained at first from the Radaelli compressor fitted with a lung of three bottles of 52 litres at 200 atmospheres (the supply was barely enough); then from a Jenbach low-pressure compressor with a capacity of 1,000 litres a minute, which was completely satisfactory.

TECHNIQUE

Order of work

The work of survey and recovery was organized in the following chronological order:

1. *Location of the wreck and marking by means of a small buoy.
2. Laying two floats and two buoys for mooring.
3. *Laying out the first grid (A–Q).
4. *Driving in the stakes (twelve) and fastening the grid.
5. *Laying out the second grid (AA–QQ).
6. *Driving in the stakes (ten) and fixing the second grid.
7. *Photographing the plan of each square of the two grids; one for every four squares and for each square outside the grid along its outer edges
8. Transferring the photographic survey to a plan and numbering the amphorae.
9. *Transferring the numbers to the amphorae, square by square.
10. *Removing the first grid, fixing the replacement stakes (inner and marginal).
11. *Starting the recovery of the amphorae from the first section.
12. *Starting excavation with the air-lift on the edges of the deposit.
13. *Plan and photographic survey.
14. Transfer of the underwater survey to plan.
15. *Removing the second grid, fixing the inner stakes; continuation of the work of recovering the amphorae.
16. *Continuing excavation with the air-lift in the bow-section, and relative survey.

            * Indicates underwater operations.

Notes

The grid was excellent in principle. The squares, however, were found to be too large (2 m. by 2 m.): to frame them well, the cameraman had to place himself at a height of 4 m., to the detriment of detail (particularly as the water was not very clear).

To carry the grid lines underwater, they were wound around a long pole which was held by three men in a boat; two divers took the ends of the grid and, swimming backwards on the surface, unrolled it. When the grid was entirely spread on the water, two more divers, waiting near the boat, took the other two free ends and helped the first two to carry the outstretched grid down to the sea-bed.

4. Stakes appeared to be the most suitable way of fixing the grid. By means of them the grid was kept at the required height, which could not be done with weights or by tying the lines to stones or such-like. Wooden stakes, however, tend to float free, and it is therefore necessary to drive them in very deep (50 cm. at least).

7. Photographic planning is the most exhausting job for a diver to carry out, particularly if he is disturbed by the current. For the survey about 100 photographs were needed, and these had to be taken from a horizontal, spread-eagled position.

In theory the problem is simple: once the object has been lined up in the view-finder (for instance, one of the squares within the frame of the reflex view-finder of a Rolleimarin camera), the camera has only to be focused. Thereafter it is sufficient to line up the frame again for the subsequent squares, since the correct focus has already been set. A camera with a reflex view-finder is indispensable. A camera with an automatic trigger, of the Robot type, may prove useful for a survey of what might be termed the film type; the cameraman swims at a certain distance from the sea-bed and keeps on taking snapshots in a regular sequence; the mounting must afterwards be done painstakingly, but it will give good results.

The photographic planning of a deposit of amphorae, or of any archaeological area, must be carried out at a height of not more than 3 m. above the field: only then will a satisfactory reading of the details be possible. In turbid or very deep water (I refer to the experience obtained from the exploration of the Albenga Roman ship), the distance must be reduced to 2 m. or even less.

The film must be of as fine a grain as possible. Moreover, since it is necessary to use a large diaphragm-opening in order to get the most detailed view, the exposure time must always be in the order of 1/30. For this reason, the photographer should have a very steady hand. This, along with the concentration needed to take a regular and accurate series of pictures, the effort of keeping still at a given distance, in spite of the current and the instability of the free-diver poised horizontally in water, are all factors which require of the photographer uncommon skill and psychological and physical endurance.

9. The numbering of the amphorae was one of the most complex problems. At

first the free-diver took down to the sea-bed the photographic enlargement of one
or more squares, on which the amphorae had been numbered in indelible ink; he
then checked their lay-out in the given square before marking them with the little
plaques, according to the numbers on the photograph. This method proved uncertain because of faulty details in some photographs. It is, however, better when
the squares are smaller (for example 1·50 m. by 1·50 m.) and the photographs are
consequently more readable.

As a second stage we replaced the photographs with blackboards, on which the
amphorae had been drawn and numbered in chalk, as on the photographs. This
method proved to be of uncertain value, since it was difficult for the diver to
interpret the rough pattern of the drawing when he had to deal with a heap in
which amphorae were mingled with sherds, stones, and various other objects.

At the third stage it was left to the diver to number the amphorae sketched on
the blackboard in chalk, according to the tags which he attached to those in a given
square. This was a good system, but it was imprecise.

From these experiments we have drawn some basic conclusions:

(a) A diver on the sea-bed can only with difficulty identify precisely a complex of
many disparate objects which have been transferred on to a diagrammatic
plan (photograph or drawing). The sea-bed is less easily deciphered than
a surface field for many reasons which it would be tedious to list.

(b) The slightest displacement of an object on the sea-bed may materially alter its
aspect, particularly when the sea-bed is composed of many heterogeneous
elements.

(c) The mere displacement or removal of a couple of amphorae in a deposit may
cause the heap to become displaced and alter its aspect enough to confuse the
diver.

(d) For the numbering of a deposit, all the amphorae must be numbered before
handling a single one.

(e) It is too much to expect perfect numbering, since, particularly for the first
layer in a deposit, the amphorae do not appear like books on a shelf, but
overlay one another in such a way that it may sometimes be uncertain whether
they belong to the first or second layer; one must therefore be content with
a fair approximation.

10. It was found to be almost useless to replace the grid with stakes when the
former was removed to begin the recovery of amphorae. Once the divers started
lifting and carrying away the very heavy amphorae, the sea-bed was stirred up, the
other amphorae shifted, the silt slid away, and the divers' fins displaced everything as they groped around. It has therefore been found by experience that when
the recovery of the amphorae has begun, markers on the deposit are of no further

use. These markers can be moved away from the deposit or can be replaced (for example, by sinking the grid again when a whole layer has been recovered). In particular, the slender iron stakes at the edges were found to endanger the divers' safety.

12. The plastic air-lift we invented proved excellent in all respects, not least because of its lightness. We tried removing one of the segments of the steel nozzle at its head, to facilitate suction, but this led to stoppages in the pipe, caused by the mixture of weeds and amphora sherds. The pipe was cleared by ramming it from above with an iron bar, but this wasted a lot of time. The filter-nozzle was, therefore, replaced and the operator accustomed himself to working with one free hand below the suction head to keep it clear of tangled weed or overlarge sherds. The suction on the hand was unpleasant and very strong, but harmless. One day half the writer's arm was sucked in and jammed, but he succeeded in turning off the tap and got himself out of the predicament without any ill effects.

The diameter of the pipe (122 mm.) proved very good for rough work: the quick removal of sand and stones. Regulation of the flow also made it possible to do delicate work on the wood and on the leaden sheets studded with nails. A larger-diameter pipe would, however, have been needed for a thorough clearing of the bottom and of the weed-covered bed.

Results

Professor Nino Lamboglia, Director of the Istituto Internazionale di Studi Liguri, was the scientific director of the undertaking. In an article, from which I quote the main passages, he has summarized the results as follows:

'No expedition for the recovery and exploration of ancient ships, even though it may have made invaluable contributions to knowledge and brought to light a notable quantity of objects, had as yet succeeded in solving one central archaeological problem: the exact survey on the sea-bed of an ancient ship's hull wrecked suddenly while under sail, or at least of those remains which have survived the wear and tear of time and sea.

'Going to Spargi to initiate this new experiment in the history of underwater archaeology, we had firmly decided to sacrifice all allurements of an incidental nature to the perfecting of working methods, and to test the co-operation between archaeologists and free-divers. The results warrant our saying that a decisive step has been taken on the right lines in this difficult and quite new field opened to archaeological research. . . . The task from the start was to photograph and survey the ship on the sea-bed, to interpret the meaning of every detail, first fully loaded and then after removing the cargo.

'The field of amphorae which appeared on the sea-bed neither showed clearly the outline nor the position and orientation of the ship; due to a stroke of luck and to intelligent observation it was possible to make them out at the end of the first expedition. This was planned to be limited to the surface layers and to the recovery of the first layer of encrusted amphorae, which lay scattered as the results of the shipwreck.

'From the chronological standpoint the choice of the Spargi ship for this first experiment was particularly happy, because by good chance it proved to belong (from the typology of the amphorae (Fig. 43) and other materials, among which was the typical glazed Campanian ware (Fig. 44)) to an intermediate stage, almost linking the Marseilles (Congloué) and the Albenga ships, separated by a century from each other; the former belonging to 180–160 B.C., the latter to 80–60 B.C.; the one typical of the second century and the other of the first century B.C. The Spargi amphorae in effect stand not only halfway between these two periods, about 120–100 B.C., but the wine types show two varieties: one is a little more developed than the Marseilles amphora, and the other rather more archaic than the Albenga type.

'It is specially fortunate that the Spargi ship lies on the sea-bed in an almost horizontal position, and is covered with sand. Her cargo remained in position, and, except for the portion which sticks up and is exposed to currents, it can be surveyed and recovered systematically, as if from an intact store. With greater reason, all that remains of the hull and its internal fittings, which have not been removed or displaced by the action of the sea, is *in situ*, which will make it possible for the first time to get an exact idea of shape and proportions.

'So far we have discovered a length of about 10 m. of the hull, which corresponds to the framework of oak ribs, held together by longitudinal timbers and covered with planks, the whole being sheathed with lead, which extends over the whole external surface. In the last days of our work we thought we caught a glimpse of the bow, towards which the timbers (vertical and horizontal) converged obliquely, following its curves. The orientation and length of the wreck have now been determined: it was a ship about 30–5 m. in length and about 8 m. beam. Roughly, from theoretical calculations which can be made, it carried a total freight of 150 tons and 3,000 amphorae. Such was, in fact, the average carrying capacity of the freight ships sailing the seas in significant numbers during the Republican period.

'On the uppermost level of the amphorae, and on the first traces of the hull, the underwater method of archaeological survey, indispensable in such explorations, was now tried for the very first time. We have had to solve innumerable problems of a practical and not only a geometric character. By trial and error, we have found the best ways of marking out the sea-bed, and in making underwater drawings and measurements, perhaps most difficult of all, we have formulated a system of communication between underwater workers and surface directors, co-ordinators, and recorders. We can affirm we have progressed towards a solution of survey problems; we must now solve the problem of making sections.

Bronze Agôn

3: MAHDIA

[Musée Alaoui, Le Bardo, Tunis]

Herm of Dionysus by Boëthos

Marble crater B1: Maenad with tambourine

Bronze hermaphrodite carrying a lamp

4: MAHDIA

[Musée Alaoui, Le Bardo, Tunis]

Marble crater P1: dancing Maenad

Bronze cornice with figure of Ariadne

5: MAHDIA

[Musée Alaoui, Le Bardo, Tunis]

Marble capital with griffon

Types of amphorae

6: MAHDIA

[Musée Alaoui, Le Bardo, Tunis]

Air-lift derrick and workshop

7: GRAND CONGLOUÉ

[F. Clouzot]

Cargo and part of the hull
during excavation

The *Sestius* amphorae in the store of the Musée Borély

8: GRAND CONGLOUÉ

[Musée Borély]

Amphora neck with clay stopper

Clay stopper with *L. Titus* stamp

Campanian goblet with inscription

The pile of amphorae when first discovered

The keel and ribs

9: TITAN

The side of the mound of amphorae

Section through the cargo, showing the stacking of amphorae and the hull

Work with the air-lift

10: DRAMONT

[Y. Girault]

Part of the wreck before excavation

11: SPARGI

[G. Roghi]

Stretching the tapes for the grid

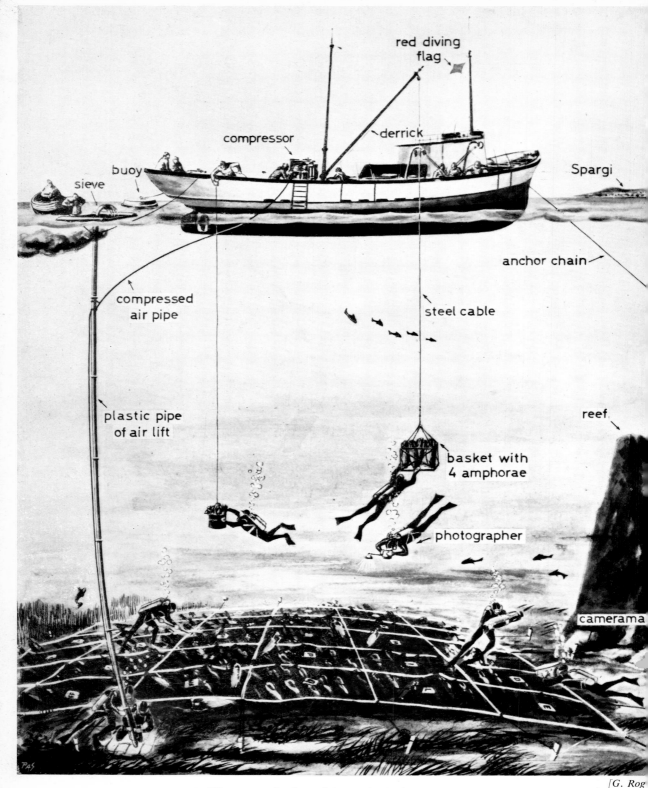

red diving flag

compressor

derrick

buoy

Spargi

sieve

anchor chain

compressed air pipe

steel cable

plastic pipe of air lift

reef

basket with 4 amphorae

photographer

camerama

[G. Rog

Diagrammatic view of the method of excavation

12: SPARGI

Schematic drawing of work on the Spargi wreck, 1958. For convenience, individual operations are all shown at one time, but it is clear that the photographs must be taken before beginning the recovery of the amphorae, that work with the air-lift must take place in the last phase, and so on. The bow of the ship lies towards the bottom left-hand corner, the stern at the opposite corner of the grid.

[G. Roghi]

The first grid laid out

13: SPARGI

The second metal grid in use

The *Lufti Gelil* anchored directly over the wre

14: GELIDONYA

[Pennsylvania Expedition]

Triangulating on the sea-bed

Cutting a cargo-filled lump
from the concretion

15: GELIDONYA

[Pennsylvania Expedition]

Raising a lump of cargo
with a cable

16: GELIDONYA

[*Pennsylvania Expedition*]

Raising a lump of cargo
with a balloon

Ingots from area G being cleaned on beach

Photographing a diver at work

17: GELIDONYA

[Pennsylvania Expedition]

Wood in area G, from north

18: GELIDONYA

[Pennsylvania Expedition]

Diver drawing remains of hull
on sheet of plastic

Clearing sand with air-lift

19: GELIDONYA

[Pennsylvania Expedition]

Raising ingots of area P, from north-west

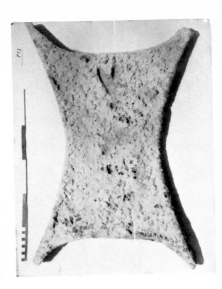

Copper ox-hide, and other ingots

20: GELIDONYA

[Pennsylvania Expedition]

Stone mace-head
with metal lining in perforation

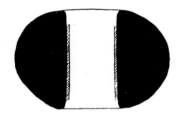

Basket bottom from area P

Stone tripod mortar

Rock crystal

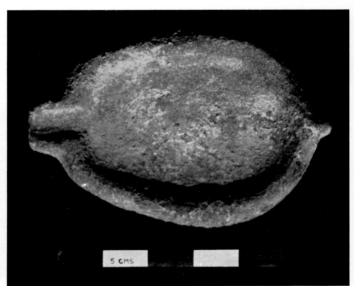

21: GELIDONYA

[Pennsylvania Expedition]

Qedet weights

Scarab with falcon-headed Re

Cylinder seal showing deity with
atef crown

Bronze swage block

Lamp from 'captain's quarters'

22: GELIDONYA

[Pennsylvania Expedition]

Roadstead: air-view from the north

[French Institute, Beirut]

23: TYRE

The south harbour from the air

[Université St. Joseph, Beirut]

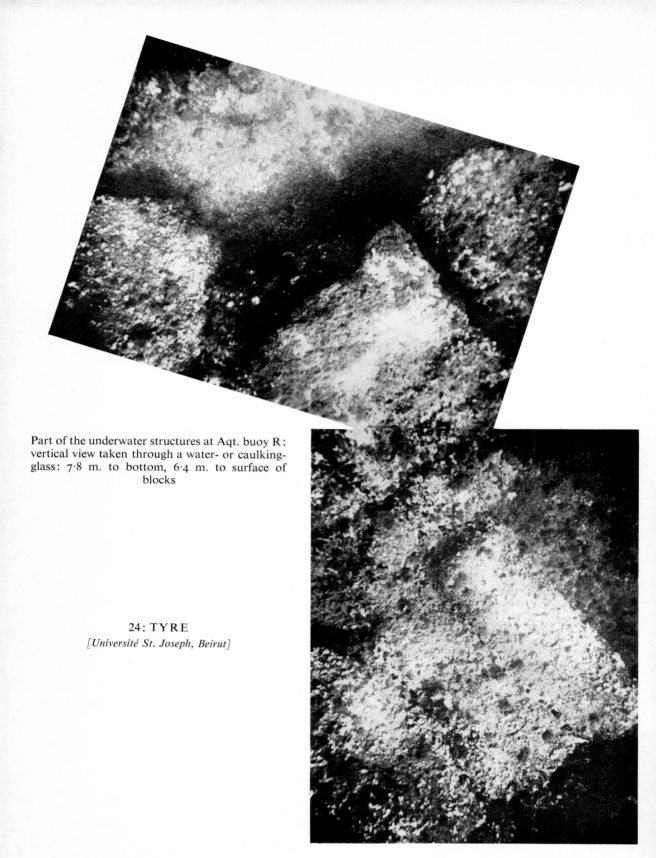

Part of the underwater structures at Aqt. buoy R:
vertical view taken through a water- or caulking-
glass: 7·8 m. to bottom, 6·4 m. to surface of
blocks

24: TYRE

[Université St. Joseph, Beirut]

General air-view from the north

25: SIDON

[Université St. Joseph, Beirut]

The inner harbour from the west

View from Gebel Akdar: Apollon
on extreme right, New Island secon
from left

26: APOLLONIA

[N. Flemming]

Fish-tanks on New Island

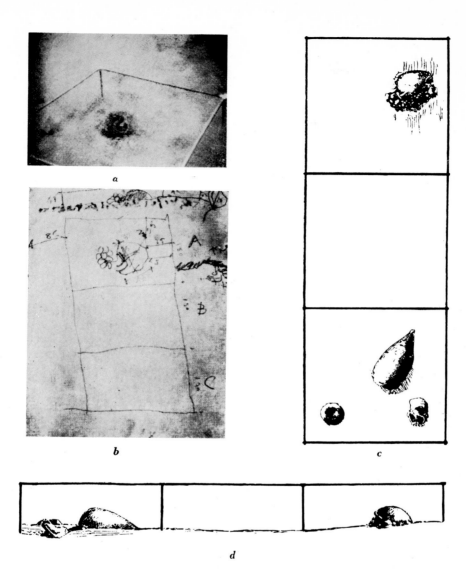

The new system of rigid grid used experimentally for the first time
on a group of amphorae near Gallinaria Island (Albenga):
a. The grid established on the bottom
b. The underwater measurements written on the plastic sheet
c. Scale drawing made from measurements and photograph
d. Section drawn up from grid

27: RIGID GRID SYSTEM

[Instituto Internazionale di Studi Liguri]

The *Daino* at Baia, lying off Punta dell'Epitaffio (in the foreground, the launch used while making the plan)

28: BAIA

[Instituto Internazionale di Studi Liguri]

The grid over the submerged area of Baia, laid out during the *Daino*'s 1956 season

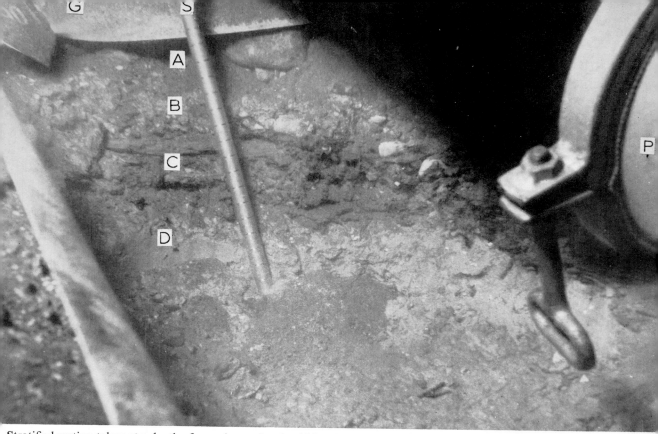

Stratified section taken at a depth of 3 m. A: sand and pebbles. B: gravel. C: archaeological layer of Bronze Age IV. D: lacustrine chalk. G: grid net and serial number of metre square. P: pipe of air-lift. S: scale graduated in centimetres

29: CHAMPRÉVEYRES

Air-lift discharging into sieve   [*W. Haag*]

Bronze bracelet

Part of a mould for pins

Button, rings, glass bead, spirals from a necklace

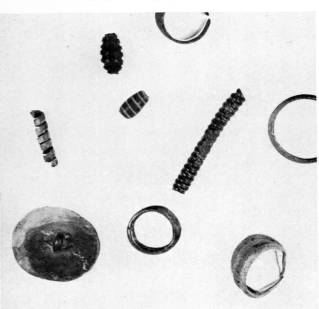

Bowl of black pottery

Pottery cup

30: CHAMPRÉVEYRES

[W. Haag]

[N. Flemming]

Stone fisherman's anchor being brought up
at Apollonia

[C. Chiapetti]

Cargo of tiles, Frioule

31: MISCELLANEOUS FINDS

Lead anchor stock lying among amphorae from a
wreck at Cape Graziano, Filicudi, Aeolian Islands

[G. Roghi]

[F. Benoit]

Lead movable stock and junction piece
of anchor from Syracuse

32: *a.* Dolium in Agde Museum; on the left, M. Fonquerle and M. Dumas

[*F. Clouze*

b. Large stone base from Herault River, possibly a mast step

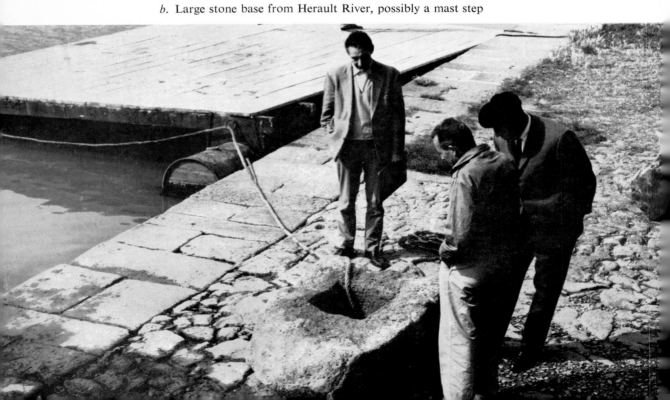

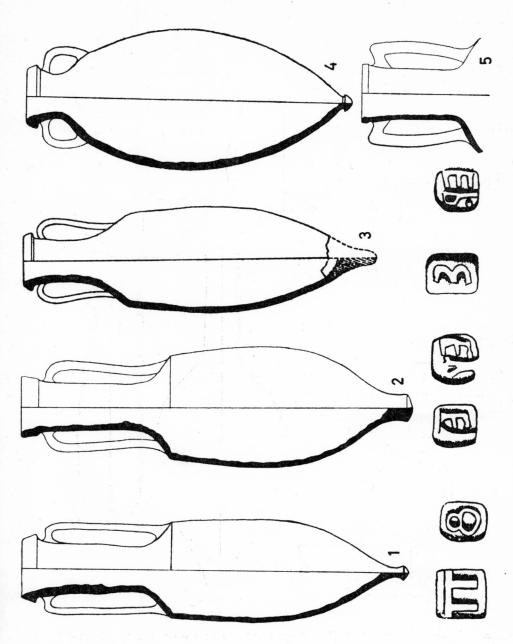

FIG. 43. Wine amphorae: 1. Dressel 1A with stamps below; 2 Dressel 1B; 3 Dressel 1C; 4 oil amphora; 5 neck of Rhodian amphora   (after *Atti* . . . Albenga, 1958)

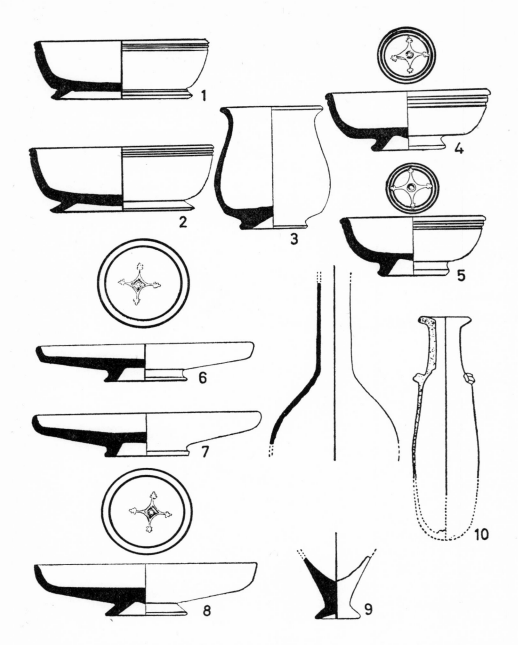

FIG. 44.   Types of Campanian B pottery: 1, 2 form 1; 3 form 13; 4, 5 form 1/8;
6, 7 form 5; 8 form 8; 9 fusiform unguentarium; 10 unguentarium of multi-coloured glass
(after *Atti* . . . Albenga, 1958)

'The system of recovery of the cargo which has been tried is also strictly archaeological: all that could be detected on the sea-bed was photographed in detail and transcribed on an exact plan to a scale of 1 : 20, before excavation and removal; lastly, all the amphorae have been numbered and classified and the position of all other objects has been accurately determined and marked before hauling them up to the surface. By this means we shall have for the first time exact statistics of the various types of amphorae, of the pottery, and of the lay-out of both cargo and equipment.

'The Roman ship at Spargi is so far the most ancient ship to have been seriously studied in this manner on the sea-bed; it constitutes therefore one of the most important stages reached in archaeology, and there is reason to be proud that it has taken place in Italy.

'The material recovered consisted of about 300 amphorae (all belonging to

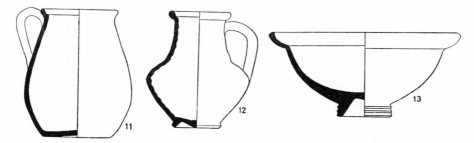

FIG. 45. Domestic pottery   (after *Atti* . . . Albenga, 1958)

the top layer), of which about 100 are intact, some 100 paterae and other pottery (Fig. 45); parts of an altar (the first to have been discovered on a ship), and various objects, among which was a precious ointment-pot of vitreous paste (Fig. 44.10). Almost all the amphorae had stamps with Greek characters. On one amphora we noticed the syllable SAB (perhaps from Sabinus, the shipowner or the maker of the amphorae). In the lead sheathing of the Spargi ship were found copper nails, also coated with lead to preserve them from electrolysis.

'All the material was taken over by the Soprintendente alle Antichitá at Cagliari, Professor Gennaro Pesce. Professor Mario Mirabella Roberti, Soprintendente alle Antichitá of Lombardy, was very helpful in supporting and co-ordinating the preparations for the expeditions.'[1]

The second season

The first and most concrete test of archaeological work made by the *Daino* in 1959 was in the sea around Sardinia when we returned to the wreck off the isle of

Spargi (La Maddalena), which the year before had been the object of the most important season of submarine excavation up to then carried out in Italy.

The plan of exploration of the wreck at Spargi was viewed as a long-term undertaking, staged in a series of successive seasons. The aim was to carry out the methodical removal of the whole cargo, to explore and, ultimately, to recover the remains of the ship. In 1958 the first stage of the plan was undertaken—namely, the survey of the position before excavation or recovery and, immediately after, the systematic removal of the first layer of amphorae (Fig. 46).

The *Daino*'s programme, in a stay at Spargi of barely twelve days between 16 to 30 August, was to accomplish the second phase in the operation. For the first time, the system of the survey grid was applied to a complete amphora field, and thus the second layer of amphorae was to be surveyed *in situ* before removal (Fig. 47). Once on the site, this work was preceded by a more accurate survey of the bow section of the ship, where the most obvious and regular traces of the ship had been previously discovered. When the squares of the survey grid had been collated by orienting them to the ship's longitudinal axis, the first inspection brought a disconcerting surprise: nothing, or almost nothing, of the wooden remains of the ship which had been revealed the year before was now visible. The action of the currents, and perhaps divers and prowling fishermen, too, had radically altered the situation. A new survey was therefore made and superimposed on the earlier

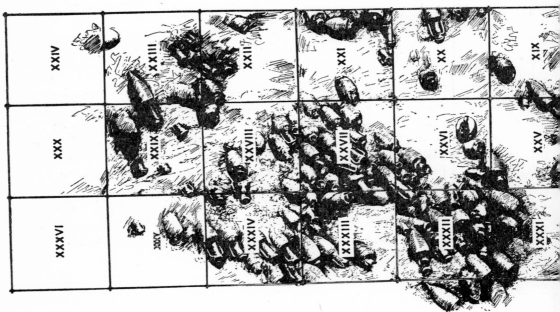

FIG. 46.   Survey of the second layer of the cargo of amphorae made in the 1959 season two shadings showing appreciable differences between each season's survey. The irregular

one without it being possible to establish where they coincided. The air-lift was also used extensively, digging systematically within the grid squares, which facilitated precise working on the plan. During this excavation new material and valuable chronological data were found. Among these was an exceptional curiosity: a human skull with clear traces of a helmet on the cranium. This is the first concrete relic of a member of the crew of an ancient ship that has yet been brought up.

After concluding the survey of the bow section, the second layer of the cargo of amphorae was given a general clean-up, and then the survey grid was laid out and a photograph made of the whole. With the same system as the year before, but now perfected in this way, it was possible to make a complete survey much more quickly than in 1958 (nine working days out of twelve days away). It is thus ready for the third season, which should prove conclusive in the exploration of the ship.

NOTES

This report was published under the title 'Note tecniche sul rilevamento e lo scavo della nave romana di Spargi' in *Bollettino e Atti* (Centro Italiano di Ricercatori Subacquei,

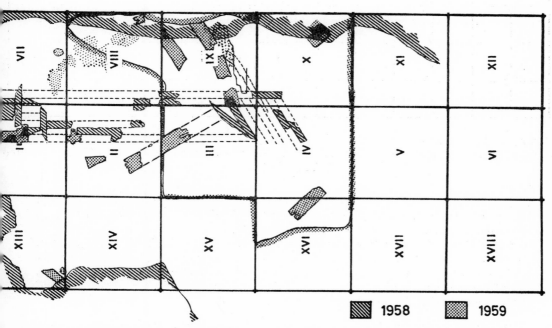

of excavation with the new system of rigid frame, survey grid. The wood is marked in hatched lines mark the limits of excavation with the air-lift   Scale 1 : 60

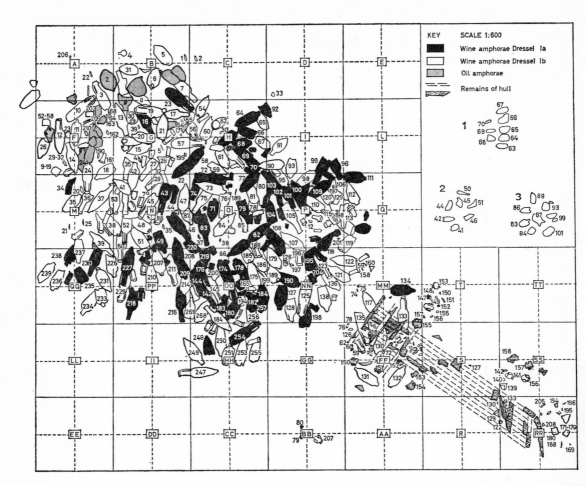

FIG. 47. Plan before the removal of the upper layer of amphorae. To the right the first traces of wood discovered during excavation. The numbers refer to the inventory of objects recovered (*Atti* . . . Albenga, 1958)

1958–9), 9ff.; the second season appeared in 'La seconda campagna di scavo sotto marina sulla nave romana di Spargi (Sardegna)', *Rivista di Studi Liguri*, 25 (1959), 301 (Forma Maris Antiqui, II).

Other reports include: 'Una nave romana con tutto il carico', *L'Europeo* (Milan, 20 October 1957), 627. G. Roghi, 'Esplorazione archeologica nell' arcipelago della Maddalena e scoperta della nave romana di Spargi', *Bollettino e Atti* (C.I.R.S., 1957), 20ff.; 'La nave romana di Spargi (La Maddalena): Campagna di scavo 1958', *Atti dell' II Congresso Internazionale* (Albenga, 1958), 143ff.

1 'Un impresa che rivoluziona l'archeologia sottomarina' in *L'Europeo*, No. 26 (29 June 1938).

(h) Cape Gelidonya

PRELIMINARY REPORT[1]

Just off Cape Gelidonya, in south-west Turkey, is a row of five tiny islands, the Bes Adalar group (Fig. 48). The current which runs around the cape and between these islands is especially treacherous, being not only quite strong, but reversing its direction in a single day for no apparent reason.[2] The rocks in the area are jagged, and some are hidden just beneath the waves; on the whole, it is a likely spot for the wreck of a ship sailing along the southern Anatolian coast. That the cape lay in a shipping route for copper and bronze traders in the Late Bronze Age might have been suggested by the discovery, about 1913, of two bronze ingots in the neighbouring Bay of Antalya.[3]

During 1958 and 1959, Mr. Peter Throckmorton spent the summer months searching for ancient wrecks along the Carian and Lycian coasts, using as his

A.E.P. Nov. 1960.

FIG. 48. Map showing relation of Cape Gelidonya to Cyprus

main source of information the sponge-divers of Bodrum, the sponge centre of Turkey. While diving with these men, Throckmorton heard of a wreck full of copper, and was later able to direct the Cochran expedition to the site at Cape Gelidonya.[4] There the ship lay between the two islands closest to the mainland; it had probably broken on the north edge of the more southerly of these, perhaps at night or in a storm (Pl. 14). The narrow passage between the two islands may have been chosen to avoid the stronger current that runs around the cape.

In the spring and summer of 1960, the University Museum of the University of Pennsylvania sent an expedition to excavate the remains of this ship.[5] The location of our camp was dictated by the nearest supply of fresh water, combined with a suitable anchorage for our diving boats. This combination was found in a small, cliff-enclosed cove about an hour's sail from the wreck. Here, on a beach about 7·5 m. wide, we were able to set up an adequate camp with living quarters, kitchen, dark room, and areas for drafting, repairing machinery, and filling air tanks. Most important, we dammed up a small spring, making a large, fresh-water basin in which to soak the finds after they had been raised from the salty Mediterranean.

Method of excavation[6]

We worked from two Bodrum boats: the *Mandalinci*, a sponge-diving boat 9 m. long, captained by Kemal Aras, the discoverer of the wreck, and the *Lutfi Gelil* (Pl. 14), somewhat larger and not a diving boat, captained by Nazif Goymen. A dinghy with an outboard motor was also with us as a safety measure, to pick up divers who might be swept away by the current; fortunately, it was never necessary to use it for that purpose. Each morning we sailed out to the site, where we moored to a permanent oil-drum buoy anchored directly over the wreck. A descending line, tied to a rock within the excavation area, allowed us to swim down to the wreck quickly, and always showed the shortest route to the diving boat in case of an emergency on the bottom. We dived, normally, in groups of two or three; the area of the wreck was too small to accommodate more conveniently. Diving equipment included aqualungs, glass face-masks for clear visibility, rubber suits for warmth, foot-fins for propulsion, belts with lead weights for ballast, and knives with serrated edges to cut through entangling seaweed or lines. Additional equipment included depth-gauges, which were not needed after the various depths on the wreck were known, underwater compasses, and underwater watches. The watches allowed divers to time their dives, although one member of the expedition kept a constant check on the surface and signalled the ends of dives by hitting two pieces of metal together just under the water. It was essential to keep a log of diving times for each excavator. Underwater, the blood absorbs pressurized nitrogen, the amount depending on the depth and duration of each dive. If a diver absorbs too much nitrogen, and rises too quickly, this gas will come out of solution, causing crippling and often fatal bubbles in the blood-stream. To prevent this divers' disease, familiarly known as the 'bends', it is necessary to allow the nitrogen to leave the body before the diver rises to the sur-face. Tables give fairly reliable rates of ascent for dives of varying length at each depth. At Gelidonya, each excavator was able to dive for forty minutes in the morning and twenty-eight minutes in the afternoon, allowing at least three hours between dives. Each dive was concluded with a six-minute decompression period on the descending line, just 3 m. below the surface.[7] The difficulties of an excava-tion where each excavator can visit the site for only an hour and eight minutes a day may be imagined; on deeper wrecks, the time would be much less. Another difficulty was the current, which normally presented no problem. At times, how-ever, we dived with air hoses rather than with compressed-air tanks, and the drag on these hoses was considerable. It was possible to descend and ascend only by climbing the descending line, and movement on the wreck was limited. Further-more, kinks in the hoses occasionally cut off air on the bottom, forcing two divers to share one mouthpiece.

When work began, divers photographed (Pl. 17) and mapped the area. An 'aerial survey' of the wreck was taken by a photographer using an absolutely level camera and swimming at a fixed distance over the bottom; a level and a plumb line were attached to the camera to make this possible. Two-metre measur-ing rods in each picture allowed the photographs to be printed at a uniform size before being cut up and glued together. The photographic records served only as a check on the drawn plans. For these plans, small groups of objects were drawn on translucent plastic sheets with ordinary pencils (Pl. 18). Measurements for the overall plan were made from spikes driven into the surrounding rock bottom, but no more than thirty or thirty-five points could be accurately tri-angulated in a single dive (Pl. 14). For any future wrecks, we plan to use a metal frame equipped with calibrated sliding members, which will allow a single diver to note co-ordinates and levels quickly and accurately.[8]

Little of the wreck was visible on the bottom, most of it being completely covered by lime deposits, which were sometimes several inches thick and always extremely hard. It would have proved unduly time-consuming to cut away this concretion underwater; thus it was decided to raise the remains in large, concreted lumps, which were cut loose with hammer and chisel (Pl. 15). Sometimes an automobile jack was used to free large pieces, but only after a breaking line had been cut deeply with a chisel (Pl. 19). On no occasion were objects damaged by what might seem an unusually rough technique. Once free, the lumps were raised to the surface with a cable running from a winch on the *Lutfi Gelil* (Pl. 16). On one occasion, as may be seen, it was necessary to wrap the lump in a sheet to prevent fragile material on its underside from being damaged by the current. On another occasion, wood was noticed under a lump weighing several hundred kgs. If the *Lutfi Gelil* had rolled or pitched while raising this piece, the heavy mass would easily have crushed the wood below. To prevent this, two large plastic balloons were attached to the concretion and were then inflated from the diver's air hose (Pl. 16). The lifting force was perfectly controlled and the piece floated gently to the surface. Such lumps, which had been plotted on the bottom before being raised, were carried back to the camp, where they were joined together and cleaned in place. The results showed the arrangement of the cargo exactly as it had been on the sea-bed (Pl. 17, Fig. 49). The cleaned

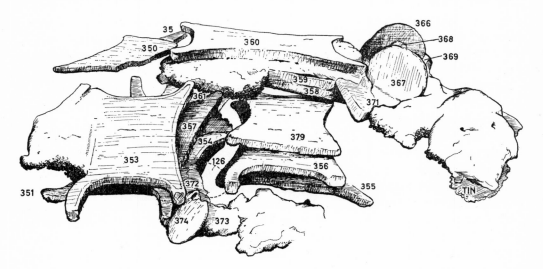

FIG. 49.   Ingots in area P from south. Drawn by Eric Ryan

groups were drawn on land and, by matching points plotted on the bottom, were added to the overall plan. Single objects were simply marked with plastic tags and, after having been photographed and drawn, were lifted in a steel-wire basket.

In order to locate small, single pieces, divers often cleared sand from the wreck by hand and raised it in buckets. For areas around the wreck, however, we used two air-lifts. The larger, about 15 cm. in diameter, carried the sand only 14 m. away, where it was caught in a bag tied to the upper end of the tube. The smaller was only 7·5 cm. in diameter, but 30·5 m. in length, which allowed it to carry the sand to the deck of the *Lutfi Gelil*, where it was dried and sifted. The air-lifts were seldom used directly on the sand, for fear of sucking up and breaking a fragile object. Instead, one diver held the tube while another fanned sand gently towards its mouth (Pl. 19). Another tool for searching under sand and concretion was an underwater metal-detector. This located several hidden deposits which might otherwise have been missed, and assured us that no metal was over-looked. Still another searching device, a core-sampler, would have been of no use at Cape Gelidonya because the bottom was covered by only a thin layer of sand. Later during the season, however, we took a sample of the mud near a Byzantine wreck at Yassi Ada, and such samples may prove of some use in finding the various parts of a hull before air-lifting begins, but it is a very slow process.

The ship

The natural contours of the sea-bed broke the wreck into easily defined areas, which were labelled accordingly (Fig. 50). Area G was the Gully between a large, fallen Boulder (B) and the base of the cliff which ran up to form the rocky edge of the island. Just west of G and B was a flat, Sandy area (S), which separated the Gully from a rocky Platform (P), about 1 m. higher than S. When several objects were discovered still further west, this new area became E, for Extension, and objects scattered by the current over a large area to the north of all previously named areas were simply from M, or Miscellaneous. There was no need, on this wreck, for a grid system.[9] Most of the wreck lay in 26–28 m. of water; depths below sea-level are given on the plan, but detailed sections remain to be checked later. Although some of the cargo was scattered, the ship seems to have settled between the large sponge, at the west, and the triangular rock, pierced by a round hole, at the east. The rock was natural and was not, as at first appeared, a form of early anchor. The positions of the largest pieces of cargo, copper ingots, are shown on this plan, but smaller objects usually lay under these or under rocks (note arrows) and are represented only by their inventory numbers.[10] Several of these copper ingots are represented by broken lines. These had been removed during the summer the ship was discovered and had been placed in Bodrum. Their impressions were still clear, however, in the concretion from which they had been pulled. Indeed, these impressions show far more clearly on the montage than do the actual ingots, which were mostly covered by sea growths and lime deposits.

Little was preserved of the structure of the ship, for the sea-bottom on to which it sank was rock covered by only a few centimetres of sand. With no protective coating of mud, most of the hull had disappeared. Tiny fragments of wood turned up in area P, but little could be made of them, and none seemed to be part of the hull. From G into part of S, however, traces of planks could be followed under the lumps raised from the southern edge of these areas. These planks were in a fragmentary state, badly broken on the rocks, but most of them ran in an approxi-mate east-west direction, pressed hard against the base of the cliff. They were from 10 to 15 mm. thick and from 5 to 15 cm. wide; none was preserved to any

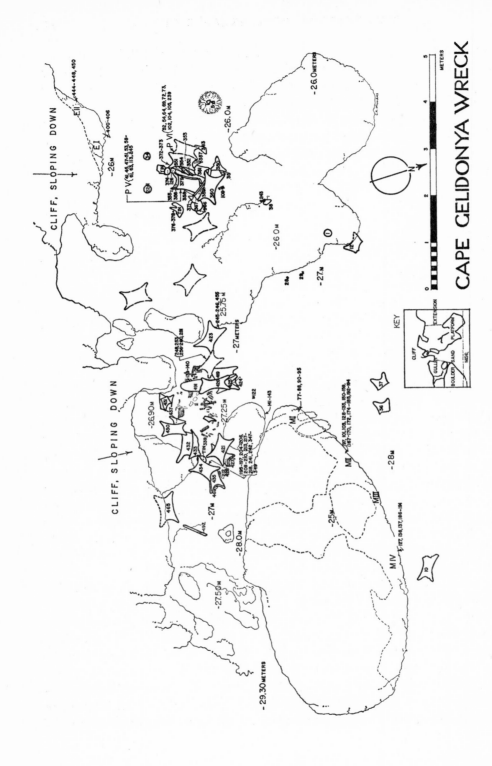

FIG. 50. Plan of wreck site

great length. Neatly cut dowel holes, from 1·5 to 2 cm. in diameter, were found in several planks, and the actual dowels were in place in a few instances (Fig. 51). The area containing most of the preserved wood was raised in one piece, after we had spent three weeks cutting under the rock to which it was attached. Before being moved, each piece of wood was pinned with a numbered plastic tag in order to allow underwater and land records to be accurately matched (Pl. 18). The photograph was taken from the north, and shows in its centre the ingot handle which lies in the midst of the wood of area G on the plan. Several plank ends protrude below and to the east of this handle. Running parallel

FIG. 51. Plank fragments showing dowel holes

to the planks was a much larger piece (just west of ingot 437 in area G, seen barely protruding from the sand in the upper left of the photograph). Until a more thorough study of several hundred photographs and drawings of this area is made, it would be premature to speculate whether this was part of a gunwale; there is some evidence to indicate that the ship had tipped part way over in the Gully, putting this large piece in the position of the keel. Over the planks, and perpendicular to them, lay a large pile of sticks. They varied in size, but none was probably ever more than 1 m. long; their ends were often preserved, cut diagonally across as if by an axe. Bark and twigs remained on most of them. Their purpose remains uncertain, but Gottfried Gruben, who drew each stage of the disassembly of this lump on land, noted that they might have served to protect the hull against the heavy metal cargo; they surely had nothing to do with the construction of the ship. His restorations (Fig. 52)[11] also show a transverse plank with three dowel holes.[12] All traces of ribs have disappeared, but have been restored tentatively in two possible fashions.

It should be noted how well our ship fits the description of the small boat (not, it would seem, a raft) built by Odysseus with the aid of Calypso.[13] We have planks with bored holes and dowels, and at least two of our planks were jointed

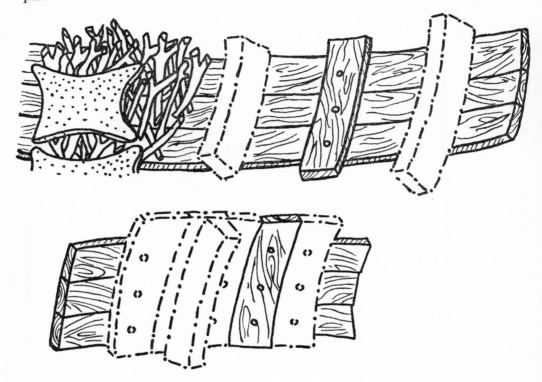

FIG. 52.   Possible restoration of wood in Pl. 18.

together at their ends. On board, perhaps only as part of the cargo, were also the main tools used by Odysseus: axes and adzes. One part of this passage had previously presented difficulties in translation:

φράξε δέ μιν ῥίπεσσι διαμπερὲς οἰσυΐνῃσι
κύματος εἶλαρ ἔμεν· πολλὴν δ' ἐπεχεύατο ὕλην.[14]

The ὕλη has often been considered part of the wattle fencing against the waves, or at least a backing for it, and has even been called ballast. It now seems that a literal translation is required, for brushwood may have been a normal covering for the interior of a hull.[15] The pile of sticks on the Gelidonya wreck was almost certainly not part of the wattle fence, for cargo was lying on it; even if the cargo fell on the sticks during the tipping of the ship in area G, there is no evidence that the sticks were woven or attached to each other in any way.[16] There remains the possibility that this was only firewood, for in this area were found traces of a meal: olive pits and bones of fish and, possibly, a bird. (An *astragalos* from the same area was probably only for playing knucklebones, for no other large animal bones were found.)

The length of the ship may not have been much more than 8 or 9 m., judging from the distribution of the heavy cargo, which lay more or less *in situ*. This size compares well with that of the *Mandalinci*, which is quite at home following the coasts of the Mediterranean. The width is harder to estimate. The portion of the cargo preserved *in situ* in area P is 1·6 m. wide, but this gives only the minimum breadth for one end of the ship, and no indication of the beam. These minimum dimensions give us a ship quite capable of carrying the cargo, which weighed approximately 1,000 kg.; in addition, there were 116 kg. of ballast stones, similar to, but individually larger than, those used on our diving boats.

The cargo

The ship carried a wide variety of goods. The pottery awaits a final cleaning and mending, after which most pieces must be redrawn and photographed; pottery was especially hard to remove from the concretion, as the deposits had soaked into the pores of the fabric. Several distinctive pieces, however, including stirrup jars, a base-ring jug, and large storage jars, are best placed in the thirteenth century B.C.; several of these tend to be late in that century. As Aegean parallels have not yet been thoroughly explored, it would be misleading to present here only the comparisons found from Cyprus, Syria, Palestine, and Tarsus.[17]

The greater part of the cargo consisted of copper ingots. Forty of these, including ten of which only half of each is preserved, are of the so-called 'ox-hide' shape.[18] These averaged in length and width from 60 by 45 cm., and in weight 20·6 kg. For the convenience of continuity, they will be classified following the divisions made by Buchholz,[19] although his dates for these divisions seem untenable.[20] We have distinguished three shapes among our ingots, all of which fall within the limits of his type II. The Gelidonya ingots are designated, therefore, as types IIa, with thick, slightly incurving handles (Pl. 20 left), IIb, sometimes longer and narrower, with a very pronounced raised rim around the edge of the reverse (Pl. 20 centre), and IIc, with more widely spaced, slightly pointed handles (Pl. 20 right).[21] Twenty-seven of them bore what must be considered foundry marks, all but one made while the metal was still soft. With the exception of the one ingot on to which the mark had been scratched, all marked ingots were stamped on the rough side; some of these carried a second mark, usually a circumscribed X, impressed in the centre of the smoother reverse. The significance of these marks has not been determined. Identical marks are found on ingots of varying type and weight. Combinations of marks are also irregular; the circumscribed X is found on the backs of ingots of different types, weights, and bearing different marks on their obverses. Until a complete analysis is made of the material of each ingot, it is not possible to say whether there is a connection between the marks and the quality of the metal.[22]

It has been stated that these ingots were a premonetary form of currency and that originally one ingot weighed one talent and equalled the price of one ox; because of this the shape and surfaces of each ingot were moulded so that the ingot would resemble a dried ox-hide.[23] It is more likely that the resemblance to an ox-hide is purely fortuitous; the 'legs', which do not appear on all ingots, were merely handles for ease of porterage.[24] It has also previously been denied that the rough side of an ingot represented the hairy side of a hide, or that the rim on the smoother side represented the curling of a dried skin. Although this is true, the earlier explanations for these features seem incorrect, for it is stated that the rim is caused by shrinkage during the cooling of the copper, and must always be on top in the mould, while the rough side is formed by the mould itself.[25] Actually, the rough side must in every case be the top, made irregular by the dross and bubbles rising to the surface of the molten metal, and the rounded rim of the reverse is the result of a deep outline in the sand mould. (After the outline of an ingot had been drawn deeply in clayey sand, the space within this outline would have been pressed down to form a mould. If the bottom of the mould was not then smoothed, a number of shallow concavities might be left, explaining the convex areas that we found on the reverse of each of our ingots.) Furthermore, the draft of each of the Gelidonya ingots showed that the rough, bubbly side was on top in the mould (Pl. 20 lower right).[26] Indeed, it seems that the ingots were not a form of currency at all, ox-hide-like or not. Discrepancies in weights of previously known ingots had sometimes been ignored or explained as local variations in the standard used.[27] From Cape Gelidonya we have a closed group, equalling in number about half of all ox-hide ingots previously discovered, and we have no apparent standard of weight. The ingots vary between 16 and 27 kg., and few of them are equal in weight to each other, even when variations due to damage and corrosion are considered. Also we found, as did Wace at Mycenae, irregular pieces of ingots which had been cut or broken from whole ingots.[28] These are only left-overs, and represent no particular part of a talent or even the weight of a complete piece.[29]

Stacked neatly beside piles of ox-hide ingots were more than twenty bun ingots, discs of copper, slightly convex on one side, and averaging almost 4 kg. apiece (Pl. 20). Again the variance in weight is such that no standard is apparent. Dikaios found a mould for ingots of this type at Enkomi,[30] and an actual ingot has been raised from the sea near the Soli mines in Cyprus.[31] Representations of bun ingots occur alongside ox-hide ingots in Egyptian tomb paintings.[32] Several pieces of another shape were thought to be blanks for making tools, when first excavated, but it now seems that these were also ingots (Pl. 20). Although much larger, they are identical in shape to somewhat earlier gold ingots from Egypt.[33] As in the case of the ox-hide and bun ingots, these slab ingots vary greatly in size, most being between 25 and 30 cm. in length. Most of them came from area G, where they were lying in several stacks. Other flat, rectangular pieces, of the same size and smaller, may have been still other forms of ingots.

With the copper ingots was found a number of piles of white, powdery tin oxide.[34] The pile found beneath ingots 433 and 434, in area G, was raised in one mass in a plastic bag. When dry, it weighed 8 kg., which was approximately half of what had been preserved on the wreck. This tin oxide was found only where it had been covered and preserved by heavy masses of copper and sea concretion, and it would be impossible to estimate the amount that might have been washed away from more exposed areas. It represents the earliest industrial tin found, although small tin objects have turned up from earlier periods,[35] and must strengthen the identification of certain white ingots on Egyptian tomb paintings as tin.[36] It should also have some effect on the interpretation of various Near Eastern texts.[37]

Lying throughout the wreck, in groups which suggest that they had been originally in bags or baskets (Pl. 21), were numerous bronze tools, weapons, and household utensils. Two such groups, P V and P VI, were trapped beneath the ingots in that area.[38] In P VI were such objects as a bronze double-axe with an oval shaft-hole and a central groove running along the underside of the blades Fig. 53a), and a bronze adze (or lugged or trunnion axe) (Fig. 53c). In P V were a small axe-adze (Fig. 53b) and a bronze mirror. Throughout the whole wreck, the most common objects were agricultural implements. A large number of socketed picks (Fig. 53e), hoes or plough shares (Fig. 54 a, b, c), and one socketed spade (Fig. 53f) were found.[39] Weapons included spearheads, one with rounded midrib and flat, triangular tang with two rivet holes (Fig. 53d), and two tiny halberds or billhooks, with pointed ends and rectangular blades (Fig. 54e). Household utensils included a *kebab* spit, exactly like those still used in Turkey, several bowl fragments, and pieces of rod tripods (Fig. 54f).[40] Some of these objects were intact, but many more were broken and were found in groups with ingot fragments, indicating that they were being transported, not for their functional use, but for the metal of which they were made. Previous evidence had indicated that in this period bronze objects were commonly melted down for re-use, and founders' hoards on land are made up of possible bagfuls of broken tools,[41] sometimes with ingot fragments.[42] Other

I

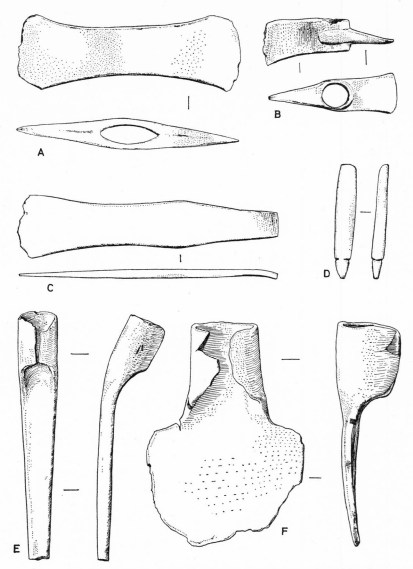

FIG. 53. Bronze tools: (a) double-axe; (b) axe-adze; (c) adze;
(d) whetstone; (e) pick; (f) spade   Scale 1 : 3

tools were in fine condition and could have been for trade or for use by the crew;
an adequate supply of whetstones was on hand to keep them sharp (Fig. 53d).

A merchant must have weights, and forty-eight of these were found, forming three sets. Those of the ovoidal, or 'sphendonoidal', class (Pl. 22) are
approximate multiples of nine and a fraction grams and the smallest of these,

marked with a unit sign on its top, is exactly 9·3 gm., an Egyptian *qedet*.[43] This is a standard also used in Cyprus[44] and Syria.[45] Other weights were cylindrical and domed, but their standards have not yet been determined. Most were of haematite. With few exceptions, the weights came from area G, which we sometimes called the 'captain's quarters' because of the quantity of such personal possessions. Here were found three complete scarabs, one fragment of a scarab,

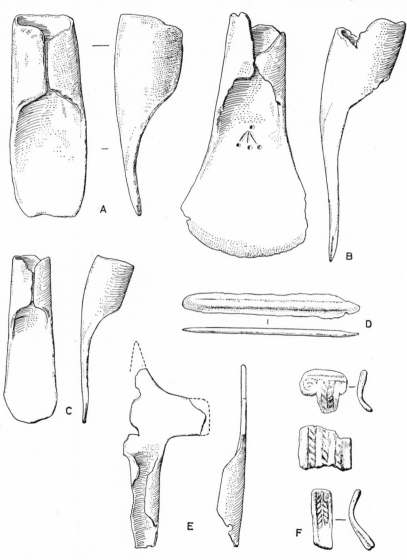

FIG. 54. Bronze objects: (a, b, c) hoes or ploughshares; (d) spearhead; (e) halberd or billhook; (f) tripod fragments   Scale 1 : 3

and a scarab-shaped plaque which was inscribed on both faces. The latest of these (Pl. 22); length 1·8 cm.), which depicts the god Re with falcon's head and a human's body, the left arm of which terminates in a uraeus-serpent, can be dated with almost complete certainty to the Nineteenth Egyptian Dynasty; the greater number of those scarabs with parallel motifs and iconography seem to come from Palestinian sites.[46] Probably from the same area, but swept into area M IV, was a finely carved cylinder seal, showing two worshippers facing a deity wearing the *atef* crown (Pl. 22; length 2·6 cm.; diameter 1·2 cm.). It seems to have been made in North Syria some time during the eighteenth or seventeenth century B.C.; that it was still in use some centuries later is not unusual.[47] In area G were also two polished stone mace-heads, one with a metal lining in its perforation (Pl. 21) and the other with a collar carved around the perforation on one side. It is interesting to note that similar perforated stone hammers were sometimes used for metal working in the Bronze Age,[48] and the occurrence of these may suggest that our merchant was a tinker who dealt both in raw metals and finished products. If this is the case, several problems of our wreck may be solved. A large stone in area S (Inv. No. 491), which was found lying on part of the hull, but which was not a stone native to the area in which we worked, could have been a simple anvil; large metal anvils do not seem to have appeared before the development of iron-working.[49] There is also some evidence to suggest that lugged axes (Fig. 53c) were used by smiths in shaping certain articles. The blades were fastened securely in a vertical position, and sheet metal was moved around on them while being beaten.[50] These blades could, however, have been wood-working tools, the stone hammers might have been weapons or ceremonial mace-heads, and the large stone 'anvil' might have been a crude anchor. Also against the tinker theory is the complete absence of moulds, although several lumps of unworked clay were in the cargo. The strongest evidence for a smith having been on board is the bronze swage block (length 10 cm.) found in area E I (Pl. 22). Such blocks are still in use; pins are drawn out in the variously sized grooves on the sides, and the tapering holes are used for hammering heads on rivets and bolts.[51]

There were other items of trade besides the metal. Several pieces of crystal (Pl. 21) were found near the scarabs, and a jar of glass beads was found in area P. A lamp (Pl. 22; diameter 11·7 cm.) and two stone mortars were probably for the crew's use. One of the stone mortars has a peculiar duck-tailed end opposite its spout (Pl. 21).

Conclusions

The ship appears to have sailed and sunk around 1200 B.C. We may suppose that it was sailing from east to west, carrying a load of copper from the mines in Cyprus.

It is interesting to note that some years ago W. F. Albright speculated that the biblical Tarshish ships were not ships from Tarsus or Tartessos, as had been speculated earlier.[52] Deriving the word 'tarshish' from an Akkadian word meaning smelting plant or refinery, he believed that these ships were the Phoenician ships which carried metal from mines. Although these references are from a slightly later period, our discoveries prove that such ships, dealing almost exclusively in metals, did sail.[53] Whether or not our ship was Syrian, Cypriot, or Helladic, however, is still difficult to say. The fragmentary portion of the ship's structure tells us little. As we have seen, it reminds us of the ship built by Odysseus, but there is nothing that could prove it was not a Syrian ship.[54] Even Egyptian sea-going vessels, differing greatly in construction from Aegean vessels, had all of the members which we have found preserved in our hull.[55] The final analysis of the wood of the Gelidonya wreck will tell us only where the wood may have come from, not where the ship itself was constructed.

The cargo gives more evidence on which to speculate about the nationality of the ship, but it is no more conclusive. The pottery finds parallels from the Greek mainland to the coasts of Syria and Palestine, including Cyprus and Tarsus in between; if, from a closer examination of the fabric, we are able to determine exactly where the pottery was made, there will remain the possibility that it was part of a cargo picked up *en route*. The sole exception is the lamp, the only one on board, which must have been the ship's lamp; unfortunately, it might have been a foreign replacement. The scarabs and cylinder seal must be discounted, for the possibility that they were trinkets picked up during the voyage is considerable. The copper and bronze were almost certainly from Cyprus. Many of the marks on the ingots are identical to potters' marks from Cyprus and from the Cypriot colony near Ras Shamra in Syria. While it must be admitted that most of the marks are simple linear designs which are often common to Linear B as well, the marks on the tools seem to be exclusively Cypro-Minoan. The shapes of the tools seem also to be Cypriot,[56] although some of their closest parallels come from the Acropolis hoard in Athens.[57] This would suggest only that these latter objects had been brought to Greece in a vessel such as ours.[58] The tin could be from a number of places. Ox-hide ingots appear in Sardinia,[59] suggesting voyages at least that far west. There is no reason to suppose, however, that Spain, which supplied so much of the tin in later antiquity, was the source of our tin. Closer sources include Byblos,[60] and perhaps Crisa near Delphi,[61] although the occurrence of tin at the latter site is not universally accepted.[62]

Even though we may conclude that the tools and ingots were Cypriot, it is possible that they were being transported by traders from other lands. Ox-hide ingots were associated with Syrians in Egypt, as in the tombs of Rekhmire[63] and Huy,[64] and even on Cyprus itself we have the small figure of a man in Syrian dress carrying an ingot.[65] Other representations, earlier than our shipwreck, show

Keftiu tribute bearers carrying ingots,[66] but if the *Keftiu* were truly Minoans, the Mycenaeans would surely have captured this trade by now. Further study will answer some of the problems raised, but even more enlightening will be the re-location and excavation of the other ingot-carrying ships which have been reported in the Mediterranean.

NOTES

1 This report was first published in the *American Journal of Archaeology*, 65 (1961), 267. Other accounts have appeared in *Expedition*, the Bulletin of the University Museum of Pennsylvania, 3, No. 2 (1961), 2; *Archaeology*, 14 (1961), 78, and the *National Geographic Magazine*, 121 (1962), 697.

2 A more detailed description of the islands and current may be found in *Sailing Directions for the Mediterranean*, IV (U.S. Hydrographic Office Publication 154 A; Washington, D.C., 1951), 174.

3 Stefan Przeworski, 'Die Metallindustrie Anatoliens in der Zeit von 1500–700 vor Chr.', *Internationales Archiv für Ethnographie*, 36, suppl. (Leiden, 1939), 92, with Pl. 13, Fig. 2; C. T. Seltman, *Athens, Its History and Coinage before the Persian Invasion* (Cambridge, 1924), 3, note 3.

4 Peter Throckmorton, 'Thirty-three Centuries Under the Sea', *National Geographic Magazine*, 117 (1960), 682–703; Stanton A. Waterman, 'Three Thousand Years Under the Sea', *Explorers Journal*, 38 (1960), No. 3, 28–35; Machteld J. Mellink, 'Archaeology in Asia Minor', *A.J.A.*, 63 (1959), 73, *A.J.A.*, 64 (1960), 58; Honor Frost, 'Two Carian Wrecks', *Antiquity*, 34 (1960), 216–18; J. M. Cook, 'Greek Archaeology in Asia Minor', *Archaeological Reports for 1959–60* (*J.H.S.* suppl.), 28–9; C. Picard, 'Découvertes sous-marines de l'âge du Bronze au Sud de la côte d'Anatolie', *R.A.*, 2 (1960), 88–91, with Figs. 2–3; George M. A. Hanfmann, 'Roebuck, Ionian Trade and Colonization', *Gnomon*, 32 (1960), 701. I wish to thank Mr. Throckmorton and Arthur Steinberg, respectively, for these last two references.

5 The excavation was sponsored by the University Museum, aided by the Littauer Foundation, Mr. John Huston of the Council of Underwater Archaeology, the American Philosophical Society, and two individual contributors. The preservation and recording of finds was undertaken by the Institute of Archaeology of London University, with funds from the British Academy and the Craven Fund. Our diving equipment was acquired through the generosity of the U.S. Divers Company in America and La Spirotechnique in France. The British School in Athens also lent all of its diving equipment to us, but, unfortunately, this did not reach us during the season because of Customs difficulties. Our high-pressure air-compressor was made available to us at a greatly reduced price by Bauer Kompressoren of Munich. Photography was made possible by loans of the latest underwater camera by the Nikon Company of New York and of a Polaroid Land Camera with film by the Polaroid Corporation of Cambridge, Mass. An underwater case for the Polaroid camera was designed and constructed by the French Navy's Undersea Research Group (O.F.R.S.). Special polythene bags, for preserving perishable finds, were supplied by Anglo-American Plastics, Ltd., of London, and Araldite for treating wood was a gift of CIBA (A.R.L.) of Cambridge, England. For preserving cloth,

we were given a supply of Gelvatol 1–30 by the Shawinigan Resins Corporation of Springfield, Mass., but our cloth proved to be a mirage this season. For various illnesses and poisonous fish stings we had drugs from the Wellcome Foundation Ltd. of London, and anti-histamine creams from Scientific Pharmacals Ltd. of Cambridge. Our fine, large dinghy was lent by Baskin Sokullu of the Turk Balik Adamlar Kulubu. The underwater metal detector which we used during the last few days of the season was brought by Luis Marden of the *National Geographic* staff.

The staff consisted of G. F. Bass, director; Peter Throckmorton, technical adviser and photographer; Joan du Plat Taylor, in charge of preservation and records; Frederic Dumas, chief diver; Claude Duthuit and Waldemar Illing, divers; Herb Greer, underwater photographer; Honor Frost, Eric J. Ryan, and Yuksel Eğdemir, underwater draughtsmen; Terry Ball, object draughtsman; Peter Dorrell, object photographer; and Ann Bass, in charge of cleaning and cataloguing during the last third of the season. Hakki Gültekin and Lütfi Tuğrul represented the Turkish Antiquities Department, and were a constant source of aid and advice. All of the above, with the exceptions of Miss Taylor, Ball, Dorrell, and Tuğrul, worked on the wreck underwater. Visitors who also dived and worked on the wreck were Mustafa Kapkin, Rasim Diwanli, Roland J. Lacroix, Gernolf Martens, and Luis Marden. At the conclusion of the season, Gottfried Gruben came to Bodrum in order to draw the only preserved section of the hull, as it was being disassembled. John Dereki, captain of the *Haji Baba* of Beirut, visited us for a day and took a series of depth readings with his electronic sounding devices. Miss Susan Womer has assisted in the preparation of some of the drawings for publication.

The formation of such a novel excavation, involving divers and equipment from five countries, took an unusual amount of paperwork. That Mr. Throckmorton's work was continued on a large scale was due especially to the foresight and planning of Mr. John Huston of the Council of Underwater Archaeology in America, and Miss Taylor in England. In Turkey, we were grateful for the technical advice given by Mr. Daniel Siglin and Mr. Kenneth Sprague. My excellent course in diving was under the instruction of David Stith, of the Philadelphia Depth Chargers, who is now training several other archaeologists to dive. A special word of thanks must go to Dr. Rodney S. Young, whose guiding hand from beginning to end made the entire project a success.

6 G. F. Bass and Peter Throckmorton, 'Excavating a Bronze Age Shipwreck', *Archaeology*, 14 No. 2 (1961), deals almost exclusively with our methods.

7 These decompression times are longer than the tables require. The only cure for the 'bends' is immediate recompression in a special chamber, but, because of various difficulties, our recompression chamber never reached Gelidonya.

8 G. F. Bass and Peter Throckmorton, op. cit. (*supra*, note 6).

9 The plan was drawn by C. K. Williams with measurements taken by the author, assisted by Duthuit and Eğdemir; positions of small objects were added from Miss Frost's working plans. It should be noted that on this plan, and on the photographic montage, north is at the bottom; this was for the convenience of divers, who sometimes took tracings to the bottom and who normally approached and studied the wreck from the open north side.

10 On a plan of this scale it was impossible to show exact positions of small objects. Also, to prevent confusion, most of the wood, which was in several layers, and many of the inventory numbers are not shown here in area G because of the very crowded conditions. The ingot and three ingot halves in area M were not *in situ* when the

plan was made, having been moved, probably from area P, by the discoverers of the wreck.

11 Drawings by Maude de Schauensee from sketches in a letter from Herr Gruben.

12 This transverse plank, which may have had five dowel holes, was actually found under some of the side planks of the hull. Ballast stones and pieces of copper were found with it, however, showing the badly twisted state of the hull; we have assumed that it must be restored within the ship.

13 *Odyssey*, 5, 233–61.

14 Ibid., 5, 256–7.

15 '. . . and he heaped up a great deal of brushwood', now seems the simplest and best translation of the last part, although it loses the basic ideal of spreading, which was quite clearly warranted by the evidence at Cape Gelidonya.

16 Cf. the fencing on the Syrian ships from a slightly earlier period in Norman de G. Davies and R. O. Faulkner, 'A Syrian Trading Venture to Egypt', *J.E.A.*, 33 (1947), Pl. 8, and Lionel Casson, *The Ancient Mariners* (New York, 1959), 19. This also appears, less clearly, in August Köster, *Das Antike Seewesen* (Berlin, 1923), Pl. 11.

17 Miss Taylor, who is studying the pottery for the final publication, has supplied the information concerning the Near Eastern parallels, but has added that she has not yet fully studied the possible Aegean relations. I wish also to thank Miss Taylor for many suggestions and notes which will aid greatly in the final analysis of other parts of the cargo.

18 Hans-Günter Buchholz has made the most complete study of ingots of this type in 'Der Kupferhandel des zweiten vorchristlichen Jahrtausends im Spiegel der Schriftforschung', *Minoica*, Festschrift zum 80 Geburtstag von Joh. Sundwall (Berlin, 1958), 92–115, and 'Keftiubarren und Erzhandel im zweiten vorchristlichen Jahrtausend', *P.Z.*, 37 (1959), 1–40. Miss Mellink referred me to these two works before the expedition took place, and Miss Taylor has brought to my attention the mention of ox-hide ingots on cylinder seals in Olivier Masson, 'Cylindres et cachets chypriotes portant des caractères chypro-minoens', *B.C.H.*, 81 (1957), 7–8, with Fig. 1; a number of these possible ingot representations may be seen in William Hayes Ward, *The Seal Cylinders of Western Asia* (Washington, 1910), 349–50.

19 Buchholz, *P.Z.*, 37 (*supra*, note 18), 7, and *Minoica* (*supra*, note 18), 96.

20 Buchholz, in *Minoica*, 93–5, and *P.Z.*, 37 (*supra*, note 18), 4–6, has dated his three types from stratified examples and examples on Egyptian tomb paintings, and has shown a continuous evolution in the ingot shape. Although there may well be a distinction between type I and types II and III, the last two types are proved to have been used contemporaneously by their appearance together on the west side of the north wall of the tomb of Huya at el Amarna, shown in N. de G. Davies, *The Rock Tombs of El Amarna, III: The Tombs of Huya and Ahmes* (London, 1905), Pl. 16. Before noticing this painting, I had not readily seen the distinction between the ingot in Nina de Garis Davies, *The Tomb of Huy, Viceroy of Nubia in the Reign of Tutankhamun* (London, 1926), Pl. 19, carried by a Syrian, and the ingots of Buchholz's type II. Now we may be sure that type III ingots were used between 1400 and 1200 B.C., a period previously assigned only to type II.

21 Types II*a* and II*b* may be accidental variations of the same type (*infra*, note 26); they are quite similar to ingots from Cyprus (Claude F. A. Schaeffer, *Enkomi-Alasia* [Paris, 1952], 32, with Pl. 63, Fig. 1; and Buchholz, *P.Z.*, 37 [*supra*, note 18], 29, with Pl. 3, Fig. 3) and the Greek mainland (I have not yet seen the original publication of the complete ingot from Mycenae, which is well illustrated in Seltman,

op. cit. [*supra*, note 3], 4–5; Buchholz, *P.Z.*, 37, p. 36, with Pl. 5, Figs. 1–2, gives the bibliography for this). Type II*c* seems much more like one of the ingots from Serra Ilixi, Sardinia (Buchholz, *P.Z.*, 37, p. 38, with Fig. 12*b*, Fig. 12*a*, from the same site, more closely resembles our type II*b*).

22 Except for areas that had come into contact with tin, which caused considerable decay through electrolysis, the copper ox-hide ingots were usually solid and well preserved throughout. The bun and slab ingots, discussed below, were so poorly preserved that they often crumbled under the slightest pressure.

23 Seltman, op. cit. (*supra*, note 3), 1–5.

24 Buchholz, *P.Z.*, 37 (*supra*, note 18), 2–4. Although we have shown (*supra*, note 20) that there can be no chronological distinction between types II and III, the lugless type I ingots do seem to be earlier. The theory that the ingot 'legs' were only handles was previously held by H. R. Hall, *Aegean Archaeology* (London, 1915), 67, with Fig. 13; and Schaeffer, op. cit. (*supra*, note 20), 33.

25 Buchholz, *Minoica* (*supra*, note 18), 95. Seltman, op. cit. (*supra*, note 3), 4, note 2, while believing that the ingots were in the form of ox-hides, had also explained the physical characteristics in this way.

26 After noting the bubbly surfaces of lead diving weights that the sponge-divers cast at our camp, I was led to the belief that the rough sides of the ingots were caused by such bubbles. I would like to thank Robert Barnes, who has much experience in bronze-casting, for confirming this, and for explaining the causes for the other features. Mr. Barnes made a small mould in the manner that he would use to cast similar ingots, and the rounded ridges and convex areas would have resulted had an actual ingot been cast in it. That the ridges were neither functional nor representational, but merely the result of chance, would explain why they did not appear on all ingots. I cannot explain the occurrence of ingots whose rough sides are smaller than their smooth sides (Buchholz, *Minoica* [*supra*, note 18], 95) and feel that these must be re-examined.

27 Seltman, op. cit. (*supra*, note 3), 3.

28 A. J. B. Wace, 'Preliminary Report on the Excavations of 1952', *B.S.A.*, 48 (1953), 7, with Pl. 2(*a*).

29 Further evidence that the ingots were not currency, but were simply blocks of raw metal, is the scene showing an ingot about to be melted down and cast in Norman de Garis Davies, *Paintings from the Tomb of Rekh-mi-rē' at Thebes* (New York, 1935), Pl. 23, and Davies, *The Tomb of Rekh-mi-rē' at Thebes* (New York, 1943), I, 54, and II, Pls. 52–3. I would suggest that the Knossos tablets which show ingots with scales tell only how many talents a number of copper ingots *of no standard weight* weighed, and did not equate copper or bronze talents with a gold unit, as in Arthur J. Evans, 'Minoan Weights and Mediums of Currency, from Crete, Mycenae, and Cyprus', *Corolla Numismatica* (Oxford, 1906), 361, with Fig. 14; nor are average weights valid, as in Michael Ventris and John Chadwick, *Documents in Mycenaean Greek* (Cambridge, 1959), 355.

30 Hector Catling has supplied me with this information. He writes that it is mentioned in A. H. S. Megaw, 'Archaeology in Cyprus, 1956', *Archaeological Reports, 1956*, (suppl. to *J.H.S.*, 77 [1957], 25), without being described as that particular type. I would like to express my special gratitude to Mr. Catling for generously supplying me with a vast number of references to Aegean and Cypriot bronzes which he has gathered over some years.

31 O. Davies, 'The Copper Mines of Cyprus', *B.S.A.*, 30 (1928–30), 78. My thanks

to Mr. Throckmorton and Miss Taylor for each bringing this ingot to my attention.

32　Buchholz, *P.Z.*, 37 (*supra*, note 18), 15, Fig. 7. These ingots had formerly been identified as loaves in N. de G. Davies, *The Rock Tombs of El Amarna* (London, 1903), I, 37, with Pl. 31. In the casting scene from the Tomb of Rekhmire (*supra*, note 29) are shown two men carrying baskets of what must be copper bun ingots, for they are the same colour as the ox-hide ingot in the same scene (Davies, *The Tomb of Rekh-mi-rē* [*supra*, note 29], I, 54, with II, Pl. 53, row 3). G. A. Wainwright, 'Egyptian Bronze-making Again', *Antiquity*, 18 (1944), 101, believed these latter ingots to be of tin.

33　F. Bisson de la Roque, *Trésor de Tod, Catalogue Général des Antiquités Égyptiennes du Musée du Caire* (Cairo, 1950), Pl. 4, No. 70,505.

34　Analysed by Turyağ Laboratories of Izmir.

35　R. J. Forbes, *Metallurgy in Antiquity* (Leiden, 1950), 232, 252, 254; G. A. Wainwright, 'Early Tin in the Aegean', *Antiquity*, 18 (1944), 57.

36　G. A. Wainwright, 'Egyptian Bronze-Making', *Antiquity*, 17 (1943), 96–7, theorized that one of the two ingots in the *Tomb of the Two Sculptors* (Norman de Garis Davies [New York, 1925], Pl. 11) was tin, although Davies had identified it as lead.

37　W. F. Albright has suggested that the Gelidonya tin provides an additional argument for identification of *anāku* in the old Assyrian documents from Cappadocia as 'tin' rather than 'lead', although he does point out that these documents are considerably older than the shipwreck.

38　Other groups designated by Roman numerals, in areas E and M, were not *in situ*, but were formed in natural pockets into which small objects had been carried by the current. The objects in E were probably from P, and those in M could have either drifted through small passages under the Boulder, or could have been carried from G and S. It was noted that the current, when running westward through the Gully, tended to sweep objects around the west end of the boulder. A change in direction of the current, a common occurrence, would have then moved these pieces eastward and deposited them along the north edge of the Boulder in area M.

39　There is some disagreement over what the various tools were. An interesting attempt to identify such tools with biblical names is in G. Ernest Wright, 'I Samuel 19–21', *Bibl. Arch.*, 6 (1943), 33–6.

40　Miss Taylor recognized these fragments as being from tripods of a type found at Ras Shamra. J. L. Benson has collected and illustrated other tripods in 'Bronze Tripods from Kourion', *Greek, Roman, and Byzantine Studies*, 3 (1960), 7–16; all of these tripods with features similar to our pieces are dated later than the shipwreck. (However, see H. W. Catling, 'Bronze Cut-and-thrust Swords in the Eastern Mediterranean', *Proc. P.S.*, 22 [1957], 111, note 7.)

41　John C. Rolfe, 'Discoveries at Anthedon', *A.J.A.*, 6, Old Series (1890), 107; H. W. Catling, op. cit. (*supra*, note 40), 104; references to other such hoards may be found here, note 10, and 109, note 5.

42　Wace, loc. cit. (*supra*, note 28).

43　Flinders Petrie, *Ancient Weights and Measures* (London, 1926), 13 and 20.

44　Evans, op. cit. (*supra*, note 29), 349–51.

45　Claude F.-A. Schaeffer, 'Les fouilles de Ras Shamra-Ugarit, huitième campagne', *Syria*, 18 (1937), 150. Here was found a weight of 18·7 gm. with two parallel strokes on its top, along with many unmarked multiples.

46　I am indebted to Alan Schulman for these data, which are from a paper he delivered on the scarabs at the 171st Meeting of the American Oriental Society in Phila-delphia, 1961.

47 Miss Edith Porada kindly studied this seal and suggested the information given.

48 H. H. Coghlan, 'Metal Implements and Weapons', *A History of Technology* (Oxford, 1954), I, 609, with Fig. 401 A. I have not yet seen the evidence on which this is based.

49 *ibid.* and Forbes, op. cit. (*supra*, note 34), 121.

50 R. Maxwell-Hyslop, 'Bronze Lugged Axe- or Adze-blades from Asia', *Iraq*, 15 (1953), 71.

51 I wish to thank Paul W. Shaw, an expert metal worker, for making this identi-fication. Previously I had assumed that it was a metal-working object only on the basis of its similarity to the tiny anvil in John Evans, *The Ancient Bronze Implements, Weapons, and Ornaments, of Great Britain and Ireland* (New York, 1881), 182–3, with Figs. 217–18.

52 W. F. Albright, 'New Light on the Early History of Phoenician Colonization', *B.A.S.O.R.*, 83 (October 1941), 21–2

53 Another piece of literary evidence, presenting the possibility of smiths travelling on ships, has just reached me thanks to Hugo Mühlestein. He has theorized that the *oka*-tablets from Pylos refer to ships, saying that the word *oka* designates a ship (ὁλκάς) in *Die oka-Tafeln von Pylos* (Basel, 1956), 36–41, with additional evidence in *Estratto dall' Athenaeum*, New Series, 36 (1958), 366–7. If this is the case, it is interesting to note that almost every ship has as one of its leaders a man who has also turned up as a smith in one of the Jn tablets (*kirijijo, komawe, atijawo, perino, erikowo*, etc.), but it seems that in no case are two smiths on board. This had led Mühlestein to pose the question of whether smiths were indispensable on military transports during the Bronze Age, and had offered evidence, previous to the dis-covery of the Gelidonya wreck, that smiths travelled on ships at all.

54 For the scanty evidence we have of the appearance of Bronze Age ships, mostly from fanciful and inaccurate drawings and carvings, see Spiridon Marinatos, 'La Marine Créto-Mycénienne', *B.C.H.*, 57 (1933), 170–235, and G. S. Kirk, 'Ships on Geometric Vases', *B.S.A.*, 44 (1949), 116–17, which includes several of this period. To the bibliographies found in these articles may be added James Mellaart, 'The Royal Treasure of Dorak', *I.L.N.*, 235 (1959), 754, with Fig. 2, and the crude graffiti at Enkomi, Schaeffer, *Enkomi-Alasia*, 102, with Fig. 38, and on Malta, Diana Woolner, 'Graffiti of Ships at Tarxien, Malta', *Antiquity*, 30 (1957), 60–7. An example of a Syrian ship has been mentioned (*supra*, note 17).

55 Although it is generally believed that Egyptian ships lacked ribs and keel, James Hornell points out the probability that 'a few ribs are inserted after the hull plank-ing has been assembled and in place', and shows that a keel plank was used, in 'The Sailing Ships of Ancient Egypt', *Antiquity*, 17 (1943), 28 and 30.

56 Mr. Catling states that out of 302 recognizable pieces of bronze, 232 have close parallels in Cypriot hoards. The 302 are made up of forty-one forms, twenty-seven of which have close parallels in Cyprus. The most common objects are also those which are most common in hoards.

57 Oscar Montelius, *La Grèce Preclassique* (Stockholm, 1924), 152–6.

58 It has been suggested by Ventris and Chadwick, op. cit. (*supra*, note 28), 356, that Pylos tablet Ja 749 may refer to the total weight of metal (copper or bronze?) that has been distributed to local smiths, as recorded on a series of tablets. The total equals 1,011 kg. (Ventris and Chadwick give 1,046 kg., using only approximate values for the standard of weight, as explained on p. 57). This is almost exactly

the weight of the copper and bronze from the Gelidonya wreck. Is it too fanciful to suggest that Ja 749 was written up on receipt of a normal shipment of copper and bronze?

59 *Supra*, note 21.
60 Forbes, op. cit. (*supra*, note 35), 239.
61 O. Davies, 'Two North Greek Mining Towns', *J.H.S.*, 4 (1929), 92–3; G. A Wainwright, 'Early Tin in the Aegean', *Antiquity*, 18 (1944), 59.
62 Forbes, op. cit. (*supra*, note 34), 244.
63 Davies, *Rekh-mi-rē* (*supra*, note 29), Pl. 22, *Paintings* (*supra*, note 29), Pl. 12.
64 Davies, *The Tomb of Huy* (*supra*, note 20), Pl. 19.
65 R. D. Barnett, 'The Nimrud Ivories and the Art of the Phoenicians', *Iraq* (1935), 209, with Pl. 28; the ingot is here identified as a skin of wine. Schaeffer, *Enkomi-Alasia* (*supra*, note 21), 31, with Pl. 66.
66 Davies, *Rekh-mi-rē'* (*supra*, note 29), Pls. 18–20; *Paintings* (*supra*, note 29).

4

Underwater Surveys

The wrecks which have been described were found in several cases by chance. But it is to the helmeted sponge-divers, who walk about the sea-bed as a farmer does his fields, that we owe the earliest discoveries. They cover the ground time and again and know the irregularities of rocks and gullies to a depth of 30 m. or more; in such a way the Cape Gelidonya wreck was discovered.

But the large body of free-divers now operating along the Mediterranean shores is rapidly discovering wrecks, anchors, and many other objects, most of which remain unrecorded before they are looted; but some wrecks have been reported and listed in French, Spanish, and Italian publications. The record is very unequal, but it does at least indicate the distribution along the coast and the range of period to which the ships belonged. To give a true picture of the hazards and the sea-routes and so forth, detailed exploration, section by section, of the coast would be required.

Without doubt, the persons best able to do this are the divers living on the coast, visiting the bays and reefs regularly in all types of weather and light, after storms and floods, seeing the sea-bed in all its changing aspects. Such a survey is being undertaken by the Agde Club (Groupe de Recherches Archéologiques et de Plongée d'Agde), led by M. Denis Fonquerle. With the support of Professor Gallet de Santerre, Director of the Antiquities Department, the members are preparing a report on the coastal and river area, from which they have recovered amphorae, anchors, pottery, and many new types of object. Together with the wrecks, these are carefully charted. From the study of objects on the files an interesting cross-section of the trade of the port, not only in Roman times but in the later centuries, has been obtained. At the same time, by regular inspection of the coast, they act as unofficial guardians of the sea-sites.

'In spite of the urge for discovery and a passion for research, each member of the team is a disinterested and devoted worker in the service of archaeology. At Agde, the "hunt for souvenirs" no longer takes place, no one will abstract a find, and the smallest sherd is taken to the Museum for registration and filing. Able to identify their finds *in situ*, the divers become valued colleagues of the archaeologists, who supervise their explorations in the most friendly fashion.'[1]

A corpus of over 200 amphorae has been prepared, drawn to the standard scale of one-fifth established by Professor Lamboglia. The first series to be published, comprising thirty-six amphorae, is of service to both land and sea archaelogists.[1]

In Italy the first organized survey of an area was made by divers of the Centro Italiano Ricercatori Subacquei of Genoa in the summer of 1957 around the island of Gallinaria, near Albenga.

Archaeological survey of the sea-bed near Gallinaria Island (Alessandro Pederzini)[2]

The proposal to make a systematic exploration of the small island of Gallinaria, between Albenga and Alassio, was accepted by Professor Nino Lamboglia, Director of the Istituto Internazionale di Studi Liguri, who undertook to carry it out under his personal supervision. The chance archaeological finds, made by fishermen and free-divers, had for many years led to the belief that there might be traces of ancient wrecks on the sea-bed surrounding the island.

The work was carried out in nine days' diving during the months of April and May 1957 by one or more teams of divers. The divers were: Gianni Roghi, Felice Motta, and Renzo Ferrandi from Milan, and Giacomo Divizia and Idelmino Callegaro from Alassio. The operation was the first of its kind in Italy. It has particularly demonstrated the possibility of a useful collaboration between archaeologists and divers.

Equipment

All divers worked with aqualungs of large capacity (about 4 cu.m.) and diving suits of winter type. When necessary, the aqualungs were refilled by a portable compressor or by the S.I.O. at Vado Ligure.

Special items of equipment which were used included plastic boards with a special pencil; marker buoys made of two plastic spheres welded to a central spool, on which was wound a thin nylon cable 50 m. long (having tied the loose end to the object or made it fast to the point to be marked, the buoy was freed and, as it was very buoyant, it quickly rose to the surface, unfurling the cable); flexible baskets of galvanized wire-net, which were easily handled and moved (they were used for carrying small objects and as containers for small finds); small painted metal balls to be fastened on the sea-bed as markers for areas or objects; special plastic balloons (polyvinyl chloride), to be inflated on the sea-bed by means of compressed-air bottles (for lifting heavy objects, on the lines of hydrostatic balloons); waterproof tapes 25 m. long, made of brass and leather, for measuring large areas; and, lastly, a set of ropes of varying lengths, and large jute bags, for storing various finds. The divers were also equipped with coloured celluloid balls, which, when released in water, enabled them to communicate by code with the support-boat. The underwater photos were taken with a Robot camera, without a flashlight.

Recompression, always necessary because of the long duration and the depth of dive, was carried out in the shelter of the reef on those few occasions when the men found themselves near the shore after their dives, or by seating them in special iron rings filled with lead. These rings, weighing 18 kg., were lowered from the support-boat at an agreed signal, made by releasing to the surface a celluloid ball of a given colour.

Two launches with inboard motors were used for the trips and as support to divers. Alassio was the operational base.

Plan of work

The chief aim of all dives was the finding and locating of archaeological deposits. The intention of the first stage of the operation, as planned with Professor Lamboglia, was to locate objects without removing them.

The sea-bed surrounding the island was divided into seven sectors, each marked with a letter from A to G (Fig. 55). The sectors were explored by one or two teams, and when there was the least indication that a particular section might be of special interest several days' diving were devoted to it. Directed by a team leader, each team made notes on the board, surveyed the area, took photographs, and marked the objects of chief interest with buoys. On the surface, the marked positions were noted down by the leader in the boat.

Recovery

After exploration work and the survey, various objects were recovered, with the main purpose of establishing if there was a chronological link between them. Of particular importance was the recovery of an intact Roman lead anchor stock. This was the second official find of its kind in Italy. From its dimensions (length about 80 cm., weight about 50 kg.), it must have belonged to a ship of no great size. The stock was found on the top of a coral reef, to the west of the island, in which the anchor had obviously become caught some distance from the shore and at a depth of 30 m. (Sector F).

The hydrostatic-balloon arrangement did not give good results in the case of recovering the anchor stock; after having risen quickly to the surface, it burst, due to an inadequate vent for the surplus air in relation to the rapid drop in hydro-

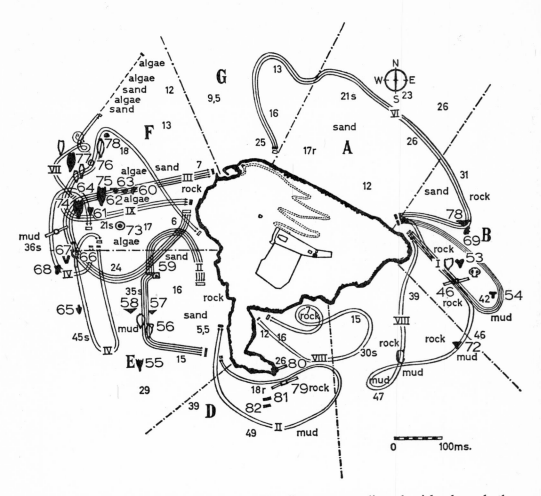

FIG. 55. Map of Gallinaria island. The lines surrounding the island mark the underwater routes. Each line traces one diver's course; the direction is shown by the black rectangles at the start and by the white at the end. The Roman numerals indicate the day the dive was made. All other details are marked on the plan itself. The innumerable sherds of scant interest, present chiefly in sector F, are not marked. Arabic figures indicate the serial number of the finds.

static pressure (from 4 to 1 kg. per square centimetre). The stock was later lashed with ropes and slowly hauled up by the support-boat, while two divers supervised the operation.

For the amphorae, the following system was used instead: two divers swam to the spot with two or three jute sacks, some balls, and a marking buoy. The amphora to be recovered was put into a sack, and after a ball had been released they waited

144

for a cable to be lowered from the boat. They firmly tied the mouth of the sack with the loose end of the cable, and another ball of a different colour signalled that the boatman might start hauling. When there was a strong tide, or the work was carried out at a greater depth, so that the ball might surface at a point far from vertically above the divers, the coiled cable was carried down by one of the divers. One end of it was then tied to the mouth of the sack and the other to the nylon line of the signalling buoy. From the boat, by hauling up the buoy-line, the loose end of the cable was hoisted up and the load was hauled on board.

The use of sacks is certainly not very sensible when a great number of amphorae have to be recovered—for example, in the case of a sunken cargo—but for hauling up isolated pieces it is the ideal system, both because the danger of breakage is reduced to a minimum and the contents of the amphora or of any other container are not lost and can therefore be examined.

Fragments and small sherds of pottery were put in the wire-net baskets.

Conclusion

The systematic exploration of the sea-bed at a maximum depth of 45 m. has proved that there are no wrecks in a belt 200–300 m. out from the island's cliffs. In two zones, however, there were scattered deposits of ancient objects. One of these zones is to the east (sectors B and C), and principally along the line of reefs of the easternmost point. Here were found small fragments of amphorae. In this zone, in 1956, Victor De Sanctis, Roberto Mero, Idelmino Callegaro, and Giacomo Divizia recovered the large stock of a Roman anchor weighing about 200 kg. The point and its reef, the island's largest, have been carefully explored by us. The fragments are scattered widely and are situated at varying depths. The absence of a deposit proper, even at the base of the reef (40–45 m.), indicates that there was no shipwreck on that spot. It is probable, however, that a big ship in difficulties would have endeavoured to slip into the shelter of the point in search of a berth, and that through heavy rolling she may have lost an anchor and a small part of her cargo. Pursuing this hypothesis, it might have been the ship discovered at Albenga, whose wreck is situated exactly on the same line to the east, at the same distance from the coast (one mile), and about two miles from the island. It could be thought that the ship, in serious difficulties from a south-westerly gale, after a last attempt to run for shelter on the east side of Gallinaria Island, put out into the open sea, again eastward, and sank not long afterwards, perhaps through being holed against this reef. No anchor from the large Albenga wreck has so far come to light, nor have we ourselves seen any during our exploration. It is, on the other hand, improbable that a ship of that size would be equipped with only one anchor.

The other area of archaeological interest is situated to the west of the island

K

(Sectors E–F). Here the high, steep cliffs standing above water form a bay sheltered from north-east, east, and south-east winds. This patch of calm sea, as far as we have been able to ascertain, was for the ancient Albingaunum (Albenga) an anchorage for ships arriving or departing from the *Vadino* harbour of the town, the only important one between Vado and Monaco. The various objects observed, marked, and recovered in a very limited quantity, such as broken amphorae, pieces of cups, paterae, and other pottery therefore must have been thrown away as useless, or had fallen overboard accidentally. The fact that these ships called at that place even though there was a harbour nearby may be explained both by the lack of room for mooring and the consequent necessity of awaiting one's turn (as still happens today in all busy ports), and by the sea often being rough in the so-called channel between the island and the coast, which would have made entry into the harbour difficult.

The objects recovered are of various dates. We have found objects of the second century B.C. and of the first A.D. only a few metres apart from each other, while the anchor stock which was found confirms the hypothesis of an anchorage. To support this hypothesis, a third, very small, anchor stock and the fragment of a fourth stock, also very small, were found in June 1957 by underwater fishermen from Albenga, led by Guiseppe Cecchetti, in water only a few metres deep in the south zone (Sector D), which is in the bay sheltered by the Falconara promontory from the westerly winds.

The total number of diving hours was forty-two. All the objects recovered have been sent to the Museo Navale Romano at Albenga.

Inventory of Finds (Figs. 56—61)

1. Sector E.66.   Lead anchor stock found in 1956.
2. Sector F.69.   Lead anchor stock found in 1957, with a retaining bar across the socket for the wooden stock. The moulding is perfectly rectangular. Complete. Length 0·90 m., weight 25 kg.

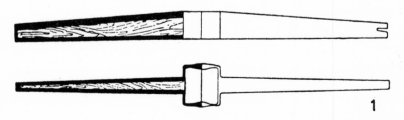

FIG. 56.   Lead anchor stock   Scale 1 : 20   (*Atti* . . . Albenga, 1958)

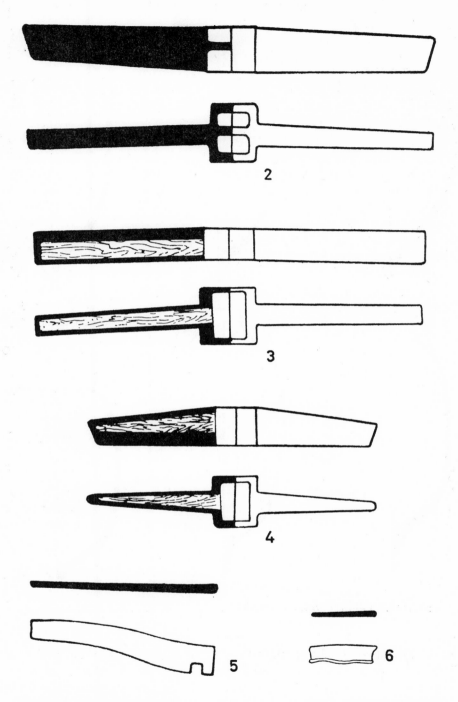

FIG. 57. Lead anchor stocks   Scale 1 : 6   (*Atti* ... Albenga, 1958)

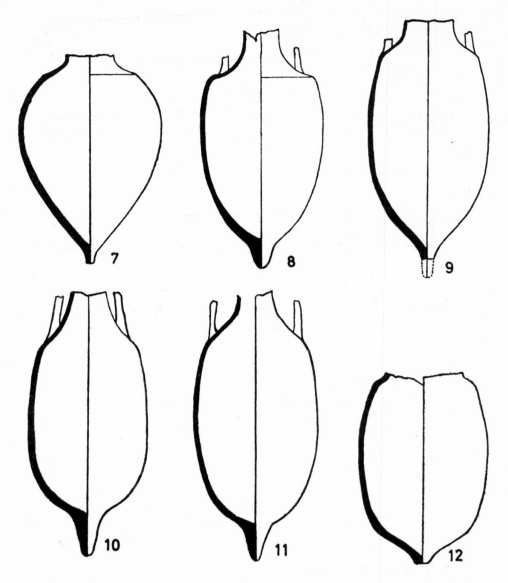

FIG. 58.   Oil amphorae   Scale 1 : 10   (*Atti* . . . Albenga, 1958)

3. Sector D.80 (1957).   Lead anchor stock, medium size, but only half preserved
(actual length 0·43 m., estimated total about 0·92 m., actual weight 12 kg.;
total about 25 kg.). Similar to the preceding, but without retaining bar in
socket and with traces of wood within the arm covered with lead.

148

4. Sector D.79 (1957).   Complete lead anchor stock of small size (length 0·63 m., weight 15 kg.), without bar in the socket, but with traces of wood attached to the lead. The mould is not only tapered, but slightly bent upwards.

5–6.   Pieces of lead, 0·41 m. by 0·075 m. by 0·028 m. and 0·19 m. by 0·065 m. by 0·036 m., belonging probably to the movable stock of two anchors.

Republican period (Figs. 58–59).

7. Sector E.17 (1953).   Oil amphora of the type first defined as Graeco-Italic (form 4 = Benoit's Republican I); neck missing, but rather similar to those from the Marseilles ship. Dated to the first half of the second century B.C.

8. Sector E.11 (1953).   Oil amphora similar to the last, more ovoid, and shorter; neck missing. Second century B.C., but rather more developed.

9. Sector F.74 (1957).   Oil amphora of form 2, similar to the three specimens from the Roman ship from Albenga, but in a more elongated form; neck missing. Dated to the second half of the second century B.C.

10. Sector F.75 (1957).   Oil amphora of form 2, similar to the last. Dated to second century B.C.

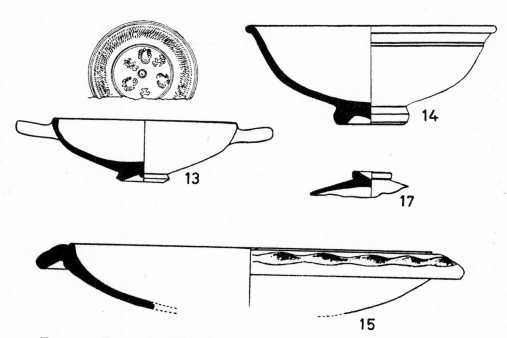

FIG. 59.   Campanian B bowls 13, 14; mortar rim 15; terra-sigillata lid 17
Scale 1 : 3   (*Atti* ... Albenga, 1958)

11. Oil amphora similar to last, without neck.
12. Sector F.71 (1957).   Oil amphora, ovoid, shorter and more squat, without neck. Dated to first century B.C.
12*bis*.   Sector E.56.   Neck of amphora of form 1 (or more probably form 4, from the rather curved sides), with short, rather oblique rim. Dated mainly in second century B.C.
13. Sector E.1 (1952).   Campanian B handled cup of second century B.C. A new type, belonging generally to Campanian B classification and characterized by two handles extending horizontally from the rim. Belongs to the first phase of Campanian B with very stylized palmettes reproducing an early motif. Can be dated to 200–150 B.C.
14. Sector F.73 (1957).   Imitation? Campanian bowl, reproducing perhaps form 8 of Campanian B with thick or bead rim. Glaze entirely worn away which does not allow of a more exact opinion. Complete. Dated to second–first century B.C.
15. Sector E.59 (1957).   Mortar with wavy edge to rim, rather characteristic of second–first century B.C. Sherd only.

Imperial times (first–second century A.D.*)* (Figs. 59–60).

16. Sector B.54.   Everted neck of amphora. Perhaps datable to first century A.D.
17. Sector E.45 (1953).   Part of a lid in Gaulish terra-sigillata with well-preserved glaze. First century A.D.

Late Roman period (Figs. 60–61).

18. Sector E.10 (1955).   Amphora with spherical body, outcurved neck and thickened rim, of uncertain Late Roman date. The whole of bottom half is missing.
19. Sector E.3 (1953).   Neck of spherical amphora, similar to No. 18.
20. Sector E.7 (1953).   Small amphora with grooved body, rather thin, with upright ridged neck; rather characteristic of fourth–fifth century A.D., the lower part missing. Cf. a reconstruction among the amphorae of the fifth century preserved in the Bapistry of Albenga (Lamboglia, 'La datazione del Battistero di Albenga', *Miscellanea Paribeni Calderini* (1956); an almost identical example from Terracena is in the possession of Dr. A. Pederzini.
21. Sector F.76.   Dish of light terra-sigillata D; one half complete of a form already known and typical of fourth century A.D. at Albintimilium, and which represents the main characteristics of this class of pottery. Cf., for instance, *Gli Scavi di Albintimilium e la chronologia della ceramica romana I* (Bordighera, 1950), 29–30, 144 *passim*.

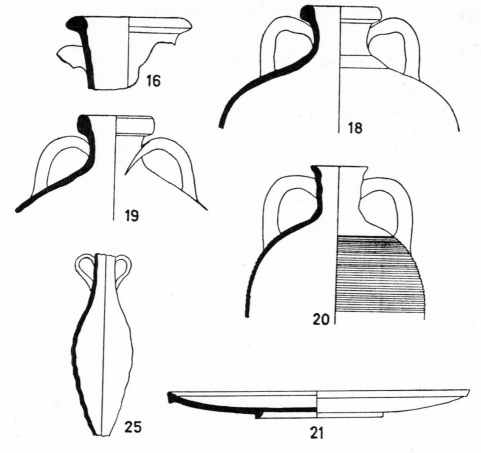

FIG. 60.   Roman amphorae 16–20; terra-sigillata dish 21; small ribbed amphora 25
Scale 1 : 6   (*Atti* ... Albenga, 1958)

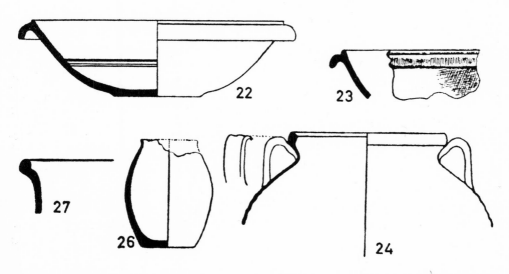

FIG. 61.   Terra-sigillata bowls 22, 23; *olla* with ribbed body 24; small pots 26, 27
Scale 1 : 3   (*Atti* ... Albenga, 1958)

22. Sector E (1953). Bowl with flange rim of light terra-sigillata D; a form recognized at Ventimiglia and attributed to fourth century A.D.
23. Sector E. (1953). Fragment of bowl similar to No. 22, of smaller size.
24. Sector E.42 (1953). *Olla* with ribbed body, lacking the lower part; in light grey pottery, typical of the Late Roman period at Albintimilium (op. cit., 152ff.).
25. Sector E.6 (1953). Small amphora with ribbed sides, fusiform body, and two handles of irregular section; imitates a form of glass vase well known and dated to fourth century A.D.
26. Sector E.12 (1953). Small pot without handles; presumably Late Roman from the shape.
27. Sector E.32 (1953). Rim of pot or decanter, in fine pottery of Late Roman type.

Underwater research was set on a more professional basis in Italy following the second International Congress of Underwater Archaeology at Albenga in 1958. In the spring of that year the Centro Sperimentale di Archeologia Sotto-marina had been inaugurated under the direction of Professor Nino Lamboglia of the Istituto Internazionale di Studi Liguri, and incorporated the group of divers of Centro Italiano Ricercatori Subacquei of Genoa, who for several years had been developing underwater techniques.

Government support was obtained, and a naval vessel, the *Daino*, an ex-German mine-sweeper of 700 tons, was seconded for a part of each year for experimental work in underwater archaeology. She was specially fitted up for diving, and was based on Albenga, where the Museo Navale Romano had been established in the Palazzo Peloso-Cepolla. Both the original C.I.R.S. group and professional divers worked side by side in the *Daino*.

Carrying the members of the First Experimental Course in Underwater Archaeology in the summer of 1959, the *Daino* began her working cruise in June.

Research and experience in the sea off Albenga[3]

When the *Daino* arrived off Albenga on 14 June 1959, she was, like the *Artiglio* in 1950, met by Professor N. Lamboglia and piloted by the fishing-boat *Prain* to the site of the Roman ship off Albenga, where Signor Renzo Ferrandi made the first trial dive from on board.

The *Daino*'s first outing at sea on 25 June to the Albenga ship was made with the purpose of locating the wreck and fixing its position with the ultrasonic scanner and other navigational instruments with which the ship is equipped. A float was placed to mark the wreck, and then the *Daino* crossed the spot several times on various bearings with the scanner in action (Fig. 62). The recorded signals

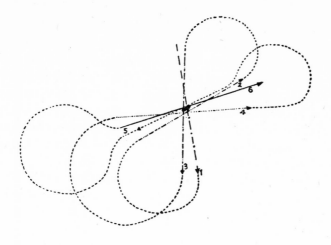

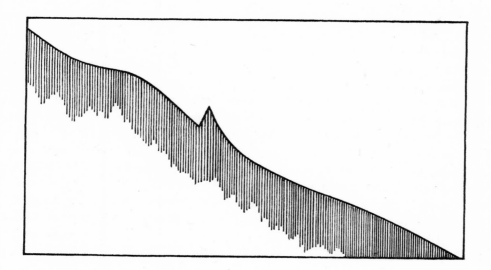

FIG. 62. Diagram of the routes of the *Daino* across the *Albenga* wreck, a drawing from the ultrasonic graph and the resulting section across the sea-bed

showed a hump on the sea-bed corresponding to the shape of the ship and the pile of amphorae lying on the bottom. The enlarged drawing, made to a single scale, of the ultrasonic reflections reproduced in different proportions in the direction of the axis and ordinates (Fig. 62), made it possible to construct the geometrical section of the wreck along one of the routes which lay across it. This also demonstrated the close resemblance of the drawing obtained in this way to that already prepared from the first summary measurements made *in situ*. This experiment was particularly important, because it was shown to be possible to identify and survey any kind of obstacle or relief existing on the sea-floor by means of the *Daino*'s instruments. It will naturally always be the diver's task to ascertain whether there is a natural or artificial disturbance, and to recognize its nature and importance.

A whole week was then devoted to Albenga, from 9 to 14 August 1959, after the training period offshore from Ventimiglia, to conclude the first season in Liguria. Thus the ship's excavation and recovery equipment, and in particular the air-lift and sand-clearing pump, were tried for the first time in the sea around the isle of Gallinaria. It was, above all, used in an experiment for excavating an isolated object deeply embedded in sand—a large iron anchor, attributed to the medieval period, which stood out about 1 m. high in front of the island's anchorage. After two days' work, the unusually large anchor was freed from sand, hoisted on board and left as an ornament on the mole of the harbour at Alassio.

Near the north-east coast of the island, where the sea-bed is richest in ancient objects, and which suffers a constant process of silting and unsilting by the action of the currents, a reconnaissance made by the divers revealed the presence of a new group of amphorae. The apparatus of detachable surveying frames, studied and produced for the first time by the Centro Sperimentale di Archeologia Sottomarina for surveying and measuring on the sea-floor, now makes it possible to take photographs to scale and to make a corresponding drawing on land (Pl. 27). The point where the object is found, produced at the surface by means of a buoy or float, is marked exactly by rings and then transferred to paper with the exact co-ordinates. When this operation has been carried out, the amphora (or any other object) can be lifted on board with the recovery cage, which can hold from four to six amphorae. One of these, surprisingly enough, was found to be unusually rare—a Massaliote amphora of the fourth century B.C., the first underwater record of Graeco-Ligurian trade in the pre-Roman period.

The exploration of the sea-bed between the Balzi Rossi (Red Rocks) and Ventimiglia

The most serious and taxing methodical work done by the *Daino* in the training period which lasted from 5 July to 7 August was that undertaken in the stretch of sea between the French-Italian frontier (Ponte San Luigi) and the Nervia torrent beyond Ventimiglia. Here we face the preliminary and fundamental theme of sub-marine exploration: the preparation of the map of submarine archaeology (*Forma Maris Antiqui*), which is to be gradually extended round all Italian and Mediter-ranean coasts on the basis of a systematic survey of the sea-bed and the topo-graphical interpretation of every detail of archaeological interest.

The only system which today permits the rational organization of such work (until we have at our disposal submarine transport endowed with absolute free-dom, not only of movement, but also able to follow a properly mapped course) is that of using the underwater glider (aquaplane). In this system a diver lies on a light support drawn by a motor-boat, and releases a buoy or float directly he catches sight of an object of interest, so as to fix its position immediately. Naturally, the same or another diver has then to go down to explore the bed more closely so as to be able to fix the position better and to advise on the significance of the discovery.

The principal difficulty met with in this method (apart from a great deal of time taken up by the various manœuvres) is that of recording on the surface the course actually followed, whether it is of interest or not. To obtain relative pre-cision in mapping and to ensure the most complete observation possible, the solution adopted was that of dividing the sea into sectors marked out on the sur-face by floats, which were placed at measured intervals; thus a sea-surface grid was made, as for a land survey. With the grid completed and the floats placed in position with the aid of an azimuth and a sextant, the underwater glider was towed on a set course, roughly plotted on the chart by the assistant, who followed the diver in the motor-boat and collated the information.

This work-plan was applied and tested in practice by tracing a series of sectors of 1 sq. km. from the French frontier and parallel to the coast (Fig. 63). With the aid of a buoy, the motor-boat was manœuvred in a series of tacks from north to south and vice versa about 25 m. apart, so as to give a view of all the intervening space. The difficulty in towing the diver at a level more than 25 m. deep led to the decision to limit this kind of exploration to the 25 m. contour, subdividing the 1 sq. km. sector into two halves; that near to the shore (up to 25 m.) and that beyond from about 500–1,000 m. out and up to 50 m. deep. The latter outer zone was explored, not only with the underwater glider, but also by the ship itself with the ultrasonic scanner in action. The ship followed a series of multiple tacks on courses carefully plotted by the use of an azimuth and sextant. Naturally, each prominent signal recorded on the scanner's screen had then to be checked by a diver. In con-trast to what happened in the case of the wreck at Albenga, rocky outcrops were invariably met which could never be distinguished by the scanner from any remains having a human origin.

When a good trial had been given to this double system, combining the diver's direct vision with the ship's scanner, the whole sea-floor was regularly 'raked', tracing on the chart three sectors of 1 sq. km., parallel to the coast between the frontier and Cape Mortola, and tests were made to show the time taken and the results achieved. It was shown that, however much organization there may be at the beginning, the practical difficulties of such systematic work exceed all expectations. To be carried out quickly, the work requires invariably ideal meteorological conditions, the perfect functioning of all instruments, and perfect co-ordination and endurance on the part of the men, whether underwater or on the surface. In about one month's stay in the area, and with ten days of effective work, it was possible to make an exhaustive study of two sectors (A and B) of 1 km. each, as well as a third, smaller, sector up to Cape Mortola.

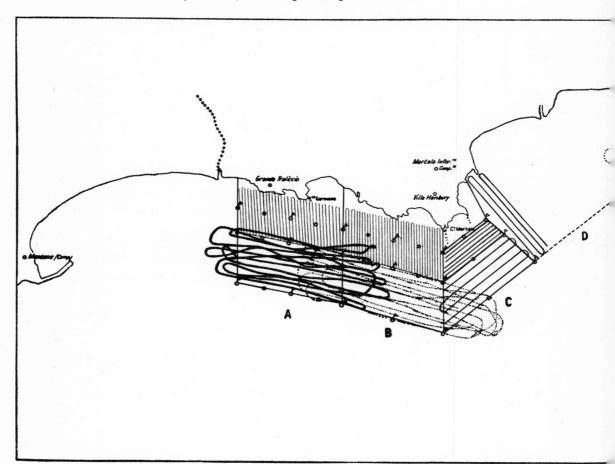

FIG. 63. First attempt at a systematic exploration of the sea-bed between Balzi Ross water glider for the first 500 m. from the coast and with the *Daino*'s scanner beyond that Scale 1 : 54,000

The results of training were highly valuable for all those who took part in the operation, but there were no sensational discoveries. The hope of making fruitful submarine observations on the sea-floor in front of the famous Balzi Rossi caves was not realized, owing to the non-participation of Professor Alberto Carlo Blanc and other expert geologists and palaeontologists. Nor were any traces discovered of ancient relics in the first zone along the Italian Riviera. The only locality that should have shown something, and where more extensive investigation has also been made from on land, is the promontory, Cape Mortola, a classic place for storms and shipwrecks. Fragments of Roman amphorae, all of the Republican period, exist there in considerable numbers, broken by the waves and caught in

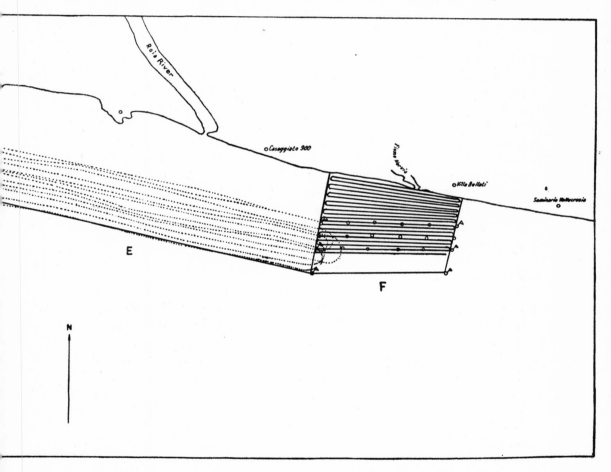

nd Ventimiglia. The sectors A, B, and C (1 sq. km. each) were covered by the under-
ne sectors D, E, F, were only partially surveyed either by one system or the other

the rocks. However, no concentration of these was found which could be taken as evidence of the presence of a wreck—even one that has disintegrated and disappeared. The extensive fields of algae which collect round the promontory have proved an unforeseen hindrance to an extension of the area under observation, and so the quest remained fruitless.

The work of research was then shifted towards Ventimiglia, and the intervening stretch was rapidly sounded with the scanner (with only negative results) as far as the mouth of the Roia. There began for the first time the exploration of the sea-bed in front of the Roman city of Albintimilium, between the mouths of the Roia and Nervia. Here came the test, and also clear proof of the inanity of the systematic research on a part of the sea-bed which is liable to massive outflows of alluvium of torrential origin and to the continuous process of silting. The sea-floor off Ventimiglia comprises an endless spread of sand and mud, continually raised and renewed by the river.

In spite of the results and experiences of a methodological character, a negative conclusion was deduced from this first month of training. The submarine archaeological map of the coasts of Italy cannot, for the time being, be based on a systematic search, done yard by yard, but must be for the most part *in vacuo* and at the expense of a great deal of time and energy. It must still depend (as archaeology does on land) on chance and on fortuitous indications, limiting detailed investigation to those zones which, whether from their history, their situation, or from particular events, give *a priori* guarantees of certain, positive results. For such zones, the system of exploration applied for the first time with the *Daino* remains valid, with the use both of the ultrasonic scanner and such other more perfect means as may be discovered in the future.

Reconnaissance off San Remo

During intervals in the preparatory training campaign off Ventimiglia, the *Daino*, which was moored in the harbour at San Remo, was used as the base for a series of exploratory exercises on the sea-floor off San Remo.

Here, too, we vainly sought a wreck and a field of amphorae which some divers from the town had indicated as likely, on the grounds of the discovery of some fragments of amphorae; again these were amphorae of the Republican period, but they seemed to be isolated pieces. Advantage was taken of the search here to complete a number of dives to take the measurements of recent objects on the bottom, thereby perfecting methods and the use of the survey grid.

On a reconnaissance further from the harbour towards the shore near Capo Verde, between San Remo and Bussana, a stray find was made of an isolated fine vase of medieval ware, attributable to the fourteenth or fifteenth century, with stylized motives and figures of fish.

Lastly, an attempt was made with a mass dive by all those taking part in the First Experimental Course of Underwater Archaeology to check the truth of a local tradition. This was that there existed pieces of wall in front of the mouth of the Foce Torrent, indicating that the remains of a Roman villa preserved on land continued in the sea, and that there must consequently have been a retreat of the coastline in historical times. No trace of walling was found, even though the water was very clear. This chapter may therefore be taken as definitely closed, even if on negative grounds.

NOTES

1 *L'Aventure Sous-marine* (January 1962), 278.
2 This article was published in *Bollettino e Atti* (Centro Italiano Ricercatori Sub-acquei, 1957) and entitled 'Catasto archeologico dei Fondali dell' Isola Gallinaria ed esplorazione del relitto della nave romana di Albenga'.
3 This report by Professor Nino Lamboglia appeared in *Forma Maris Antiqui, II, Rivista di Studi Liguri*, 25 (1959), 294, under the title, 'L'attivitá del Centro Sperimentale di Archeologia sottomarina nel 1959'.

Other reports on finds from the sea may be found in the following articles: F. Benoit, 'L'archéologie sous-marine en Provence', *Rivista di Studi Liguri*, 18 (1952), 237ff.; 'Épaves de la côte de Provence; typologie d'amphores', *Gallia*, XIV (1956), 23ff.; 'Nouvelles épaves de Provence', *Gallia*, XVI (1958), 5ff.; XVIII (1960), 41ff. A. Bouscaras, 'Recherches sous-marine au large d'Agde', *Rivista di Studi Liguri*, 20 (1954), 47ff. F. Braemer and G. Mercadé, 'Céramique antique et pièces d'ancre trouvées en mer à la pointe de Kynosoura (baie de Marathon)', *Bulletin de Correspondence Hellénique*, 77 (1953), 139ff. L. Casson, 'Sea Digging' and 'More Sea Digging', *Archaeology*, 6 (1953), 221; 10 (1957), 248. S. Casson, 'Submarine Research in Greece', *Antiquity*, XIII (1939), 80. R. Demangel, 'Fouilles et recherches sous-marine en Grèce', *Bulletin de Correspondence Hellénique* 74 (1950), 271–3; 75 (1951), 198ff. Honor Frost, 'Two Carian Wrecks', *Antiquity*, XXXIV (1960), 216; *Discovery* (May 1960), 194ff. George Karo, 'Art salvaged from the Sea', *Archaeology*, I (1948), 179. N. Lamboglia, 'Mise au point sur l'archéologie sous-marine en Ligurie italienne', *Rivista di Studi Liguri*, 21 (1955), 162ff. P. Throckmorton, 'A Bronze Age Wreck', *National Geographic Magazine*, 117 (May 1960), 682ff.

5

Ports, Harbours,
and other Submerged Sites

Marine archaeology is not confined to the study of ancient shipping and routes, but must include ports, harbours, and roadsteads.

It has been possible for archaeologists to gain some knowledge of ancient harbours, for many which were situated at river mouths have become silted up and have been excavated by normal land methods. Two well-known examples are the Roman harbour built by Tiberias at Ostia at the mouth of the Tiber,[1] and Leptis Magna in North Africa, a Severan port excavated by Bartocini[2] in 1952–8.

Lehmann-Hartleben,[3] in his survey of ancient ports, found many to be silted up, while others are now partly submerged and their moles and breakwaters destroyed. In addition to personal observation, he only had plans made in the course of hydrographic surveys and some more detailed reports, such as that of Delos, on which to base his conclusions.

These studies were only an extension of land methods, but it is to Gaston Jondet,[4] Chief Engineer of Ports and Lights in Egypt, that we owe the first real survey of an ancient harbour. He was able to study in detail the area west of the Pharos (Fort Kait Bey), before the construction of the breakwaters of Alexandria's new harbour in 1916 (Fig. 64). There he discovered a range of ancient breakwaters along the reefs, extending westward across the Bay of Anfouchy, past Ras el Tin Island, as far as Abu Bakr Rock. Later reports mentioned by Weill indicate that traces of construction existed even further west, and may have enclosed a much larger roadstead now included in the modern harbour. The principal entrance appears to have been from the south, ships having to round Abu Bakr and then turn north under Ras el Tin promontory, where there was deep water. To their left were solid quays, some 700 m. long, reaching to Abu Bakr, now included in the foundations of the modern mole. To the right was a small quay with a jetty at the north end, protecting the harbour entrance. These were built of blocks each measuring about 1 m., and cut to fit, with small stones filling the joints.

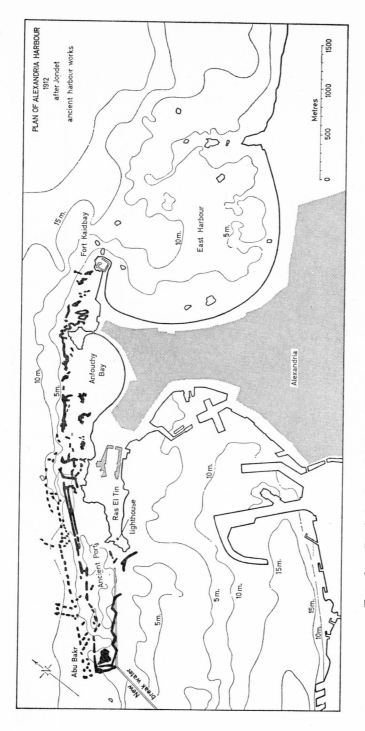

Fig. 64. Jondet's plan of Alexandria Harbour. Ancient structures are shown in black

Inside the present harbour is an islet covered with ancient remains. Some are tombs, but there are also the submerged foundations of a rectangular structure. A flight of steps and small rock-cut channels lead out of it.

The great outer breakwaters, which were in parts double, extended for some 2,000 m. to protect the harbour from the north and west. They enclose the western basin, which is 2,360 m. long by 300 m. wide.

The report is a detailed study of all artificial works in the ancient harbour, accompanied by plans and sections across the more important breakwaters and quays. As the structures lie only a few metres beneath the surface, they are still easily visible. Nevertheless, in a few cases divers were used to record the sections.

No mention of these ancient harbour works is to be found in the historical records, and though it was originally considered that they might be earlier than the time of Alexander, no evidence exists to support this hypothesis. Indeed, in comparison with the extensive works at Tyre, they may well be of Roman date.

The first strictly archaeological study of a harbour was undertaken by Père Poidebard, following his air survey of the Roman *limes* (frontier forts) of Syria.[5] In the course of several flights along the coast, he noticed that reefs and moles were clearly visible underwater off the ancient cities in suitable conditions, and the possibility of finding the port installations became apparent. It was obvious that ground and underwater exploration was needed to complete the details.

During three seasons, 1934–6, with the help of local sponge-divers as well as French naval helmeted divers, he explored and planned the ancient harbours, breakwaters, and other installations off Tyre, one of the best-known Phoenician ports of the Near East (Pl. 23).

With the support of the French and Lebanese authorities, as well as the Navy, Air Force, and harbour engineers, Père Poidebard developed a thorough and detailed method of recording the underwater structures. The problem was both technical and archaeological, and the difficulties of obtaining clear photographs both from the air and underwater had to be overcome.

The method employed was to check the plans of structures located on the air photographs with the aid of the free-divers, and then to consolidate the information by underwater photographs, taken through the glass-bottomed bucket or water glass, or with underwater cameras (Pl. 24). The principal points were marked by buoys and tied into a separate survey.

Detailed exploration of the moles and their structure was undertaken by helmeted divers, who measured depths, worked with hammer, chisel, and crowbar to clear structures of concretion, and made small excavations when required. The divers' reports were taken down from dictation, and sketch-plans and sections were prepared from them.

The results of the exploration revealed the existence of two roadsteads, one to the north and one to the south of the island (Fig. 65), sheltered by hitherto

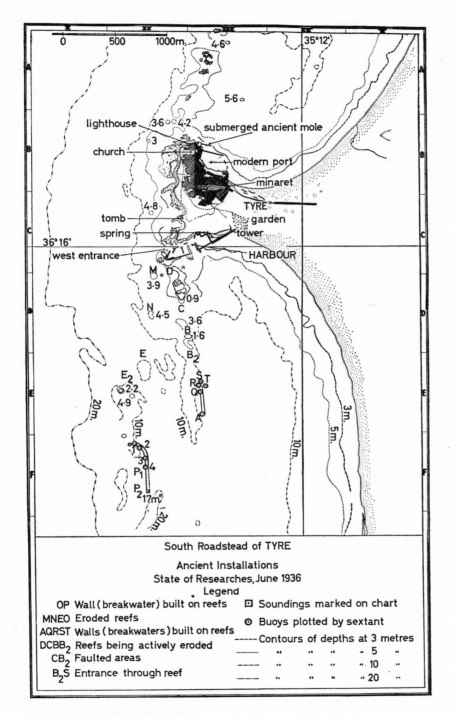

FIG. 65. Plan of Tyre Harbour (after Poidebard. *Tyr*)

undiscovered breakwaters of substantial construction, joining up and reinforcing the natural reefs. Most of the work was concentrated on the southern side, where the harbour works adjoined the town. The harbour proper (Pl. 23) consisted of two basins enclosed by moles constructed of large blocks set on the natural rock. The entrance was on the south side. Substantial quays bordered the shore.

Outside the harbour, the natural bay was enclosed by breakwaters, following the line of the reef, to form a roadstead some 1,200 m. long, protected from the winds and swell from the west and south-west. The arrangement of inner and outer harbours is similar to that planned by Jondet at Alexandria. No specific evidence emerged for the dating of these works, but by comparison with those of other historically known ports they are probably of the Graeco-Roman period.

In 1945 Père Poidebard started his survey of the ancient port of Sidon.[6] This was partly occasioned by the silting of the modern port on the same site. A jetty had been built in 1939 and the enclosure had silted up within a few months. Sidon, to the north of Tyre, is on the same flat coastline with dunary reefs (Pl. 25). The ancient town was built on a promontory which looks on the map like a fist

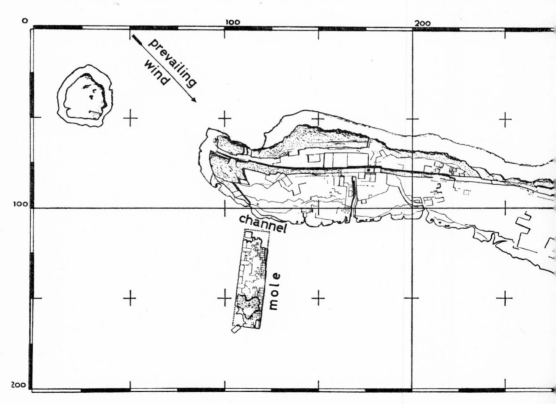

FIG. 66.   Plan of Outer Anchorage at Sidon

emerging from the coastline, with a spur of rock as the index finger pointing seawards to the north-west. A rocky, offshore island to the north is an extension of this same dunary formation. As at Tyre, the exact positions of the 'open' ports, beyond the city's defences, were in doubt. Renan suggested that the two bays to the south of the town might have served, but the larger is exposed to the heavy local swell while the other is too small.

Poidebard (Pl. 25, Fig. 66) showed that the rocky island was an adequate anchorage for foreign merchantmen; big ships could lie along the sheltered eastern side, and their cargoes would be transferred by lighter to the landing quays, of Roman construction, which were found on the beach to the north of the town.

The rock of the island had been flattened by excavation on the landward side to form quays, while a wall, part built, part excavated, running the length of the island, separated the quays from the seaward slopes. From the southern tip of this rock, a jetty 50 m. long and 15 m. wide ran landwards. A gap of 8 m. separated it from the island. The exposed face of this jetty was constructed from colossal blocks;

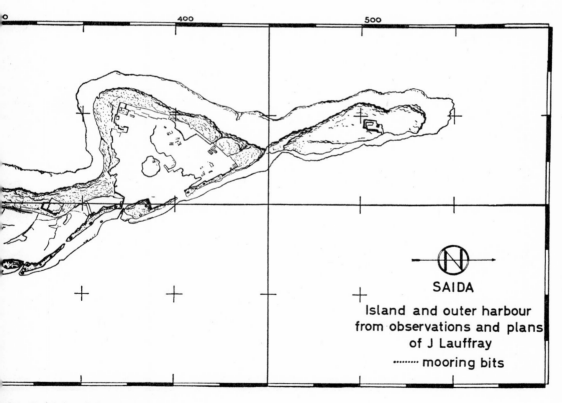

SAIDA

Island and outer harbour
from observations and plans
of J Lauffray
········ mooring bits

after Poidebard & Lauffray. *Sidon*)

those on the inner face were much smaller. Roman sherds were found in the concrete binding the rubble core of the masonry together.

The closed port (Fig. 67) within the city's walls is bounded on the south by the rock spur, which is levelled on the inside, like the island, to form quays. From the tip of this spur, moles built on shallows form a triangular enclosure with the present shore-line, the mouth being at the apex. Remains of defensive towers were found at the base of the spur, at the juncture of spur and mole, and at the tip of the mole. This enclosure was divided into two docks by a jetty running out from the shore and stopping short of the seaward mole. The docks were connected with the Roman landing quays opposite the island anchorage by an artificially deepened channel. Both wall and channel were buried under silt, and only showed up on aerial photographs (Pl. 25). Indeed, without the heavy dredging machinery which was being used to deepen the modern port, the dividing mole could not have been

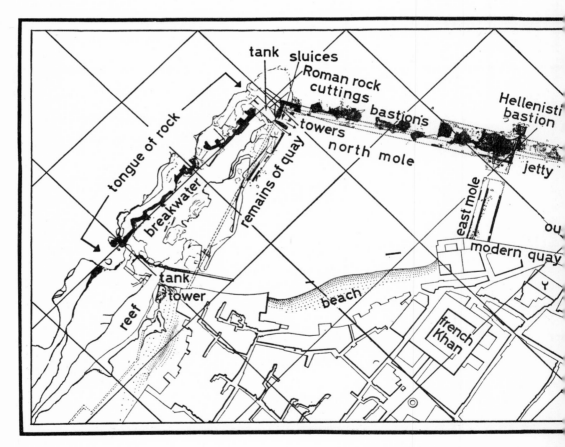

FIG. 67. Plan of Sidon Inner Harbour

examined. The most important discovery at Sidon was the two large rock-cut tanks on the spur; these were connected with the enclosure, and one of the four sluice gates belonging to them is preserved. Behind these tanks, which are like large swimming baths, are gaps in the sea-wall, allowing the swell to break through and fill the tanks. This water could be released into the harbour itself by means of the sluices. The rock-cut grooves and holes, into which a wooden gate fitted on the extant sluice, cannot be dated, but the masonry and hydraulic concrete on this spur are known to be hellenic and Byzantine. The Crusader castle, Château de la Mer, built on a rocky island near the mouth of the closed port, was at that time joined to the land by a causeway. There are traces of early rock-cutting on the island itself, but the causeway can never have been on the earlier foundations, since it runs across the artificially deepened channel connecting the inner port with the island's landing quays.

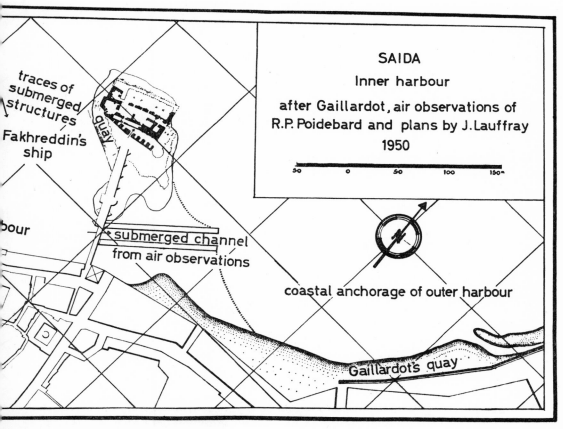

(after Poidebard & Lauffray. *Sidon*)

In the last decade, since the advent of the aqualung, several surveys of ports have been undertaken. The British School at Athens organized two exploratory parties of divers with equipment supplied by the *Sunday Times*: first at Chios and then at Crete, in conjunction with land excavations. Both expeditions were experimental.

In Chios the south and east coasts were explored and traces of amphora cargoes were reported.[7]

In Crete[8] the main work was directed to planning the Roman harbour of Chersonesos, and the enclosing moles and remains of quays along the shore. Parts of the moles were well preserved, and in places stumps of stone bollards were still to be seen. Outside the moles were breakwaters of large, rough blocks. Traces of the hellenistic harbour works were found outside the Roman harbour. Here, and also at Mochlos, plans were made of the ancient fish-tanks cut in the rock. Exploration at Pseira Harbour revealed the remains of a Roman mole, and amphorae and other sherds were recovered from the bay outside.

The study of the ancient installations at the port of Narbonne made by M. Guy[9] is a good example of the combined use of air photography and land survey, supplemented by some diving. He gives a reasoned account of the development of the port, based on former records, his personal observations of the terrain, and excavation. Such a topographical study is an admirable preliminary to further exploration of the area, both on land and in the sea, which should fill in the details of the history of the port.

More recently, in 1958–9, a Cambridge expedition led by Mr. Nicholas Flemming studied and planned the Greek harbour at Apollonia, in North Africa.[10] We are indebted to him for the following preliminary note:

'The purpose of the 1958 expedition was to survey accurately the partially submerged city of Apollonia on the coast of Cyrenaica, and to discover the cause and date of its inundation. It is at present submerged to an average depth of 2·50 m. In the year before our visit, Captain D. Forrow, R.E., had made a rough survey. During our four-week stay, most of the city was planned, but, because of bad weather during the last few days, we were unable to extend the survey to the eastern limits of the site, and to plan in detail the *piscina loculata*.

'In ten days during September 1959, we surveyed the eastern part of the city, checked the position of the sea-walls, established the existence of two harbours, defined the true entrance to the harbours, discovered the foundations of a lighthouse, planned the *piscina loculata*, discovered a ruin-covered island to the west of Apollonia, made a rough survey of Phycus, and established the probable cause of subsidence.

'Behind Apollonia, the Gebel Akhdar is 1·5 kms. from the shore. From the foot of the hills a plain slopes gently to the sea, and continues with no break of slope to 3 kms. out and a depth of 76 m. From this point the slope increases rapidly.

'At the present waterline are two lines of Pleistocene sand dunes which have been calcified. The inner line of dunes forms the present shore, while the outer line forms a chain of islands and promontories some 360 m. from the shore. Between the two there are many basins, which made excellent natural harbours. At Apollonia the part of the city which is still on land is on the inner line of dunes; the two harbours and their surrounding buildings are in the basin, with a few buildings on the islands.

'Apart from some imported marble columns, all the building-stone for the city was quarried from the calcified dune ridges.

'The Gebel Akhdar as a whole is a very stable structure, and there is no evidence for major tectonic movements. Dr. Hey levelled a 6-m. beach from Derna to Benghazi, and has shown clearly that there has been no large movement over this stretch. However, Mr. P. Howard, a petroleum geologist of the Esso Oil Company, who has just completed an intensive survey of the area, informed us that there were several minor faults near Apollonia which could easily account for the subsidence. From this we conclude that there is no evidence for eustatic change of sea-level, and that the subsidence was probably due to local faulting.

'The submerged area of the city, lying between the islands and the shore and measuring about 0·4 kms. from north to south, and 1·2 kms. from east to west, varies in depth from zero to 5 m., though the eastern harbour is 8 m. deep in places.

'The surf breaks up, scatters, and buries all the foundations in the beach area, and sweeps bare the rocky areas, so that the land site is divided from the submerged areas by a band, varying in width from 10 m. to 50 m., in which nothing survives. A cross-section from the land through the beach to the sea would show all archaeological strata from early hellenistic to Byzantine on land, only a few blocks scattered at random on the beach, and the earliest foundations in the sea.

'On the assumption that two or more scraps of foundation, though individually unintelligible, may seem clearly related as soon as they are plotted, we surveyed all visible foundations in the area. Many of these scraps are still incomplete, but they are left on the map in case the shifting sands should uncover related material at a later date.

'For obvious reasons, most of the submerged city sites in the Mediterranean are very close to the shore, and thus it is usually possible to do a large part of the survey from a base-line on the mainland.

'At Apollonia we marked a base-line of 900 m. from the Main Gate at the west to the Theatre in the east, which was marked with a stake at every 50 m. From this we worked with a plane table and telescopic alidade, and fixed three points on the Western Island. Since these three were to be used as base-points for the seaward part of the site, we checked their location by fixing back from them to the original base-line on shore.

'While the base-line was being set up, parties of swimmers with plastic drawing-boards were making sketches of the foundations of the city, working from west to east. For the first stage of the survey, an area was chosen which was fairly well known, and on the rough sketch each key-point was numbered. The leader of a team of four swimmers was given one copy of this diagram, and the man at the alidade took the other. The leader of the team was then responsible for positioning the swimmers in order over points 1, 2, 3, and 4, where they held ranging poles on which a sight was taken. On a signal from the man at the alidade, the team leader moved the swimmers to the next points and positioned them in the same order on positions 5–8. Since it was possible to recognize the swimmers through the alidade, the surveyor could always be sure which point the swimmer represented.

'In this way it was possible to fix thirty-five points in two hours. Since the whole survey was conducted from the same base-line, there was no cumulative error.

'The details of buildings were filled in by direct measurement with a metre rule, or with a wire mounted on a reel strapped to the diver's chest. Here follows a detailed account of the salient features of the site (Fig. 68).

'The wall to the West Reef (G1 to D3) was both sea- and city-wall. Eighty metres northwards along its total existing length of 140 m. is a small rectangular fort similar to those south-east of the Acropolis. The wall itself peters out in sand and rough water about 75 m. from the reef.

'The West Reef (B4) itself comprises a series of small islands and submerged rocks left by regular quarrying. Many of these residual masses have carefully cut parallel sides, the outer faces of which form a natural sea-wall.

'In the gap between West Reef and the Western Island (B5 to A8) there is a natural ridge running from the west reef to the Western Island, with a raised area of quarrying on its outer edge. This rock at A5 comes within ·5 m. of the surface, whereas most of the ridge is under more than 3 m. of water. There is a series of large blocks (c. 2 m. by 6 m. by 6 m.) and quantities of rubble overlying the ridge and at the foot of the slope towards the inner harbour.

'On the Western Island (A9 to B9) there are ten parallel slipways of elaborate construction and in a fine state of preservation (Fig. 69). These were formed by quarrying, and are divided by walls of unquarried stone, now 2 m. high at the top and trailing off towards the bottom end. They are cut in steps to allow a super-structure of squared blocks. The tops of these walls may have been carried up, as at Sunion, to support wooden roofs. Polybius, in his description of the destruction of Carthage in 146 B.C., states that the slipways in the harbour there had storage chambers above them for the ships' gear, and that there was a column at the foot of each dividing wall, so that the frontage looked like a portico. There are in fact four columns (4 m. by 1 m.) lying on the slipways, but whether they were part of the structure or have fallen from the land or from a ship it is

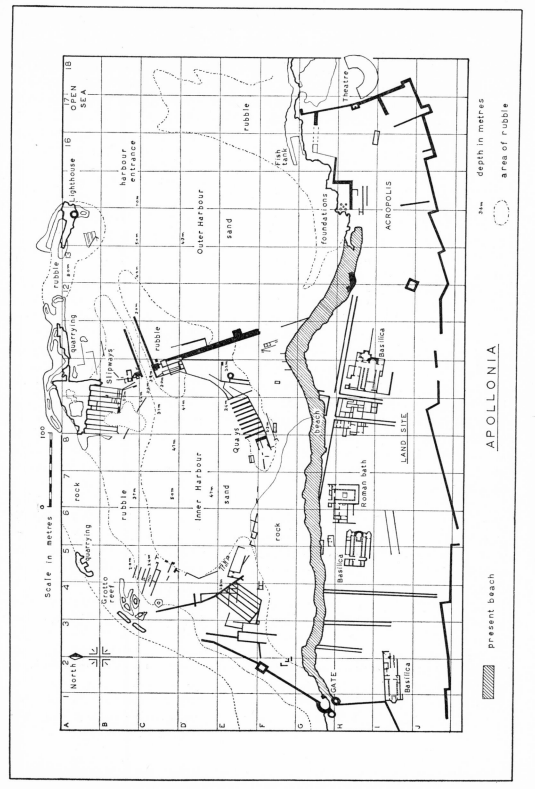

Fig. 68. Plan of Apollonia Harbour   (N. C. Flemming)

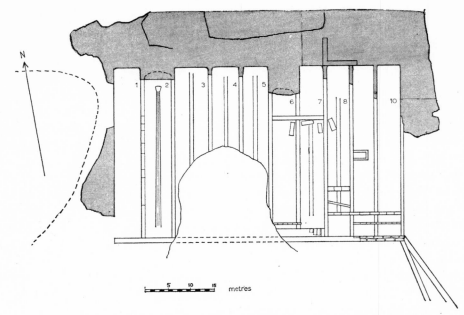

FIG. 69.   Plan of Apollonia slipways   (N. C. Flemming)

impossible to say. Three of the slipways are half covered by rubble, and there are later foundations over most of them.

'On the second slip from the west the central runner had a slot for the keel of a ship. While the slot grew shallower, but not wider, towards the bottom of the slip, the runner itself grows flatter and broader. This would facilitate the aligning of the keel in the initial stages of hauling a ship up the slip. There are five cross-sections of this on Fig. 70.

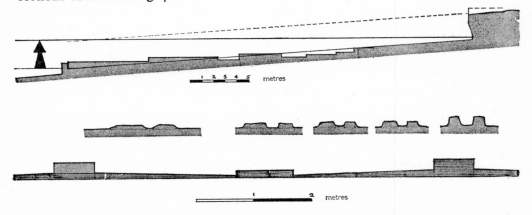

FIG. 70.   Sections across slipways   (N. C. Flemming)

'From west to east, the third, fourth, fifth, seventh, and eighth slipways have flat central runners with no slots. The first, sixth, ninth, and tenth have neither slot nor runner.

'The West Island slipways at Apollonia may be compared with those at Sunion.[11] Although the slipways at Sunion are considerably later than those on the West Island at Apollonia, their construction is worth comparing, since both were built for light vessels. The slips at Sunion were more highly developed, but the differences were dictated more by the direction in which they faced, and the consequent lack of shelter, than by their later date.

'The prevailing wind is approximately north-north-west in each case, and, while the ships at Sunion face north-east by east on to the open sea, those at Apollonia face south-south-east and into a sheltered harbour. This accounts for the great difference in gradient, those at Sunion being at 15° 50', compared with 4° at Apollonia. The steepest slope at Sunion would prevent waves carrying up the slip in an onshore wind.

'That a general rule can be made of this is confirmed by the gradient of 6° at Piraeus, which is also a sheltered harbour facing south-south-east.

'While the gentle slope at Apollonia would have enabled ships to be man-handled, this would not have been so at Sunion. (The bronze ratchet-wheel found there in 1900 by Stais, then thought to have been part of some cargo-lifting derrick, may have been part of a winch for hauling up ships.)

'The Eastern Island (A14) is quarried on all its faces, and at the south-east corner an overhanging buttress of rock has been left, which supports the edge of a circular foundation 15 m. in diameter. Some blocks, cut on the round, are still in position in recesses specially shaped for them. This is probably the site of a fortified tower or lighthouse.

'There are three simple slipways in the shallow water near the Eastern Island which are merely platforms of sloping rock. A later wall 20 m. long crosses the foot of two of these slips diagonally.

'From the inner harbour a channel (C10 to B11) leads out between two block buildings, and it is defined for 65 m. by well-preserved walls 14 m. apart. The channel is now partly silted up, and we could not establish the original depth; but the present depth graduates from 4 m. by the inner harbour to 6 m. at the outer end.

'On either side of the channel are block buildings (C10), their construction being so massive that they remain sound to within inches of the surface. These, and the sea-wall leading to them, proved on comparison of block sizes to be a continuation of the late hellenistic structures on land. There are parallels for such a channel with block buildings at Fréjus and Piraeus, and it has been suggested that in both cases they were built to take a defensive boom. The block buildings at Piraeus also link up with the city defences.

'The central sea-wall (H13 to F11 to C10) is of particularly solid construction, and when the current moves the sand in the right direction it can be traced right on to the beach. In E11 there is a platform or wharf of large blocks linked by dovetailed dowels of lead.

'This wall, which separates the two harbours, may have been constructed to act as fortification and defence against the sea before the building of the Eastern Mole. In any case, its enormous width would serve as wharf space when the Eastern Mole was built to enclose the outer harbour, and the walls in D11 and the debris of blocks and pottery testify to the fact that there was plenty of activity on the eastern side of the wall.

'The rectangular building in E11 is 7 m. by 12 m., excluding the thickness of the sea-wall. The dovetailed dowels are of lead and are 30 cm. by 8·5 cm. wide. The most common form of dowel is I-shaped, and is not earlier than the fifth century B.C., whereas the dovetailed shape occurs in the sixth century B.C., and also very much later. Most Greek examples are iron-centred, the lead filling being sometimes melted in and sometimes cold-packed. Crude forms were used in Egypt, archaic wooden dowels being followed by pure lead.

'It was impossible to say for certain whether those at Apollonia had had iron centres. The centres were in fact missing, though the gaps were large enough to have taken iron, and the lead came away in chunks, as though it had been cold-packed.

'The Eastern Mole (F17 to C17) is represented by a broad strip of rubble and blocks stretching out almost 200 m. into the sea from the foot of the Acropolis Hill, on a bottom which is otherwise white sand. At the end nearest the Eastern Island there is an accumulation of large blocks measuring about 1 m. by 2 m. by 4 m. and amongst the general mass of local sandstone there are many blocks of white marble. The rubble lies in 8 m. of water, and from it the sea-bed slopes up in a basin shape towards the Eastern Island, the Central Wall, and the mainland. The gap between the rubble and the Eastern Island is also 8 m. deep.

'In the bed-rock at the foot of the Acropolis Hill there is a fish-tank (F16), which is now completely submerged.

'The ends of these buildings (E9) are open to the inner harbour, and, as they are of exceptional breadth and solidity, they may have been used as quays for small merchant vessels. The top courses of the westernmost quays are complete, which suggests that this is the original top, and at a depth of 2 m.

'The "Shipsheds" (C5) are also hewn from the solid rock, and although at first we thought that they were slipways, they have no central runner or slot, and the rock-cut floor is horizontal. The tops of the dividing walls, however, slope down towards the harbour at about 4°. The fourth bay from the north has a series of notches, 15 cm. cube, at distances of 1 m. apart along the top of the inside edges of its sloping walls. There are also two boat-shaped hollows, each about

10 m. long, cut in the floor of the third and fourth bays, for which no explanation can be found.

'The remaining foundations (E4) comprise six parallel walls, with traces of two more on the south-east side. They are closed at the ends by contemporary walls. These walls, and the absence of gradient, show that, although they have been associated with the water's edge in the early hellenistic period, they were not slipways. (Mr. Goodchild suggests that they could have been the foundations of a warehouse. There would have been difficulty in finding timbers to roof a wide gap; close, parallel walls would have been the most economical way to cover a large area.)

'Above the "warehouse" grid lie the well-preserved foundations of a house (or office) of Roman or later date (E4). There is an apsidal end to the centre room, three courses of stone remaining at this end, while elsewhere only one course remains.

'On the seaward side of both the Western and Eastern Islands the quarrying was so conducted that a deep basin was left, separated from the sea by a wall of solid rock several metres thick. The top of this wall is now within centimetres of the surface, and would have projected about 2 m. from the water in classical times. Newbiggin reports that there is a similar construction on the exposed western side of the Phoenician island colony of Arvad. He suggests that the lagoon was excavated as a wave-trap, so that in rough weather the waves would break over the wall and plunge into the lagoon, and would not inundate the island. In spite of the change of level, the lagoon still serves this purpose admirably. The depth of the lagoon is now 3 m.

'Karl Lehmann-Hartleben[3] has made a general survey of classical harbour plans and methods of construction throughout the Mediterranean, but inevitably, since he could not see underwater, his plans are very rough. Nevertheless, the basic properties of a harbour system, one basin or several, man-made or natural, are usually clear on simple investigation, and his work demonstrates the way in which the Phoenicians, Greeks, and Romans adapted a wide variety of sites to their needs.

'There are three common patterns. The first is a partly enclosed bay with sea-walls, built to protect it from the open sea. Misenum is an example of this. The second is a headland or offshore island which provides several rather exposed harbours, each of which has to be protected by the joining of islands, reefs, and the mainland with a series of sea-walls. Apollonia conforms to this pattern. The third is represented by artificially excavated harbours, as at Carthage.

'At Apollonia the site is very exposed to the dominant north-west winds, and before shelter could be obtained for any number of ships artificial walls must have been built. From the literature, it is known that the Greeks built sea-walls in up to 8–10 m. of water, and at Syracuse we have seen the remains of a sea-wall in

10 m. of water. Thus, taking into consideration the large quantity of rubble between the West Reef and the Western Island, it is certain that a mole was built across this gap. Since the principal slipways are on the Western Island, and since it is unlikely that the material for the repair and construction of ships was ferried thither in small boats, it is probable that the sea-wall was very broad and was topped by a roadway.

'In 1958 we did not discover the rubble at the extreme east of the site, and, ignorant of the possibility of a second harbour, we supposed that the entrance to the inner harbour was between the two islands. In spite of the depth at this point, 8 m., it is now suggested that this gap was also closed by a sea-wall. The great quantity of rubble between the islands, the presence of quarries and low-lying foundations on the islands facing towards the supposed channel where they would have been exposed to the open sea, and the difficulty of entering harbour by a narrow channel with a right-angle bend in it, all suggest this.

'The rubble at the extreme east of the site testifies to the existence of the East Mole, a fact borne out by the buildings and wharves which face into the second basin so formed, and which would otherwise be facing the open sea.

'The construction of moles falls into two types: first, the solid mole formed by tipping rubble into the sea, and second that of *Opus pilarum*, formed of blocks of stone or concrete joined by arches.

'The *Opus pilarum* seems to have been developed in order to allow currents of water through the harbour, and thus prevent silting. At Apollonia there is relatively little sand, and the solid type of mole was used in all parts of the site.

'In 1820 a chart was made of the area, which shows the shoreline at Apollonia some 150 m. north of its present position. The retreat of 150 m. in 140 years is consistent with the destruction which occurred in the winter of 1958–9, but if this rate of damage has been constant since the time when the city was last occupied in the sixth century A.D., it is surprising that there is anything left at all. This may be explained by supposing that the sea-walls lasted for some time after the initial submergence of the city, and that it was only after they had been breached that the lesser buildings were exposed to the full force of the winter storms.

'The fish-tanks at Apollonia are examples of an interesting type. Most of the early fish-tanks, or *piscinae*, seem to have been constructed on lake-sides (especially in north Italy) and river-sides (especially the Nile), and must therefore have been for fresh-water fish.

'In the fifth century B.C. the Agrigentinians had built a piscina 7 stadaes (1,295 m.) long and 20 coudées (9 m. 24 cm.) deep. They led the waters of nearby rivers through it, and trapped and assembled vast numbers of fish.

By the second century B.C. the Romans had done the same in the lakes of Ombria and Toscana, Risti, Bracciano, Bolsena, and Vico. But by the time of Cicero they seem to have lost interest in fresh-water fish, and only constructed *piscinae salsae*, or salt-water tanks. From *c.* 90 B.C. onwards, private *piscinarii*, as Cicero called those of the gourmets, became a veritable passion. Vedius Pollio, a friend of Augustus whose *piscinarii* may be seen in the water off Marechiano, near Naples, threw condemned slaves to his moray eels, while Antonia, the wife of Drusus, had rings put in the gills of a favourite moray. By the end of the first century A.D. most *piscinarii* were communally owned.

'Varro compares a *piscina loculata* to a paint-box, with each kind of fish confined to its own compartment. Columella, however, makes two distinctions: Firstly, there is the use of a natural cove, with the rocks trimmed to a convenient shape and the entrance blocked with a grill. For this type, 2 m. is the minimum depth. Secondly, there is the artificially cut basin, lined with *opus signum*; but in this case the walls must be 3 m. high, with 1 m. of them above the surface of the water, and the bottom must be covered with rocks and weed.

'In both systems it is essential to keep a constant flow of clean water through the tank to prevent stagnation. Therefore canals (*rivi*) are placed not only at the open end, but also along the sides, and are controlled by sluice-gates of stone or bronze pierced with holes (*cancelli*). Aurigemma[12] found two examples of *piscinae loculatae* at Formiae in 1935 which were constructed on a rhomboid pattern, as opposed to the rectangular pattern at Apollonia. Leatham found a stone sluice-gate in Crete in 1956.[8]

'The discoveries at Apollonia provide some evidence of a change of water-level. The Romans did not use slipways, so we assume those on the Western Island to have been Greek.

'The slipways must have projected into a sufficient depth of water at their lower end to have taken the keels of the largest vessels, and, although we cannot say exactly what these would have drawn, the table below sets out the reasonable limits:

Depth at foot, m.	Dry length of slipway, m.
1·5	18
1·0	25
0·8	28
0·5	32

'While a depth of 1·5 m. would take vessels too long for the length of the slipway remaining out of the water, 50 cm. would only take such small vessels that the slipway need not have been made so long. This is based on the assumption that, since the slips are 6 m. wide, the ships must have been about 4 m. wide, but no assumptions have been made about the construction of the ships, other than nautical common sense.

'Since the present depth at the foot of the slips is 2·8 m. it follows that the sea-
M

level in the Greek period must have been relatively 2 m. lower than the present—
that is, the land has sunk 2 m. since then.

'From the plan of the fish-tank, it appears that the shelf which is marked as
being 2·5 m. below the water must originally have been meant as a terrace to walk
on, since there are steps leading down from it. The fact that the bottom of the tank
appears to be at only 3 m. is because of the debris lying in it. Thus it would seem
that the southern part of the site has sunk slightly more than the northern.

'When comparing the depths of other foundations with a proposed change of
from 2 m. to 2·5 m., it should be borne in mind that in the Mediterranean, where
there are no tides, it is common practice to build quays, roads, etc., only a few
centimetres above the water-level, provided that the water is sheltered from the
open sea.

'It is tempting to correlate the subsidence of Apollonia with the earthquake
which devastated Cyrene in A.D. 365, but for this there is no real evidence, and the
subsidence may well have been very gradual.

'We found that the quarries of the Western Island at Apollonia, the tanks on
the New Island, and many of the chambers at Phycus often contained what
appeared to be concrete. At Apollonia it was over 2 m. thick and had potsherds
and building blocks embedded in it. It almost filled the largest tank on the New
Island, and there were in it many building stones set at all angles. At Phycus several
of the tanks were half full, and the passage into which the rock-cut steps led was
filled to within 1 m. of the roof.

'In all cases the material was as hard as the local sandstone, and it had the
appearance of having been tipped into the cavities like concrete from a lorry, but
we soon realized that this was a natural formation created by the action of the
sun on a mixture of sand and sea water; it was a variety of "beach rock", an opinion
confirmed by Mr. Howard, the Esso geologist. Beach rock is fairly common,
though the process of its actual formation is not understood, and it is interesting
to note that a thickness of over 2 m. can be laid down in less than 1,500 years.'

The exploration of submerged sites other than harbours is best exemplified
by the work of Gunther in the Bay of Naples. In 1901 he observed that many submerged ruins would repay investigation, and would also supplement our knowledge of land movements since Roman times. Detailed investigation over the next
two years led to the planning of a large number of submerged structures and a
study of the shoreline from Naples west to the island of Nisidia. The report was
published in *Archaeologia*;[13] and in the *Geographical Journal*[14] he discussed the
methods used to ascertain the rise and fall of the coastline.

Recently this work has been continued by Professor Maiuri in the region
between Pozzuoli and Baia[15] with the aid of air photography and divers from the
Daino.[16] The methods used are described in the following report:

'In September 1959, at the request of Professor Maiuri, the *Daino* organization made the first attempt at a systematic plan of an entire submerged archaeological complex in the vast and important zone of Baia, of which the great baths and Imperial villas at the foot of the hill extend for more than 1 km. underwater, reaching to a depth of 16 m.

'The underwater research was preceded by an aerial survey made by the Air Force, from the results of which Professor Maiuri studied the whole submerged shore from Pozzuoli to Capo Miseno. Though the vast submerged constructions of Pozzuoli had been effectively photographed and transferred to a plan, at least in their general aspect, all attempts to make a useful aerial reconnaissance of the Baia area have failed because of its particular geographical position and of the constantly clouded water. For the same reasons, it presents equal difficulties for making underwater photographs which are illegible if taken at a distance of more than 1 or 2 m.

'The method selected was to make a direct survey with the aid of groups of divers and an aquaplane to determine at least the general outline of the topography and the limits of the submerged city. The Punta dell' Epitaffio, which forms the eastern extremity of the Gulf of Baia, was taken as a base-point from which to begin. The sea in front was divided by means of a row of buoys, 100 m. apart, into twenty-four squares, numbered in the conventional manner (Fig. 71); they were divided in their turn into six squares of 500 sq. m. each. Once the overall square is filled in with the main plan of the submerged structures, as well as with the results of the air photos, it should give in future a complete archaeological plan of submerged Baia, complementary to that of Pozzuoli.

'After the first two days of work and reconnoitring with the aquaplane, it was at once possible to ascertain that the extreme limits of the structures at the Punta dell' Epitaffio were at a depth of 16–18 m. and lie 800 m. from the shore (Fig. 72). They are marked by a fall of some 3–4 m. in the average depth of the bottom, indicating an ancient shoreline, and by a series of enormous blocks of masonry forming a mole beside the sea. Internally, lines of streets and the remains of buildings extended towards the Punta dell' Epitaffio in a chaotic mass of structures partly or wholly buried, the interpretation of which was particularly difficult for divers.

'Thanks to a long exploration by G. Roghi, it was possible to see that this line of coast, to the west of the point explored, turned sharply inwards towards the port of Baia and formed some kind of ancient inlet or artificial harbour. Unfortunately, the modern port installations, the vast accumulations of material, and the continual presence of cargo-boats being loaded and unloaded made it particularly difficult to extend the search in a useful manner.

'It was proved by experience that the survey could continue on two systems: general measurement of the main structures and their transfer to a plan without

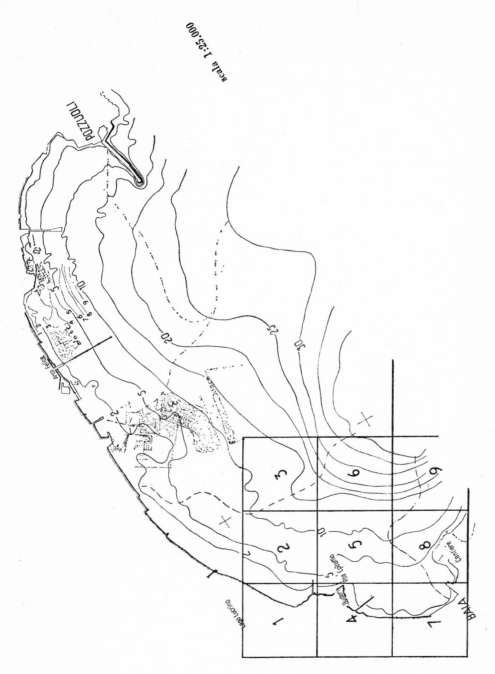

Fig. 71. Overall grid and general plan for the further exploration of the area of sea between Baia and Pozzuoli containing submerged structures. Each numbered square represents a section of the future plan of Baia. Exploration began within the limits of square 5 (cf Fig. 72)

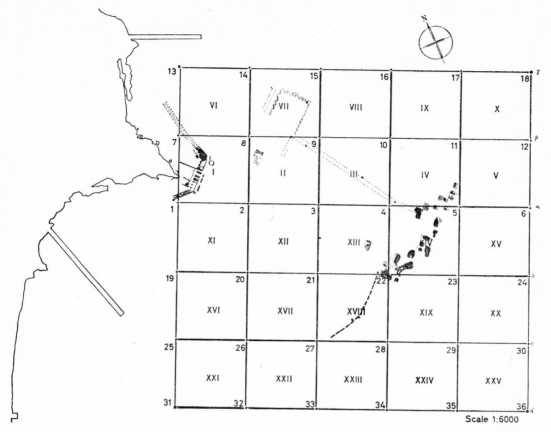

FIG. 72. Square 5 of the archaeological plan (subdivided into squares of 100 m.)
partly explored in 1959

bothering about detail; and the planning of archaeological and architectural
details as for a monument on land. The two systems were tried out by the groups
of divers reinforced by three architectural students from Naples University,
working under the Director and assistants of the Centre and assisted by the divers.

'A general survey was made of a large sector comprising the blocks of walling
of the mole (square XIV) (Fig. 73) to establish its plan, section, and true orientation,
as well as to distinguish the parts *in situ* from what had fallen and been displaced.
The grid squares proved to be highly effective, and indispensable for plotting fixed
alignments on the bottom, and for taking exact measurements and positions,
especially under conditions of very limited visibility. When the work was done, the
real plan turned out, as always, to be very different from the summary drawing
made on the basis of first impressions and approximate measurements. The greatest

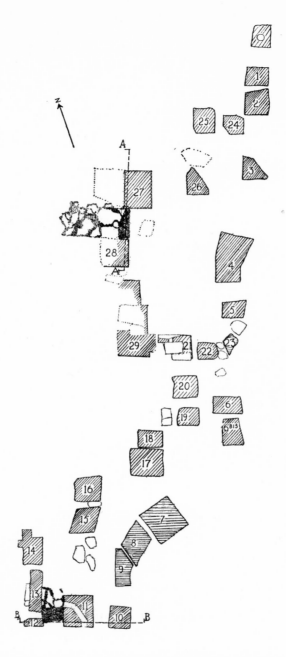

Fig. 73. Detailed plan of the scattered stones on the ancient sea-shore (square XIV) at the end of the 1959 season

1:1000

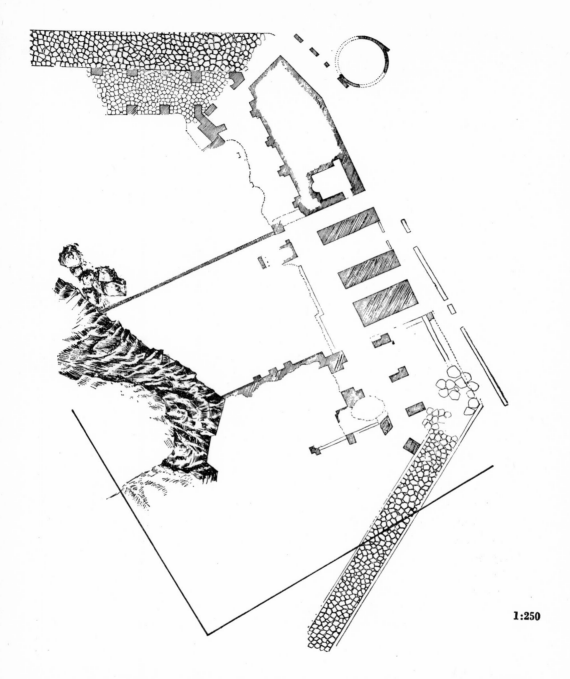

1:250

FIG. 74.   Detailed plan of the porticoed street and submerged structures surrounding
Punta dell 'Epitaffio (square I) at the end of the 1959 season

difficulty in transferring the plan on to paper concerned the buoys and basic lines of orientation originally laid down, since, owing to the variable currents, the buoys easily became displaced.

'The detailed survey was assigned to a second team, operating simultaneously with the first on the shallower and easier part of the bed lying against the Punta dell' Epitaffio (Fig. 74), where the existence of a large Roman road, running parallel to the coast, was already known, because it was visible from the surface in clear water. A kind of floating drawing office was fitted up for the purpose in the divers' launch, so that the measurements taken on the bottom could be immediately brought to the surface and be transferred directly to the plan. In twenty days it was possible to make a relatively exact plan of about half of square 1. In this way, the exact direction of the road, which runs round the Punta dell' Epitaffio in three sections, was determined. The presence of a huge porticoed zone surrounding it was also ascertained, and the principal walls noted which comprise the visible parts of submerged Baia: *opus reticulatum* and *opus latericium* alternate or combined which assign it generally to the first century of the empire.

'The results obtained in the first year were important, above all as a first essay in underwater archaeological surveying, and are therefore more valuable from the experimental and methodical point of view than for their intrinsic significance.

'Once the criteria of the work to be undertaken were determined, we endeavoured to give them a systematic character and to create a basis for continuous exploration; and for that purpose the position of the single buoys was fixed on the bottom, so that research could be resumed at a later date.

'Many sporadic dives were made in the intervening space between squares I and XIV, with the limited aim of ascertaining the importance and state of preservation of the existing ancient buildings. The results were partly contradictory, partly fragmentary. Some features were located and approximately plotted on the plan, but it was not possible to identify any complex of buildings or to find the general lines of the old streets because of the deep silting-up of the ruins and the extent of the rubble which encumbered the area. It was apparent that only a detailed, systematic, and patient survey could yield any preliminary deductions regarding the typography of the whole.

'In one place only was an attempt made to use the air-lift, at a depth of 7 m., beneath a vault of uncertain interpretation. In this way the possibility of an easy and probably fruitful method of excavation was ascertained. After a few hours' work, it was possible, not only to reveal perfectly clear stratification (underwater the colours are brighter and more vivid than on land), but many sherds were brought up, none of them later than the third century. This is a first indication, if confirmed by others, that Baia became submerged in Imperial times.

'From this first campaign of one month in the waters of Baia it was ascertained in principle that a series of similar campaigns, based on land and without the support of the *Daino*, would, by degrees, yield a complete plan of everything standing out on the sea-bottom in the area of the ancient city.

'Subsequent or even simultaneous assistance from the *Daino* might be of use for a much wider scheme of excavation to be directed at well-chosen points of particular archaeological interest. The recovery of whole objects, and possibly of works of art, can only be either a matter of chance or of a well-studied choice of site.'

Though not actually in the Mediterranean itself, the experimental excavation of lake dwellings at Neuchâtel is too valuable to omit, more especially as M. Haag has been able to observe and record stratigraphy in shallow water. In the following report on 'Archaeological Research in Lake Dwellings',[17] he recounts his experience:

'Since 1957 the Underwater Sports Centre of Neuchâtel has been interested in the excavation of the lake dwellings of Lake Neuchâtel. After having explored numerous places and studied the possibilities of using free-divers for the excavation of submerged sites, the Underwater Sports Centre began systematic exploration in March 1961 at the site of Champréveyres (Pls. 29–30), situated midway between Neuchâtel and La Tène.

'It is too soon to draw conclusions from the work. Also, of necessity, this note is brief, being designed as an introduction to the problem and to that of Lake Neuchâtel in particular.

First: chronology of the lake settlements:
Stone Age: Early, middle, and late Neolithic, from 4000 to 1800 B.C.
Bronze Age: periods I–V, from 1800 to 700 B.C.
At Champréveyres, the part actually explored belongs to Bronze Age IV and V, from about 1200 to 700 B.C.

'*History*

'In 1853 Keller made the first discoveries of lake dwellings at Meilen, in Lake Zürich. In 1882, following the diversion of the waters of the Jura, the level of Lake Neuchâtel was lowered by 2·50 m., and numerous lake dwellings, bristling with piles, were exposed.

'From that moment the rush began: hundreds of publications appeared. In 1930 120 sites were recorded in Lake Neuchâtel. In 1943 the latest major works concerning the region appeared, since when nothing more has been published. All interest was lost and the subject has been almost forgotten.

'Nevertheless, many sites remained unexplored (at least, systematically)—chiefly the most recent, those of the Bronze Age, for they were further out in 2 or

3 m. of water. Tentative excavation by land methods gave poor results. And some individuals, "Sunday" archaeologists, have recovered objects from the surface.

'Daniel Vouga wrote: "There is certainly much to be done, the study of the transition from Stone to Bronze Age, the position of Bronze Age III sites, and the exact chronology of Bronze Age IV–V, but it is *the technical means which are lacking*. In the meantime, it is better to abstain than to loot the sites, which will one day be of the utmost value."

'Two opposite theories

'Apart from the above-mentioned programme proposed by Vouga in his large and comprehensive work, one important problem persists which still divides specialists into two parties: Did the lake-dweller live on the shore or over the water?

'In his enthralling book, *Le Mythe des Cités lacustres*, Oscar Paret, an eminent German, replies humorously to this primary question. For him, without doubt, the lake-dwellers lived on the edge of the lake. As it happened, Oscar Paret could avail himself of extremely well-preserved material for study, particularly from the site of Ehrenstein, near Ulm, which is so well preserved, indeed, that we have no hesitation in adhering to the "sea-shore" party.

'Unfortunately, the case is quite otherwise on the shores of Lake Neuchâtel. The hundreds of stakes (which for Oscar Paret were stakes for huts and not piles) are planted in such a disorderly fashion on our sites that any attempt to find the shape or the outline of a hut is even today impossible. Also, the hut circles so useful for Paret's study have completely disappeared—very probably destroyed by waves.

'The possibility for free-divers

'Speaking of the material of the Bronze Age, Daniel Vouga said in 1943: "This is obtained from random 'pickings' from the surface when the water was low, or with a dredge." Either method is only a makeshift one to enrich the museums, which impoverishes and even destroys the sites, with no profit for science. And this because we lack the technical means which would render accessible the layers buried below 2 m. of water. As a matter of fact, all the sites of the Bronze Age are situated further out in the lake than those of the Stone Age, and the tentative efforts we ourselves have made to excavate them, when the waves receded, have all been abortive.

'Such is the problem. We are actually trying to resolve it by the technical methods required by Vouga, and which we now possess—the Cousteau-Gagnan free-diving equipment.

'We have chosen the site of Champréveyres partly because it was untouched, partly for its apparent richness; and also because of the easily accessible archaeological layers unencumbered by alluvium, since no watercourse debouches in the neighbourhood.

'*Method of work*

'A net 100 m. square, divided into meshes of 1 m. square, was spread over a portion of the site. It was made of yellow plastic tape, 4 cm. wide. Each mesh carried a number from 1 to 100 on treated aluminium; the numbers are in yellow on a black ground. With the aid of air photographs and a theodolite, the position of the net was marked on the plan.

'Each square was excavated with an air-lift 14 cm. in diameter, attached to 12 m. of flexible, reinforced rubber pipe of 16 cm. diameter. The material sucked up by the air-lift was disgorged on a floating sieve with a mesh of 4 mm. (Pl. 29). The compressed air necessary for working the air-lift was supplied by a large compressor giving 6,000 litres/minute at 2·5 kg./cm.²

'All this material, including the diving equipment, was installed on a pontoon 15 m. long and 3 m. wide. An office, sheltered from the weather, was established at one end.

'The diver who worked with the air-lift was instructed to keep the sand, the lacustrine mould, and chalk separate within each square metre. He made detailed observations, which were at once reported to the office, and he also noted at the bottom, on a special pad, the exact position of the stakes and crosspieces found.

'The pieces brought up bore the number of the square from which they came, in addition to a letter corresponding to the position of the net. All the worked objects in wood, bone, and horn were preserved in water with a little thymol (a preservative) until such time as their treatment in air could be assured (method: alcohol, toluene, paraffin wax).

'After the exploration of each square, the sieve was emptied and its contents minutely examined. All the bones, whatever they were, were kept by squares in a box, as were the vegetable specimens, of which the most frequent types were nuts, cherry-stones, acorns, seeds of beech, conifers, and willows.

'All sherds, however small, were collected. Those which were decorated or of special interest were numbered. The others were kept in bags for a statistical count per 100 sq. m.

'A statistical report on the pollen will also be made. By good luck the stratigraphy was simple and well preserved. In the first 50 sq. m. excavated, we had on an average: sand, 10–20 cm.; lacustrine mould (the archaeological layer), 6–12 cm.; lacustrine chalk, to 40 cm.; then the white bottom and sand (Pl. 29).

'*Advantages of the method*

'The free-diver is weightless under water. Thus there is no risk of his crushing objects, of which many are extremely fragile.

'The air-lift has a double advantage; it creates in the immediate vicinity of the excavation a stream of clean water, allowing work to be performed in good conditions of visibility; and it is also found to be a delicate working tool. One can thus expose the archaeological layer and make valuable observations *in situ* on the undisturbed surface.

'The material gathered in the sieve was automatically freed of sand and mud, and this greatly assisted sorting and prevented losses.

'*The human problem*

'Since the divers who devote the whole of their spare time to this work are people of varied talents, we sometimes found it difficult to make them understand the prime importance of the many details of our method of excavation. To alleviate this inconvenience, we have arranged archaeological lectures, followed by visits to the principal museums specializing in material from the lake settlements. Aided by practice, we have now an alert and sufficiently well-trained team. Nevertheless, we lack the active co-operation of an archaeologist specializing in the subject, an archaeologist without whom we know well such an important job cannot be properly carried out.'

NOTES

1 R. Meiggs, *Roman Ostia* (Clarendon Press, 1960), Chapter 4.
2 R. Bartocini, *Il porto romano di Leptis Magna*, Bollettino del Centro Studi per la Storia dell' Architettura No. 13, Supp. (1958).
3 Karl Lehmann-Hartleben, 'Die antike Hafenanlagen des Mittelmeeres', *Klio*, Beiheft, XIV (Leipzig, 1923).
4 Gaston Jondet, 'Les ports submergés de l'ancienne Ile de Pharos', *Mémoires de l'Institut Égyptien*, IX (1916).
5 A. Poidebard, 'Un grand port disparu: Tyr. Recherches aériennes et sous-marines, 1934–6', *Bibliothèque archéologique et historique*, XXIX (Paris, 1939).
6 A. Poidebard and J. Lauffray, *Sidon. Aménagements antiques du port de Saida. Études aériennes, au sol et sous-marines*, 1946–50 (Beirut, 1951).
7 Richard Garnett and John Boardman, 'Underwater Reconnaissance off the Island of Chios, 1954', *Annual of the British School at Athens*, 56 (1961), 102.
8 John Leatham and Sinclair Hood, 'Submarine Exploration in Crete, 1955', *Annual of the British School at Athens*, 53–4 (1958–9), 263ff.
9 M. Guy, 'Les ports antiques de Narbonne', *Rivista di Studi Liguri*, 21 (1955), 213ff.
10 Nicholas Flemming, 'Underwater Adventure in Apollonia', *Geographical Magazine*, XXXI (1959), 497; 'Apollonia revisited', ibid., XXXIII (1961), 522.

11 E. J. A. Kenny, 'The Ancient Docks and the Promontory of Sunion', *Annual of the British School at Athens*, 42 (1947), 194.

12 S. Aurigemma and A. de Santis, *Gaeta, Formia, Minturno* (Rome, 1955), 27.

13 R. T. Gunther, 'The Submerged Greek and Roman Foreshore near Naples', *Archaeologia*, 58.2 (1903), 499ff.

14 R. T. Gunther, 'Earth Movements in the Bay of Naples', *Geographical Journal*, XXII (1903), 121ff., 269ff.

15 A. Maiuri, 'L'esplorazione archeologica sottomarina di Baia', *Atti del II Congresso Internazionale Sottomarina* (Albenga, 1958), 108.

16 N. Lamboglia, 'La prima campagna di rilevamento della citta sommersa di Baia', *Rivista di Studi Liguri*, 25 (1959), 302.

17 W. Haag, 'Recherches archéologiques sur les palafittes du lac de Neuchâtel', *L'Aventure sous-marine*, No. 36 (December 1961-January 1962), 288ff.

6

The Future

It will have been observed from the foregoing chapters that the first objective of marine archaeology has been the natural one of collecting objects and excavating. But, as M. Dumas points out, excavation techniques require considerable professional skill both on the part of the archaeologist and of the diver.

Until these techniques are developed, the problems put forward by Professor Nino Lamboglia at the first conference on underwater archaeology, held in Cannes in 1955,[1] will remain only partly resolved. These problems were set out in five questions:

1   Is it possible to organize underwater excavation with the same deliberation and scientific accuracy as a land excavation without exorbitant costs and means difficult to achieve in the ordinary way?

2   Are helmeted divers preferable to free-divers?

3   What is the position of the archaeologist with regard to underwater excavation, and what must be his relations with technicians and divers?

4   Is it possible, after photographing, drawing, and recording all the details underwater, to clear a wreck completely in the same way as on land, and can one observe stratigraphy?

5   Can one achieve the aim of raising a wreck to the surface with the techniques now available, and at what cost?

In the years that have since elapsed, many of his points have been satisfactorily answered. For the first question, the work at Gelidonya has been undertaken with funds raised in the normal manner for any excavation, and at Mahdia and Dramont local organizations have been successful in dealing with this problem at no extravagant cost. Larger undertakings, such as the raising of a vessel, can obviously be achieved only with the full co-operation of naval and industrial diving resources.

For the second question, Professor Lamboglia had little experience of free-divers at the time he spoke, but since then the ability of the free-diver to float above the wreck has made it the safest method of excavation, and it is clear that he can perform most of the functions of a land archaeologist. Crumlin Pedersen, however, considers that the free-diver is best suited to reconnaissance, observation, measuring, and photography, but not for heavier jobs, for which skill and experience are required.

Nevertheless, Professor Lamboglia made the point that *all* divers who expect to work on a wreck should have a full preparatory training, both archaeological and technical, such as that being given at the Centro Sperimentale di Archeologia Sottomarina at Albenga, before setting out to excavate.

The third question—perhaps the most difficult—concerns the direction of the excavation and the role of the underwater archaeologist. Professor Lamboglia stated clearly that the ideal would be to find, among the rising generation, the diving archaeologist, but he emphasized 'the absolute priority of the archaeological over the technical factor in underwater exploration'. In his view, this amounted to asserting that the collaboration between the archaeological specialist who directs the excavation and the technicians who do the work and control the diving must not only be organized on a basis of mutual understanding and equality, but with very definite archaeological control in the conduct of the excavation.

This system worked well in collaboration with Commandant Rafaeli and the *Artiglio*; and in subsequent exploration in the Ligurian Sea the technicians and chief divers played the part of collaborators and valuable advisers, with the most satisfactory results in the limited field of sondage and in prospecting.

But the fourth, basic, question remains. Given these primary and indispensable conditions, can the principal aim of submarine research be achieved in the future, can we not merely bring up the objects, place them in their context, and decide their origin—which is at least a substantial gain—but make plans and take photographs before bringing a wreck to the surface, as was done in Italy on Lake Nemi? How far we have gone towards this has been shown in the foregoing reports, but there is still much to be done before the Lake Nemi standard is reached.

For the fifth question, regarding the raising of a wreck, in three cases only is there a report and sketch of the keels recovered, and there is considerable disparity in the reconstructions. So far reports have only referred to the preservation of the keel either under the cargo or in the hull fragments recovered from the silt of ancient harbours, as at Marseilles and Ostia. On some the lead sheathing is attached by copper nails and overlies a layer of woven material.

The problem of preservation when the timbers are raised is as yet only partly solved, and requires efficient laboratory conditions. It has not been attempted on a large scale, except in the case of the Scandinavian ships, where the wood was in exceptionally good condition. The occasions when a whole ship, such as the *Vasa*, has to be preserved are rare, and present special salvage problems; the results achieved will be of great interest.

However, it is an axiom of archaeological research and field work that *exploration* should precede *excavation*. Only in this way can the most suitable site for excavation be chosen. This aspect has been sadly neglected in marine archaeology, as is apparent from the meagre records of exploration;[2] but, archaeologically, it could be the most rewarding for the informed free-diver, provided he will adopt Professor Lamboglia's watchword, 'Look and don't touch', until such time as the evidence has been fully considered.

The most urgent need is for a record of the information collected by divers to be collated in some central, national record. Only then can the implications as regards trade routes and anchorages and so forth be clearly understood in relation to the general archaeological background. The objects found on the sea-bed will themselves furnish information not otherwise available if recorded in detail on the lines set out in the questionnaire (Appendix).

So far, the most numerous objects recorded are perhaps lead anchor stocks.[3] These have now been recovered from all over the Mediterranean, and not only in association with ships (Pl. 31); groups may well indicate anchorages or places of refuge. In quite a number of cases the lead collar or junction-piece for the arm has been found, and once only (Chrétienne) part of the wooden shank; it was broken off at the stock, and only the upper part with the square hole remained. Reconstructions based on the large wooden anchors from Lake Nemi have been made with reasonable certainty. The length between stock and junction-piece, which would give some idea of the correct proportions of an anchor, has never been recorded. The leaden stocks were cast about a wooden core (which sometimes remains) directly on to the wooden shank, as shown in the sketch (Fig. 75). A few bear inscriptions or decorative reliefs of dolphins, Medusa heads, etc.

Movable stocks (Pl. 31), sometimes of stone, of the type which could be slipped out of the shank to lie flat on the deck, as in the modern Admiralty-pattern anchor, have also been recovered. Ancient iron anchors are rarely found, for in time iron dissolves in sea water, leaving only the matrix of its shape in the marine concretion which forms upon it. These concretions may, however, be used as moulds to cast the original shape, as was done with the anchor from la Ciotat.[4]

The triangular stone fisherman's anchor occurs frequently in a number of forms (Pl. 31), usually with a round hole at the apex for the rope, and two square holes at the bottom through which wooden spars were thrust to form flukes to grip the sea-bed. A third type consists of a simple block of stone with a hole for the rope to pass through. Other objects reported from time to time which may be attributed to a ship's equipment include brailing rings, sounding leads (one still armed with tallow), lead piping, small bronze hubs, perhaps parts of small capstans, and large, pierced, rectangular stones, considered by some to be mast steps (Pl. 32), but with a fuller record of the context the interpretation would be easier.

With the exception of the copper ingots, the cargoes of ancient ships so far recorded have comprised amphorae, Campanian pottery, tiles (Frioule, Caria) (Pl. 31),

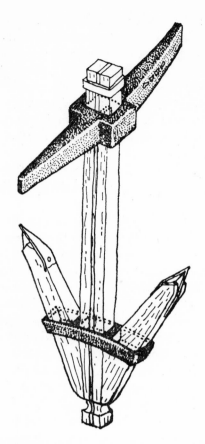

FIG. 75.   Reconstructed anchor with lead stock and collar
(*Rivista di Studi Liguri* XVIII)

or else bronze and marble sculpture, columns, and building stone (St. Tropez, Marzameni).[5] All of these are types of objects which are readily recognized and are not easily destructible, and the reasons for their transport are obvious.

Amphora wrecks have attracted most attention because the amphorae have been fairly easy to recover and are satisfying objects for the diver to possess. These ubiquitous packaging containers of the Greek, Roman, and Phoenician worlds have been found in a wide variety of types on the French, Italian, and Spanish coasts, ranging from the fourth century B.C. to the sixth century A.D. or later. The principal variants contained wine from the Greek islands, Rhodes, Thasos, and Cos, but many more came from the south Italian coast. Punic types of amphorae come from the Spanish ports, south Italy, Malta, and Sicily. Many of these contained other products.

Garum made from salt and small fish, a special flavouring much used in the Roman kitchen, was carried in a Punic type of amphora; but we know little about whence it was shipped, though the brands prepared in Leptis Magna and Pompeii were highly prized. Shell-fish, such as mussels and oysters, were also shipped. Nuts, pine cones, and olives were carried in unlined porous jars, and olive oil in distinctive, bulbous amphorae; mutton-fat was recovered from another in the Black Sea off Bulgaria. But honey, the only form of sweetening then known, which was mixed with wine to make *mulsum*, or cheese, must also have been shipped in some form of container.

Dolia, used as store jars or as the predecessor of the vat for making wine, were shipped along the French coast, and several have been recovered from Agde (Pl. 32).

Because amphorae are so easily discovered, little has been recorded of seventeenth- and eighteenth-century ships, except when cannon have been found. Records of the equipment and cargoes of ships of the later periods are equally important, for details are lacking in regard to their lay-out and construction. Interesting research on these later cargoes has in several cases led to the identification of the ship through the cargo manifests, thus opening up a whole new field in the history of shipping.

Work on harbours has made a beginning and is a projection of land archaeology, but another side, the exploration of submerged land surfaces in relation to ancient settlements and the rise of sea-level, has been insufficiently studied; and, though not directly connected with seafaring, is of considerable importance to the land archaeologist.

Dr. John Waechter writes: 'Most of the archaeological finds discussed above have been comparatively late in date, and a large proportion consist of wrecks of various periods. There are, however, classical sites, such as Epidaurus[6] and Apollonia, parts of which are now submerged, and such submergences are quite common with ancient harbour installations. This raises the whole question of land submergence or marine transgression, and opens a wide field for archaeological and geological research. Broadly speaking, the relation between land and sea is altered in three ways. Perhaps the best known is the sudden submergence of the land due to violent earthquakes, which is generally referred to as 'tectonic movement'. Such earth movement can depress the land as well as raise the sea-bed in some cases to considerable heights, though the upthrust is not our concern here. The downward direction, however, is often of considerable importance, and coastal settlements can disappear into the sea in a very short time, often resulting in underwater sites which are remarkably intact. The handling of such sites from an excavation point of view has been dealt with above.

'The two other main causes of submergence, in some respects related to each other, are a great deal less abrupt in their effect, often being processes taking

several thousands of years. The first, whose effects are world-wide, is known as
"Eustatic change". During the last million years, northern Europe was covered
from time to time by massive ice-sheets. They were four of these major glacia-
tions, with a few minor ones, the cold phases alternating with periods of very
much warmer conditions. During the glacial phases the evaporation-precipitation
cycle was, of course, disrupted and the water taken from the sea did not return,
being retained as ice. This naturally resulted in a major drop in sea-level. During
the warm periods the melting ice released the imprisoned water and the sea-
level rose again.

'The third cause of change of sea-level is "isostatic recovery". This is an
adjustment of the earth's crust after the weight of the ice had been removed,
resulting in localized tilting. Since the ice mass was in northern Europe, the effects
are mainly in this area, and the Mediterranean was hardly affected. In Britain this
isostatic recovery is still in operation and the northern parts of Scotland are
rising at the rate of about 10 cm. per century, with the south coast of England
sinking a similar amount. Since the final retreat of the ice took place about 8,000
years ago, the change of sea-level has been considerable. At the beginning of this
period, for example, most of the present North Sea was land, with south-east
England joined to the Continent. From an archaeological point of view, the significance of these changes is obviously considerable. Vast tracts of land which
were available for occupation by prehistoric man are now under the sea and are
accessible only by diving. Undoubtedly, the erosive action of the encroaching sea
has destroyed much of the evidence of such occupation, but in favourable circumstances some traces are likely to be preserved. In addition to the archaeological
possibilities, very little is known of the shore-lines of the low-level stages, though
quite a lot of those above present sea-level, whose sequence is known, have provided
useful dating evidence for archaeological material associated with them.

'In the spring of 1962 a four-man diving team, drawn mainly from London
University and Cambridge, consisting of an archaeologist, a geomorphologist,
an electrical engineer, and a photographer, undertook a survey for ancient submerged shore-lines and archaeological sites off the coast of Gibraltar. This expedition was the logical outcome of work done by the archaeological member
between 1948 and 1954, when he excavated a prehistoric cave at the base of the
cliff on the eastern side of the Rock which provided evidence of occupations
extending back some 60,000 years. Since the situation of the cave was such that it
could be occupied only during periods of low sea-level, much of the filling consisted of wind-blown sand derived from a wide strand-line now submerged. A
detailed survey of the sea-bed in the area was obviously called for, particularly as
the deposits inside the cave indicated that during the occupation the sea went
down at least three times.

'Before describing the methods used it is necessary to discuss the geological and archaeological problems involved, particularly in the case of the submerged shore-lines, since, without understanding the composition of the shore-line, they are not likely to be recognized.

'The study of shore-lines, particularly ancient ones, is extremely complicated, and varies according to the geological structure on which it is formed. Since shore-lines on soft structure are not likely to be preserved, it is more useful to describe those involving the harder and more durable rocks. Fig. 76 shows the profile from cliff-top to deep water of a typical cliff shore-line, a type which is likely to be preserved, at least in part, under water. The three main features are the abrasion platform rising shorewards to the more steeply inclined bench which abuts on to the base of the cliff. At the foot of the cliff, at its junction with the bench, a distinct notch can be seen. This is the result of the waves continually pounding at the base of the cliff. Where there is a small promontory, these notches are very easy to see

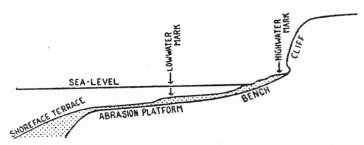

FIG. 76.   Elements of a shore.
Cross-section showing erosional features with a thin veneer of deposits
(Zeuner. *Pleistocene Period*)

at present sea-level, and they can also be seen in many places on the cliff face high above water-level, being in this case the remains of older high sea-levels. Where the cliff face lacks promontories, the notch takes the form of a long groove. On the platform and bench of a modern beach are superficial deposits of sand and shingle, as can be seen in the diagram, often spilling over the seaward end of the platform into deeper water. During periods of low sea-level these superficial deposits are often covered by consolidated dunes which themselves are an indication of a submerged land surface. Generally the ancient shore-lines above present sea-level are better preserved, as they have never been re-covered by the sea, whereas those below the present sea-level have been covered more than once, with the result that some of the characteristic features are likely to have been destroyed; but in many cases, as recent work has shown, such submerged shore-lines can still be recognized, even if not all the features are preserved.

'The archaeological problems are also considerable. Whereas sites suddenly

submerged by earthquake action are likely to be more or less intact, those which
the sea has covered during a long period are liable to be completely destroyed and
the material reduced to unrecognizable pebbles. There are some sites, however,
which afford the material some measure of protection, and the most obvious of
these are the caves, some of which, like those in Gibraltar, were occupied for
several thousand years.

'During the excavation of land caves, particularly those in limestone, the filling
tends to become consolidated near the walls as a result of dissolved calcium
carbonate. These cemented deposits or breccias often become as hard and as
resistant to erosion as the rock, and while a rising sea will usually scour out the
main deposit, these breccias will often remain clinging to the walls, particularly in
recesses protected from the main force of the sea. Since these breccias were
originally part of the occupation deposit, they will, like the remainder, contain
flint implements and bone, as well as being structurally very different from the
rock of the cave walls.

'The differences of the breccias and the rock notwithstanding, they are not
always easy to distinguish in a sea cave, particularly when both are covered by
marine growth. This necessitates taking samples throughout the cave, paying
particular attention to the recesses, the samples being taken with a hammer and
chisel; as only small pieces are required initially, this is not very difficult. If it is
found that there are breccias, then much larger samples must be detached and
broken up on the surface, with very careful notes kept of the relative positions of
the samples, since problems of stratification are naturally involved.

'The Gibraltar expedition was concerned with two problems—the identification and plotting of submerged shore-lines and the investigation of submarine
caves, but in the limited time available it was only possible to concentrate on the
first. The shore-line survey was done in two parts. Firstly, as much ground as
possible was covered, using a continuous-recording echo-sounder. This was done
by making runs out to sea at right angles to the shore and plotting to a depth of
91·5 m., thus providing permanent records of the profile of the bottom. Heavy
seas and strong currents made it very difficult to keep the runs straight, but the
boat's position was checked at frequent intervals by simultaneous readings with
two marine sextants on prominent features on shore; in this way the profiles could
be accurately positioned.

'The eastern side of the Rock showed a gently sloping bottom, with no marked
breaks in the profile, but on the western side and off the southern tip the sound-
ings showed a series of vertical cliffs. Their exact nature could not, of course, be
deducted from the echo-sounder's profile alone, and it was necessary to dive on
each feature to establish whether it contained shore-line evidence or not. Detailed
examinations of these submerged cliffs showed that there were four well-defined
shore-lines, their existence being based largely on the presence of clear wave

notches, and there is no doubt that, given more time, more would have been found and the extent of each shore-line plotted in more detail.

'The Gibraltar expedition was largely experimental, but the techniques used have since been employed elsewhere with considerable success, and, though the archaeological side had to be restricted through lack of time, this aspect is also capable of extensive development.

'The important thing about this type of underwater research is that it is within the range of the ordinary diver, it is not destructive, and it requires no equipment which is not easily obtainable or adaptable. Familiarity with shore-line features can be readily obtained by intelligent observation of existing beaches, a study which can be carried out in periods of bad diving conditions. The only technical requirements are the ability to plot an accurate bottom profile and to be able to relate the measurements to existing mean sea-level. Apart from tape-measures, plastic drawing-boards, and sample-bags, all that are needed are a mason's hammer, a cold chisel, and a $\times$ 10 lens, but it must be remembered that, as in the case of all archaeological investigations, the recognized methods of recording apply.'

This aspect of archaeological research is closely related to geology and marine biology. Of the former, M. Nesteroff writes:[7]

'Oceanography is not a science on its own, but consists of a number of distinct disciplines. There are physicists, zoologists, and chemists who study the sea, each one viewing it from his own particular angle. Their work is always interconnected, and the various disciplines cannot do without the assistance which they afford one another. Oceanography is essentially team-work.

'The discipline most nearly related to submarine archaeology is sedimentation, which aims at studying marine deposits. The links which unite these two sciences are self-evident, for it is in the marine deposits that one finds archaeological remains, which for the sedimentologist are only deposits of a special kind.

'One of the primary questions in sedimentation is the chronology of the samples brought to the surface. The samples (a sort of sausage of silt or sand called *carotte* (French) or "core" (English)) are taken vertically through the mass of sediment by a tube with a collecting centre. It is most important to be able to date the different levels. In fact, all interpretation is based on these results: rate of sedimentation, nature of the depositing sources at a given time, etc.

'The older writers held wholly empiric opinions on these problems. It is only during recent years that more precise methods have been developed. The round-the-world cruise of the oceanographic ship, *Albatross*, directed by Hans Petersson, brought back a large number of these samples, on which scientists endeavoured to develop modern methods. . . .

'These particular methods, specifically developed for deep water, cannot be applied to coastal sediments. But, all the same, the coastal contributions are very important, though irregular. The remains which would help chronologically are swamped in masses of sediment. We must therefore use other techniques. For a piece of limestone of biological origin, chronology based on radio-carbon (C.14) methods gives excellent results.

'Moreover, the discovery of archaeologically dated objects stratified in marine sediments is extremely important. In land excavations archaeologists apply to geologists to assist in the dating of soils in which they find their tools, arrow-heads, skulls, etc. In marine deposits the situation is reversed, and it is the geolo-gists specializing in marine deposits who ask the archaeologists the exact age of the layers.

'The application can be demonstrated. The rate of deposition of coastal sedi-ments is very variable, governed by their nature, geographical position, etc. Dated potsherds have often allowed us to specify this rate.

'In the same way, the Mediterranean sea vegetation, well known to divers, grows upon its own roots, which die down in course of time, enclosing sediments, sands of land origin, and remains of shells. This carpeting of roots full of sand is called *mattes*. Little-known erosional phenomena have cut sinuous channels and large basins in these *mattes*, which are called *intermattes*. On the sides which en-close the *intermattes* and which yield a natural section of the *mattes*, stratified Roman pottery has been found and it has been possible to deduce the rate of accretion of the vegetation. At the bottom of the Anse St. Roch it is 50–60 cm. in 1,600 years, whereas in front of the citadel of Île St. Marguerite it is from 1·5 m. to 2 m.

'This difference can be attributed to the geographical position and to the varia-tions in sedimentary deposition. These points concerning rate of sedimentation and the evolution of the bottom should not be neglected in research and work on ancient wrecks. At Anse de St. Roch there are two wrecks entirely embedded in *mattes*. It is only when examining the sides of the *intermattes* that one becomes conscious of their existence.

'The wreck of Grand Congloué, excavated by Commandant Cousteau, was entirely buried at the beginning of the work. Only a few necks emerged from the sand here and there on the bottom. Rocks, scree from the cliff, sand and shells, and other fine particles had covered the wreck. On the other hand, that of the Esquillade, situated in the open, in a region where no foreign sedimentary deposits reached it, was not buried. Only some shells and other debris from close by had lightly covered it.'

In this respect, he quotes an exceptional case: 'Two of my friends . . . found at Cap d'Antibes several amphora scattered at the foot of the cliff. In spite of their search, they could not locate the wreck. During a dive on that spot, I was struck by an unusual phenomenon of sedimentation; the current was no longer felt at that depth (40 m.). We found the sand on the bottom raised in a dune against the cliff. An exceptional swell, aided, perhaps, by a shelf forming a converging lens, had displaced the sand. This movement might well have engulfed the wreck, which should not be sought only on the projections of the cliff.'

Confronted by a ballooning of the bottom, he suspected a silted-up wreck. A rapid check confirmed the hypothesis.

To conclude, he summarizes the state of research at Anse St. Roch:

'The vegetation occupies the northern part of the bay, where the reconnaissances of the two clubs had identified two late Roman wrecks. The vegetation rises to 2–3 m. from the surface and the *intermattes* are some 3–4 m. deep. In addition to the Gaulish pottery, the cargo consisted of types of burial amphorae (near to Dressel 26/Almagro 50). He also saw a piriform specimen like those of Anthéor wreck (related to Dressel type 8). Caught in the *matte*, these amphorae are usually crushed or broken. The exploitation of these wrecks, in spite of their shallow depth, presents great technical difficulties, for the *mattes* covering them must first be destroyed.'

In the reports on wrecks, the presence of marine concretion covering the, deposits is frequently mentioned; in harbours there are deposits of 'beach rock' as at Apollonia, and the *trottoire* formation covers other demolished structures just below sea-level (Leptis Magna). None of these formations, chiefly due to marine organisms, is well understood by marine biologists; and, as they are usually to be found on archaeological sites, their observation and study present yet another field of research. But, as the 'handmaid of history', archaeology is the study of man in his environment, and surface archaeology cannot be divorced from its underwater counterpart. In the same way that aerial surveys and photography widened our view in the 'twenties, diving has opened to us a new field. Ships, navigation, trade routes, ports, submerged sites and land surfaces—and re-lated geological and oceanographic phenomena—all have a bearing on marine archaeology.

Underwater exploration is of necessity more costly than on land, not only in money, but also in time, due to the limited period that the diver can remain on the job. It follows that the first requisite is the careful recording of all sites, which must involve planned exploration of a much higher order than on land. Now that the technical means are available, it is for the diver and archaeologist to collaborate in studying each other's methods and to select a programme which will be suitable for the coasts available. Areas most likely to be rewarding of exploration or likely to yield an answer to a problem must be studied beforehand, and in this geology, marine biology, and archaeology must go hand in hand. Underwater research has made a useful beginning, and the finds brought up should stimulate archae-ologists to develop methods comparable to those used on land.

NOTES

1 Club Alpin sous-marin, *Rapport du premier Congrès Internationale d'archéologie sous-marine* (Cannes, 1955).

2 *Gallia*, XIV (1956), 23–34; XVI (1958), 5–39; XVIII (1960), 41–56; XX (1962), 147–76. *Cris, Revista del mar* (Barcelona, 1959), *passim*.

3 For studies on ancient anchors see F. Benoit, 'Jas d'ancre et organeaux de plomb', *Rivista di Studi Liguri*, 18 (1952), 266; 'Jas d'ancre et pièces d'outillages des épaves de Provence', ibid., 21 (1955), 117; 'Ambiances et survivances Méditerranéennes', *Ogam*, XII (1960), 176. W. Bebko, 'Rapport sur la découverte de deux jas d'ancre antiques', *Études et Sports Sous-marin*, 15 (1962), 12. N. Lamboglia, 'Un ancora romana all' Isola Gallinaria', *Rivista Ingauna e Intemiglia*, XIV (1959), 131. P. N. Gargallo, 'Anchors of Antiquity', *Archaeology*, 14 (1961), 31. H. Frost, 'From Rope to Chain', *Mariner's Mirror*, 49 (1963), 1.

4 La Ciotat, *Gallia*, XVI (1958), 25, Fig. 29.

5 St. Tropez, *Rivista di Studi Liguri*, XVIII (1952), 240. Marzameni and Isola delle Correnti, Gerhard Kapitän, 'Schiffsfrachten antiker Baugesteine und architekturteile vor den Küsten Ostsiziliens', *Klio*, Band 39 (1961), 276.

6 T. Falcon-Barker, *1600 Years under the Sea* (Frederic Muller, 1960).

7 Club Alpin sous-marin, *Rapport du Premier Congrès Internationale* . . . (1955), 48ff.

For general works applicable to marine archaeology see the following:
L. Casson, *The Ancient Mariners* (Gollancz, 1959).
J.-Y. Cousteau, *The Silent World* (Hamish Hamilton, 1953).
G. E. R. Deacon, *Oceans* (Hamly n, 1962)
P. Diolé, *4,000 Years Under the Sea* (Sidgwick and Jackson, 1954).
F. Dumas, *Deep-water Archaeology* (Routledge and Kegan Paul, 1962).
    Épaves antiques (Arthaud, 1964).
J. Dugan, *Man explores the Sea* (Penguin, 1960).
H. Frost, *Under the Mediterranean* (Routledge and Kegan Paul, 1963).
A. Guilcher, *Coastal and Submarine Morphology* (Methuen, 1958).
Istituto Internazionale di Studi Liguri, *Atti dell' II Congresso Internazionale di archeologia sottomarina* (Albenga 1958, 1961).
C. A. M. King, *Coasts and Beaches* (Arnold, 1959).
B. Landstrom, *The Ship* (Allen and Unwin, 1961).
E. G. R. Taylor; *The Haven-finding Art* (Hollis and Carter, 1956).
G. Ucelli, *Le Nave di Nemi* (Rome, 1950).

APPENDIX

In the final chapter of *Le Plongeur et l'Archéologue*, M. Dumas explained the need for the preparation of central records, from which distribution maps could be prepared. Accompanying a note by Miss Frost on how to record an ancient wreck, a questionnaire was put forward as a preliminary means of collecting information. The amended version is now being circulated in Britain.

REPORT UPON AN UNDERWATER ARCHAEOLOGICAL DISCOVERY

To be returned to: The Secretary, Underwater Research Group, London University, Institute of Archaeology, 31–34 Gordon Square, London, W.C.1.

Please cast your information in the form of answers to the following questions

1 Name, address, and telephone number of informant:
2 Name of diving club to which informant belongs:
3 Nature of find. Is it a wreck, an isolated find, etc.?
4 Region of the find:
5 Position. Specify the find spot, preferably on a tracing from a marine chart. Give the bearings. Describe the position in relation to the coast or to fixed points.
6 Nature of the sea-bed: rock, sand, mud, etc.
7 Depth of the find.
8 Appearance of the find. Did it lie upon the sea-bed or is it partially buried?
9 Size of the site. Make a sketch-map of the site, with measurements. If you cannot make a sketch-map, make as detailed a description as possible, with measurements of length and width.
10 Description of objects. Where many are found, your general sketch-map

made for No. 9 should be supplemented with drawings and measurements of individual objects. Add submarine photographs if amphorae are found; estimate approximately their number and the percentage of broken fragments. How many different types of amphorae are there? Submit sketches if you can: better still, photographs of each type represented. If the number of objects found and photographed and sketched is not too great, number each drawing and photograph and indicate by the same numbers where each was found on the general plan of the find.

Record any inscriptions found on any amphorae (these may be on lip, neck, or base of a handle, and there may be two different ones on one amphora). Send drawings or rubbings of any inscriptions.

11   General Comments. Send any information about diving conditions, currents, etc., which you think useful.

Most Important: If you know that objects of archaeological interest have been found before in the area, please send details.

DATE:.....................   SIGNED:.............................

Index

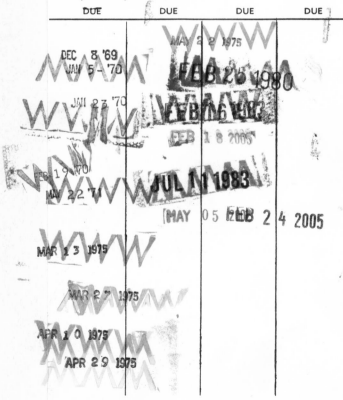